WOMEN DEVELOPMENT PROGRAMMES

WOMEN DEVELOPMENT PROGRAMMES

By

Dr. M. Lakshmi Narasaiah
M.A., Ph.D.

Professor of Economics
Co-ordinator, Dept. of M.B.A. and Commerce
Special Officer
Sri Krishnadevaraya University Post-graduate Centre
Kurnool–518 002
Andhra Pradesh

&

Smt. S.A. Haseena Sulthana
Dept. of Economics
Osmania Degree College for Women
Kurnool
Andhra Pradesh
(India)

D P H

DISCOVERY PUBLISHING HOUSE
NEW DELHI-110002

First Published-2007
Reprinted 2012

ISBN: 978-93-5056-639-8

Published by

DISCOVERY PUBLISHING HOUSE
4831/24, Ansari Road, Prahlad Street,
Darya Ganj, New Delhi-110002 (India)
Phone: 23279245 • Fax: 91-11-23253475
E-mail: dphbooks@rediffmail.com
dphtemp@indiatimes.com

Printed at:

Dynamic Printers, Delhi

Preface

Ours is a male dominated society where women are described as the 'second sex' and the 'second creature' who live on surplus. Their very existence has been considered as parasite on the men who rule them. Female subordination has been an essential feature of human life in all contemporary societies, although with a varying degree and expression of male dominance. One of the important manifestations of this women subordination lies in the division of labour which provides a cheap and ready source of labour. Division of labour between sexes is culturally imposed, and this segregated role pattern has led to a structural subordination of woman to man.

However structural subordination of women to men has not been able to prevent them from playing a vital role in the overall development of the society. Especially, their active participation in economic activities has become common in all countries, developed and developing.

Participation of women in socio-economic activities is a global issue. Women play a very crucial part in the socio-economic activities and have now become an integral part of global market.

The developed countries, many of which are now characterized by full employment, still there is room for more women in the work force. On the other hand, the developing countries which are marked by labour surplus, the income of the families by and large is low and the families require the assistance of an additional earner. This economic vulnerability of the family compels their women members to go for work supplementing the increase of income of their respective families.

Dr. M. Lakshmi Narasaiah

Abbreviations

AGS	Additional Gram Sevikas
AGM	Assistant General Manager
AIDS	Acquired Immune Deficiency Syndrome
ANP	Applied Nutrition Programme
BC	Backward Caste
CAPART	Council for Advancement of Peoples Action and Rural Technology
CC	Community Coordinator
CDF	Cooperative Development Fund
CDPO	Child Development Project Officer
CIRDAP	Centre on Integrated Development for Asia and the Pacific
CRD	Commission of the Rural Development
CSWB	Central Social Welfare Board
CV	Community Volunteers
DRDA	District Rural Development Agency
DWCRA	Development of Women and Children in Rural Areas
EAS	Employment Assurance Scheme
EDP	Entrepreneurial Development Programme
FAO	Food and Agricultural Organisation

FWPR	Female Work Participation Rate
HDI	Human Development Index
HDR	Human Development Report
HIV	Human Immuno Deficiency Virus
IADP	Intensive Agriculture District Programme
IAY	Indira Awaas Yojana
ICDS	Integrated Child Development Scheme
IFAD	International Fund for Agricultural Development
ILO	International Labour Organisation
IMR	Infant Mortality Rate
IMY	Indira Mahila Yojana
IRDP	Integrated Rural Development Programme
ISACPA	Independent South Asia Commission for Poverty Alleviation
ITI	Industrial Training Institute
JRY	Jawahar Rojgar Yojana
MCH	Maternity and Child Health
MDM	Mid Day Meals
MDO	Mandal Development Officer
MFI's	Micro Finance Intermediaries
MIS	Management Information System
MMR	Maternal Mortality Rate
MNP	Minimum Needs Programme
MRCP	Maharashtra Rural Credit Programme
MSY	Mahila Samridhi Yojana
NABARD	National Bank for Agriculture and Rural Development

NCF	National Creche Fund
NCF	National Children's Fund
NCW	National Commission for Women
NFHS	National Family Health Survey
NGO's	Non-Government Organisations
NIRD	National Institute of Rural Development
NISIET	National Institute of Small Industries Extension Training
NORAD	Norwegian Assistance for Development
NOVOK	Network of Voluntary Organisations of Kurnool
NPA's	Non-Performing Assets
NREP	National Rural Employment Programme
PAC's	Primary Agricultural Co-operative Societies
PEM	Protcin Energy Malnutrition
PD	Project Director
PMGY	Pradhan Mantri Gramodaya Yojana
PMRY	Prime Minister's Rozgar Yojana
PVO's	Partner Voluntary Organisations
RBI	Reserve Bank of India
RCH	Reproductive Child Health
RF	Revolving Fund
RLEGP	Rural Landless Employment Guarantee Programme
RMK	Rashtriya Mahila Kosh
RPR	Rural Poverty Report
RRBs	Regional Rural Banks

SAARC	South Asian Association for Rural Cooperation
SAP	Structural Adjustment Programme
SC	Scheduled Caste
SEWA	Self Employed Women's Association
SGSY	Swarnajayanthi Gram Swarozgar Yojana
SHARE	Society for Helping and Awakening Rural Poor through Education
SHG	Self-Help Group
SIDBI	Small Industries Development Bank of India
SIRD	State Institute of Rural Development
SMART	Simple, Moral, Accountable, Responsive and Transparent
SNP	Special Nutrition Programme
ST	Scheduled Tribe
STD's	Sexually Transmitted Diseases
STEP	Support to Training and Employment Projects
TBMPP	Telugu Bala Mahila Pragati Pranganam
UGC	University Grants Commission
UNDP	United Nations Development Programme
UNICEF	United Nations International Children Emergency Fund
UT's	Union Territories
VDO	Village Development Officer
WCP	Women's Component Plan
WCARRD	World Conference on Agricultural Reform and Rural Development

WDC's	Women Development Corporations
WDR	World Development Report
WHO	World Health Organisation
WTTI	Women Technical Training Institute

Contents

Preface *v*

Abbreviations *vii*

1. Women and Development—Poverty Eradication—Design and Methodology 1
2. Women Development Programmes and Five Year Plans 22
3. Origin and Progress of DWCRA and Self-Help Groups 81
4. Characteristics and Performance of Sample DWCRA and SHGs in the Study Area—Kurnool District 121
5. Income and Employment Generation and Capacity Building 158
6. Poverty Alleviation Through Social Mobilisation—the Kurnool Strategy 190
7. Problems of Women Development with Reference to the DWCRA/SHG Approach 233
8. Summary and Conclusions 243

Bibliography 275

Index 291

1

Women and Development—Poverty Eradication—Design and Methodology

Ours is a male dominated society where women are described as the 'second sex' and the 'second creature' who live on surplus. Their very existence has been considered as parasite on the men who rule them. Female subordination has been an essential feature of human life in all contemporary societies, although with a varying degree and expression of male dominance. One of the important manifestations of this women subordination lies in the division of labour which provides a cheap and ready source of labour. Division of labour between sexes is culturally imposed, and this segregated role pattern has led to a structural subordination of woman to man.

However structural subordination of women to men has not been able to prevent them from playing a vital role in the overall development of the society. Especially, their active participation in economic activities has become common in all countries, developed and developing.[1]

Participation of women in socio-economic activities is a global issue. Women play a very crucial part in the socio-economic activities and have now become an integral part of global market.[2]

The developed countries, many of which are now characterized by full employment, still there is room for more women in the work force. On the other hand, the developing countries which are marked by labour surplus, the income of the families by and large is low and the families require the assistance of an additional earner. This economic vulnerability of the family compels their women members to go for work, supplementing the increase of income of their respective families.[3]

EMPOWERMENT

Women and children who represent more than two third (67.7%) of the country's population, constitute the most important target groups in the context of the present day development planning. Thus, their concerns are placed on the priority list of the country's development agenda. Needless to say, they have the strength and support of the constitution. As per 2001 census women as a separate target group, account for 494.8 million and constitute 49 per cent of the country's total population. Depending upon the development needs of the individual age groups, the entire female population has been categorized into five distinct sub-groups, viz.:

1. Girl children in the age group of 0-14 years who constitute 37.8 per cent;

2. Adolescent girls in the age group of 15-18 years, who account for 9.5 per cent;

3. Women in the reproductive age group of 15-44 'years, who constitute 45.1 per cent;

4. Women in the economically active age group of 15-59 years, who account for 55.5 per cent;

5. The elderly women in the age group of 60+ constitutes 6.7 per cent.[4]

In India women in general are poor, rural women in particular are relatively powerless with no control over resources and little decision making power. Often the decisions are imposed on them. The prevailing patriarchal ideology which demands values of submission, sacrifice and silent suffering often undermines their capability and deprives them of their share of resources.

The process of challenging existing relations and gaining greater control over the forces of power may be termed as empowerment. Empowerment of women must be an integral part of sustainable human development.[5]

GENDER INEQUALITY

Gender inequality is now receiving greater attention. The principle of gender equality and equity and protection of women's rights have been the prime concerns in Indian thinking right from the days of independence. Accordingly, the concern of the country in safeguarding the rights and the privileges of women found its best expression in the constitution of India.

While Article 14 confers equal rights and opportunities on men and women in the political, economic and social spheres, Article 15 prohibits discrimination against any citizen on the grounds of sex, religion, race, caste, etc., and Article 15(3) empowers the state to make affirmative discrimination in favour of women. Similarly Article 16 provides for equality of opportunities in the matter of public appointments for all citizens. Yet, another Article 39 mentions that the state shall direct its policy towards providing men and women equally, the right to means of livelihood and equal pay for equal work. Article 42 directs the state to make provisions for ensuring just and humane conditions of work and maternity relief. Article 51 (A) (e) imposes a fundamental duty on every citizen to renounce the practices derogatory to the dignity of women. To make this de jure equality into a de facto one, special legislations have been enacted from time to time in support of women.

WOMEN AND DEVELOPMENT

Development today is human development. It is a process of enlarging the choices for all people not just for one section of the society. Such a development process becomes unjust and inequitable if women are excluded from the benefit of participation. The concept of women's development in the earlier phase of development planning was mainly 'welfare oriented.' Women's education during sixties received priorities along with the measures to improve maternal and child health and nutrition services. There was a definite shift in the approach from 'welfare' to 'development,' during the seventies, which started recognizing women as participants of development. The Eighties adopted a multi-disciplinary approach with a special thrust on the three-core sector of health, education and employment. Accordingly, priority was given to implementation of programmes for women under different sectors of agriculture and its allied activities of dairying, poultry, small animal husbandry, handlooms, handicrafts, small scale industries etc. Recognising the role and contribution of women in development the nineties made a beginning in concentrating on training-cum-income generation programmes for women with the ultimate objective of making them economically independent and self-reliant.

Developmental policies and programmes, both in women specific and women related sectors, put into action through various Five Year Plans, have brought forth a perceptible improvement in the socio-economic status of women in the country. The bulk of women workers have all along been engaged in agriculture and allied activities.

According to National Commission on Labour, the majority of women have been employed on unskilled jobs or on such economic activities where more simple and traditional skills are required. Vocational guidance and training of girls have, in fact, long been neglected in the economy, primarily because the girls were considered to be the bread winner in the traditional family structure. Consequently majority of girls are educated without any career planning for them. For rational distribution of women labour in economic activities it will be desirable to give preference to women for training in such trades and occupations for which they have special aptitude (National Commission on Labour, p. 381).

The Commission has also pointed out that the spread of location particularly in urban areas, has opened up more employment opportunities for women in non-manual, clerical, administrative and professional work. Employment for women is now open in business firms, secretariat, teaching, nursing and journalism etc.[6]

Contribution of women towards development of this country is comparatively a new area. Despite the fact that women constitute nearly 50 per cent of the Indian population and play a significant role both as housewives and also as workers, hardly any attention has been paid to assess their contribution to the economy.

Thus the Indian society has hardly bothered to pay attention to its womenfolk. This as well has been the case in most developing countries which women made the UN report, prepared at the time of women decade, to conclude that while women and girls contributed half of the world's population, did two-thirds of the world work hours and yet received only a tenth of the world's income and owned less than a hundredth of the world property. This very aptly sums up the status of women in a male dominated world.[7]

DEVELOPMENT POLICIES FOR WOMEN

Since the 1950s, when development planning first came into the international spotlight, a number of approaches, having different effects on women, have been tried. They may be detailed as follows:

Welfare: This was the earliest approach. It dominated from 1950 to 1970 and is still widely used. Its main purpose was to enable women to be better mothers which was seen as their main role in society;

Equity: This was the original approach of women in development and was utilized during the Decade for Women

1975-85. Women were seen as active participants in the development process;

Anti-Poverty: It aimed to increase the productivity of poor women and saw their poverty as a problem of underdevelopment not of subordination;

Efficiency: This is the most prevalent approach used today. Its aim is to ensure that development is efficient and effective;

Empowerment: An approach articulated by third world feminists since the mid-1980s. It aims to empower women through greater self-reliance and sees women's oppression as stemming not only from male patriarchal attitudes but also from colonial and neo-colonial oppression.[8]

Why Do Women Lag Behind?

Some case studies have been taken up to analyse the reasons for the backwardness of women in relation to the status of development prevalent in the country today.

1. Early marriage
2. The dowry system
3. Lack of education
4. Lack of economic independence
5. Social customs and traditions

To be a female in India is to be less than a human. She is considered a burden on her family, right from her existence in the womb. The girl child is neglected and deprived of most of the basic needs for proper growth. This attitude is rooted in the Indian social system. She is a victim of social stigma.

The degree of her miseries may change from rural to urban, from community to community and from family to family, but the basic social attitude of looking at her as an inferior being is universally the same.[9]

Why Focus on Women?

1. *Firstly:* Women constitute one half of the segment of population in India. We cannot afford to keep them out of the mainstream.

2. *Secondly:* Women are vital and productive workers in India's national economy. Women make one third of the labour force.

3. *Thirdly:* The poorer the family, the greater is the dependence on women's economic productivity. Enhancing women's economic productivity is an important strategy for improving the welfare of Indian households below the poverty line.

4. *Fourthly:* There is a significant gap between women's, especially rural women's potential and actual productivity. The productivity gap of poor women is much wider than that of the poor men. Therefore, women will gain more proportionately, if investment allocation and development efforts are shifted in their favour.

5. *Fifthly:* Women's earning have a positive correlation with children's health, nutrition levels and education. Studies have shown that Indian women contribute a much larger share of their earning to basic family maintenance than the men.[10]

Improving women's productivity, income and quality of life, therefore implies a multi-dimensional contribution to overall growth and development.

How to Focus on Women?

Women are central to the success of poverty alleviation efforts. This realisation brings women at the center stage of development efforts. The key to programming for women lies in recognizing their problems and constraints and programmes should be adaptable to suit their specific needs.

Today, the women's concern in all sectors, education and literacy, health and nutrition, training and income generation, legislative and judicial reforms—has been flag-marked. The challenge lies in converting these concerns into reality. Strategies for empowering women and rural women in particular would have to be sharpened to be effective.

1. Direct involvement of women in programming and management.
2. Effective collaboration with community organisations.
3. Organising and strengthening women's groups.
4. Sensitisation and advocacy for gender just society.
5. Prioritising women's needs.
6. Registration of new voluntary societies.[11]

Why Women Work (or) Why Do Women Seek Employment?

Causes that prompt women to enter into employment are as complex as those influencing other choices that affect their way of life. It is generally believed that socio-cultural changes play a very important role in creating a situation in which women would like to seek employment.

In one of the ILO studies dealing with women's employment, it was presumed that motives differed with marital status both objectively and subjectively. Not only the economic needs but the motivational reasons also vary with marital status. They broadly mentioned two reasons:

(*a*) Women's economic needs; and

(*b*) National necessity for increased production.[12]

Some other studies have brought to light the fact that loneliness is a powerful motive for women to seek employment outside their homes.[13]

The Ministry of Labour, Government of India has pointed out whatsoever the stage of economic or social development of a country, four factors prevail which lead women to join the work force. They are:

- The inadequate income of the principal earner which forces a women to work and supplement the income;

- Mishaps, such as incapacity of the bread winner;
- Death of the bread winner;
- A women's desire for economic independence or for securing higher standard of living; and
- There is also a desire on the part of the women to give expression to their own talents and skills.[14]

Female Work Participation Rate

The role of women in socio-economic development has undergone a marked change over the years. The world of women is no longer confined to periphery of household activities. Today they contribute in the promotion of economic development in different capacities.

Female labour participation rate in India has been much lower than in other countries. Due to awareness in women and effects of women's liberation movement etc., the female work participation rate has increased recently.[15]

Table 1.1 Area-wise Female Work Participation Rate in India

Year	*Rural*	*Urban*
1981	23.06	8.31
1991	27.90	9.34
2001 [Census Total]	30.98	11.55
NSS (1999-2000)	29.90	13.90

Sources: 1. Census of India, 1991.
2. Computed by author from National Family Health Survey (NFHS) and census estimates.

It is clear from the table 1.1 that Female Work Participation Rate (FWPR) in both rural and urban areas show an upward trend. But in urban areas, the increase in Female Work Participation Rate (FWPR) is very less when compared to rural areas during the corresponding period. Thus women are actively participating in rural areas as compared to urban areas.

Percentage of Female Workers in the 15-59 Age Group in Different States in India

In case of females, the interstate variations in urban areas were nearly half of that of rural areas. The rural female work participation rates were more than 50 per cent in A.P Karnataka, Maharashtra and Tamilnadu. On the other hand it was lower than 10 per cent in Haryana, Himachal Pradesh and Punjab. It is clear in the table 1.2.

There can be many reasons for low Female Work Participation Rate (FWPR). In many communities there is a reluctance to admit that women go out to work. One of the reason for too low a figure for Punjab can be existing social norms which prohibit women's participation in economic activity. Similarly there are certain categories of women workers like contract workers, domestic workers etc., whose services remain unquantified.[16]

Table 1.2 Percentage of Female Workers in the 15-59 Age Group in Different States in India

States	*Rural*	*Urban*
Andhra Pradesh	61.30	20.23
Assam	13.45	13.18
Bihar	19.18	9.17
Goa	26.21	25.90
Gujarat	43.64	18.92
Haryana	6.34	12.07
Himachal Pradesh	9.52	19.02
Jammu	12.09	16.16
Karnataka	54.65	25.75
Kerala	16.79	15.70
Madhya Pradesh	48.90	21.70
Maharashtra	56.22	19.40
Orissa	21.63	17.30

(Contd...)

States	*Rural*	*Urban*
Punjab	5.03	12.97
Rajasthan	24.33	10.92
Tamilnadu	54.71	28.85
West Bengal	19.22	14.20
Uttar Pradesh	13.10	9.63
New Delhi	6.57	15.76
North-Eastern States	38.80	35.01
India	28.67	19.00

Sources: 1. Census of India, 1991.
2. Computed by author from National Family Health Survey (NFHS) and census estimates.

National Machinery for Empowering Women

The Department of Women and Child Development, being the National Machinery of Empowering women in the country is made responsible for mainstreaming women into national development by raising their overall status on par with that of men. The programmes of the Department include continuing education and training, employment and income generation, welfare and support services and gender sensitisation and awareness generation.

Rashtriya Mahila Kosh (RMK)

It is an innovative venture established in 1993 to facilitate credit support/micro-financing to poor and assetless women, struggling in the informal sector, works through the medium of NGO's as its channelising agencies for identification of borrowers, delivery of credit support and also recovery. In addition, RMK also supports its NGO partners, to form women's thrift and credit societies, which are popularly known as Self Help Groups.[17]

National Commission for Women (NCW)

The National Commission for Women, a statutory body was set up in 1992 to safeguard the rights and interests of women. It also set up parivarik Mahila Lok Adalats and extended speedy justice to approximately 7000 women. The other issues taken by the commission during the plan period included welfare of women prisoners, women and children involved in the sex trade, reservation for women in parliament and state legislature, Anti-Arrack movements etc.[18]

Poverty Eradication through Women Development: Rural Women—The Key to Ending Hunger

It has now been sufficiently established that poor women's contribution towards family survival in rural areas is higher than that of men's and that the contribution of women towards the survival of the household during the periods of economic crisis in rural households goes up to 100 per cent to meet the basic survival needs of households.[19]

The ILO estimates that between one fourth and one third of all rural households in some countries are headed by females (Ghana, Malawi and Sudan) while in other countries the proportion is estimated at between 5-20 per cent.

It is pointed out that 30 to 35 per cent of Indian rural households are headed by women and thus in most cases dependent exclusively on female income. Even where there is a male earner, women's earnings form a major part of the income of poor households. Moreover compared to men, women contribute a large share of what they earn to the basic family maintenance.

These studies prove that the poorer the family, the greater is the dependence on women's income, despite the triple burden of reproduction, domestic labour and productive labour.[20]

Magnitude and Characteristics of Women in Poverty

Of the estimated 1.3 billion people living in poverty, more than 70 per cent are female. This feminisation of poverty is the tragic consequence of women's unequal access to economic opportunities.

Women face all manner of cultural, social, legal and economic obstacles that men even poor men do not. They typically work for longer hours, and are paid lower wages. A study in Nepal found that on an average, poor women worked eleven hours a day, men seven and a half hours. Poor women often have too many children spaced too close together to the detriment of their health.

The number of rural women living in absolute poverty rose by nearly 50 per cent over the past two decades. The majority of them belong to socially and economically backward communities. They are substantially less literate and more assetless than their males. Poor women provide great importance to expenditure—saving activities—through free collection of fuel, fodder and other necessities. Poor women have a very lengthy work life which starts from a very young age.[21]

Statement of the Problem

A close look at the way poverty eradication programmes are talked about clearly reveals that the task assumed is fulfilled, when programmes have reached the people. This tendency has created and perpetuated over the years, a feeling among the poor to become dependent on the feeding bottles of development agencies. The poor people are seen and made to see themselves as 'targets', beneficiaries' and recipients of development assistance. This state of affairs has left them in a very vulnerable position. Thus government and other outside agencies have instead of being supportive, acted in a directive manner. The poor may need outside help to perform catalytic and promotional functions, until such time as the poor are sufficiently organized to claim their own economic, social and political rights.[22]

What is needed is the creation of an enabling environment and evolving, supporting and strengthening appropriate institutional mechanisms, so that even poor people can explore their own creative potential.[23]

However, the poor are not 'have nots.' They have detailed knowledge of their immediate environment and development constraints. Most of them are able bodied, hard working, have some technical or entrepreneurial skills, capacity for self-organisation and a social and cultural wealth. What they lack, however, is sufficient opportunity to widen and diversify their resource base (Verhagen, 1987).[24]

They are poor because they cannot retain the genuine return for their labour. The reason for this is obvious: they have no control over capital that calls the tune. The poor work for the benefit of someone who controls the capital (Yunus, 1997).[25] Therefore the question is how can the opportunities for the poor be widened and their control over capital enhanced?

Objectives of the Present Study

The following are the major objectives of the study:

1. To study the present socio-economic status of the women under the existing social hierarchy;
2. To review women development programmes and the creation of self-employment opportunities for the educated and uneducated unemployed women in three revenue divisions of the Kurnool district;
3. To analyse the effect of women development programmes like DWCRA, SHG on the generation of additional income for educated and uneducated women;
4. To examine and analyse the structural characteristics and functions of DWCRA and SHG's across the sample mandals in the district;
5. To explore the performance of DWCRA and SHG's in terms of savings and credit mobilisation, income generation and asset creation;
6. To study the nature and extent of capacity building and social mobilisation.

Hypotheses

The following are the specific hypotheses of the study:

1. The larger the self-employment programmes, the greater the employment opportunities for women and the higher the level of development of women;
2. The larger the self-employment opportunities created for the unemployed women, the greater the scope for the generation of additional income and overall development of the society;
3. The structural characteristics and level of functions of DWCRA and SHG groups do not differ significantly among the sample mandals in the district;
4. The levels of social mobilisation by SHG's are positive to the level of development of the sample mandals in the district.

Research Design and Methodology—Universe of Study

Kurnool district has 54 mandals and 13 community development blocks. Of the total number of blocks, seven are backward blocks and the rest are ordinary.

The present study is concerned with the women development programmes particularly DWCRA and SHG in the three divisions of the district. With the help of a questionnaire, survey has been conducted to know whether these programmes are really fulfilling the objectives in generating additional employment for educated and uneducated women in Kurnool district.

Sample Design and Size

Ours is a multi-stage sample study of DWCRA or SHG's in the district. Among 28 states in India, we have chosen Andhra Pradesh not only because of our convenience and familiarity with the state but also because of the rapid strides made by the different SHG's and DWCRA groups in it.

At the second stage, we have selected Kurnool district of Rayalaseema region in Andhra Pradesh state.

At the third stage, we have randomly selected 15 mandals among 54 mandals of the district. As the district is divided into three revenue divisions, 5 mandals from each revenue division were selected.

At the fourth stage, we have chosen 10 sample groups from each mandal at random. Thus we arrived at 150 sample groups. The selection of groups themselves is based on a combination of random and purposive methods to ensure a representative picture of groups at mandal levels. Table 1.3 offers details of our samples, the basis of selection and their size at different levels.

Table 1.3 Sampling Units and Sampling Size

Sl.No.	*Sample Unit*	*Universe*	*Type of Sampling*	*Sampling Size*
1.	A.P	28 States	Purposive	1
2.	Kurnool district	Rayalaseema (4 Districts)	Purposive	1
3.	Mandals (Division-wise Selection)	54 Mandals	Random and Purposive	5 x 3=15 5 Mandals from each revenue division
4.	DWCRA / SHG	15 mandals	Random and Purposive Sampling	15 x 10 = 150 10 groups from each mandal
	Total	**15 x 10**		**150 groups**

Data Base

The present study is based on the collection of primary data and secondary data.

The primary data is collected from our sample units with the help of a structured schedule. It consists of eight parts. The first part of the schedule deals with the identification and general background of the respondents.

The second part deals with socio-economic profiles of the respondents, whereas the third part is concerned with questions related to communication knowledge and implementation of women development programmes.

The fourth part deals with the creation of employment opportunities for the educated and uneducated unemployed women in the pre-group period and post-group period. The fifth part deals with the source of finance for self-employment. The sixth part deals with the impact of group activity on the income of self-employed women. The seventh part deals with social mobilisation of the group. The eighth part deals with the opinions of the respondents regarding the quantum of financial aid provided and its proper use in the improvement of the status of the educated and uneducated unemployed women.

Further, researcher interviewed the leaders of several organisations of self-employment schemes and educated women to obtain necessary statistical data for the purpose of the study.

Secondly the study also covers secondary data from a multiplicity of agencies—national and international, official and non-official. The publication of World Bank, International Fund for Agricultural Development, ILO, FAO, UNDP, Indian Journal of Agricultural Economics, RBI, NABARD, and allied agencies provide a valuable source of data to our study dealing with empowerment of women and SHG's. The publications of the Government of India and Andhra Pradesh constitute an indispensable source. Discussions were held with the officials of NIRD, SIRD, DRDA, MDO, Offices, Banks and other organisations.

Analysis of Data

Raw data by itself may not and will not serve the purpose. Data analysis and processing are the logical steps. Analytical skills and statistical tools provide the sophistication that is needed to draw meaningful conclusions. Simple statistical tools like Mean and Standard deviation have been used for presenting the data in an appropriate manner. The significance of different variables with regard to women development programmes is highlighted through the calculation of the chi-square values. In addition to this, different types of bar diagrams (simple, multiple, subdivided and percentage), and pie diagram were used to represent the data and to make it easily comprehensible.

Design of Dissertation

The dissertation consists of eight chapters:

The *first* chapter deals in general with the development and empowerment of women. This chapter also explains about the work participation rate and employment of women. It also includes the study area, methodology used in the study, sampling technique used, objectives of the study, hypotheses, collection and analysis of data;

The *second* chapter deals with five-year plans and women development programmes in India and Andhra Pradesh;

The *third* chapter deals with the origin and progress of women self-help groups and DWCRA groups;

The *fourth* chapter deals with characteristics and performance of sample self-help groups in the study area—Kurnool district;

The *fifth* chapter deals with income and employment generation and capacity building through DWCRA and self-help groups;

The *sixth* chapter deals with poverty alleviation through social mobilisation in the study area—Kurnool district;

The *seventh* chapter deals with the problems of women development with reference to the DWCRA and SHG approach. It also includes the problems faced by women in their economic activities.

The eighth chapter covers the conclusions of the study and some policy implications as well as suggestions for increasing the employment opportunities and income earning capacity of women and for the overall development of women in the country. It also covers some suggestions as remedies in solving various problems faced by women in their group activities.

Summing Up

Indisputably, India is committed to the cause of empowerment of women. However, the journey towards progress is long and arduous.

India has witnessed great changes in the last two decades. Age-old prejudices and gender-based biases are giving way to gender equality and harmonious development. However in the present circumstances empowerment of women is possible more effectively through economic empowerment rather than through reservation of some seats in parliament or state legislatures.

All over the world so also in India poverty has got a feminine face. Since majority of women are poverty stricken they have to be made self dependent by ensuring their access to credit. They must go through training and orientation courses so that they can become independent and intelligent.

Women and development should be linked together. In the context of development, women's empowerment is a key goal but it is achieved to the extent that they strive for it. Empowerment of rural women would in real sense hasten the pace of economic development. They need to be empowered in both ownership as well as management aspects of agricultural and allied services which would help to raise their income and justify their importance and contribution to rural economy. However, the emergence and progress of the DWCRA, and SHG movement is expected to bring about greater social mobilisation through economic empowerment and capacity building.

REFERENCES

1. S. Wal, Shruti Banerji, "Encyclopaedia of Women as Human Resource in 21st Century and Beyond," (Volume 4), Woman and Globalisation.
2. Cagatay, N. and S. Ozler (1995), "Feminisation of the Labour Force," World Development Report, Vol. 23, No. 11, Nov. *Oxford.*
3. S.Wal, Shruti Banerji, "Encyclopaedia of Women as Human Resource in 21st Century and Beyond," (Volume 4), Women and Globalisation.
4. Ninth Five Year Plan, 1997-2002, Vol. II.
5. N.Lalitha, "Rural Women Empowerment and Development Banking," *Kanishka Publishers,* New Delhi.
6. G.Standing (1989), "Global Feminisation Through Flexible Labour," World Development Report, Vol. 17, No. 7, *Oxford.*
7. Mira Seth, 'Women's Development: Indian Initiatives,' *Kurukshetra,* August 1995.
8. Maithili Viswanatham, "Social Framework and Strategies in Women's Development," *Printwell,* Jaipur (India).
9. Dr.Sobha, Dr.Vijaya Lakshmi Rama Mohan and M.S.N.Reddy, 'Why Do Women Lag Behind,' *Social Welfare,* September 2001.
10. Walker and Ryan (1988), "Against the Odesi Village and Household Economies in India's Semi-and Tropics," Unpublished Manuscript, ICRISAT, Hyderabad.
11. Urvashi Gulati, Dept. Director, NIRD, Rajendra Nagar, Hyderabad, 'Women's Development in India with Special Reference to Rural Women,' *Kurukshetra,* August, 1995.
12. An International Survey of the Conditions of Working Women with Home and Family Responsibilities, Carried Out by the International Labour Office, as Quoted in Myrdal, Alva and Klein, Viola Women's Two Roles, London, Routledge and Kegan Paul, 1962, p. 82.
13. Zweig, F. "Women's Life and Labour," London, Victor Gollanz, 1952, p. 74.
14. "International Trends." Government of India, Women in Employment, Labour Bureau, Ministry of Labour and Employment, 1964, pp. 58-59.

15. Thakur, R.N. (2000), "Education and Political Status of Indian Women: Key to Economic Development," Women and Economic Development, A. Banerjee and R.K. Sen (Ed.).

16. 'Women's Empowerment in India: Evidence from NFHS,' *Economic and Political Weekly,* Vol. XXXIX, No. 7, Feb 14-20, 2004.

17. IX Five Year Plan 1997-2002, Volume II — Thematic Issues and Sectoral Programmes, Government of India, Planning Commission, New Delhi.

18. Ibid.

19. N. Lalitha, "Rural Women Empowerment and Development Banking," *Kanishka Publishers,* New Delhi.

20. International Fund for Agricultural Development (IFAI-2001), "Rural Poverty Report, the Challenging of Ending Rural Poverty," *Oxford,* New York.

21. N. Lalitha, "Rural Women Empowerment and Development Banking," *Kanishka Publishers,* New Delhi.

22. Lalit Kumar Tyagi, 'Poverty Eradication Through Self-Help Promotion,' *Indian Association of Social Science Institutions* (IASSI).

23. Ibid.

24. Rouilled d oregruil H. (1984). Cited in Verhagen 1987.

25. Yunus Muhammed (1997) "Toward Creating a Poverty-free World. Lecture" Delivered at Institute of Social Sciences, New Delhi.

2

Women Development Programmes and Five Year Plans

Introduction

It is not surprising that the development of women in India has been the centre stage of its development planning. In most South Asian countries, the status of women is low and their socio-economic conditions are much more depressed than that of men. In India, while the constitutional and legal status of women is equal to that of men in all respects, the reality, is that they suffer in all spheres of social and economic life. Poverty, in fact, is one of the aspects of their deprived condition. Low earning, lower wages, low level of skills, limited access to the factors of production, low literacy, malnutrition, poor standard of health, greater exposure to domestic violence and vulnerability to sexual crimes are some of the other dimensions of their low status.

Today, the women's concerns in all sectors—education and literacy, health and nutrition, training and income generation, legislative and judicial reforms have been flagged. The empowering strategies would need to be further sharpened to make them effective and result oriented. The vision for the future should be built on the achievements to date and fully reflect a gender perspective. There is, therefore, a need for comprehensive and holistic policy on women. This would enable the country to fulfill the constitutional mandate of women's equality and objective of women's total involvement in national development.

Women as Critical Agents of Change

Women need to be viewed not as beneficiaries but as active participants in the process of development and change. Her capacity to work, her knowledge and her skills are often the only resources to call upon for survival in poor households. Thus women become the critical actors in the process of moving their families out of poverty. The key to programming for women lies in recognising their problems and constraints and then adopting a flexible approach that permits programmes to be adopted to suit their specific needs.[1]

We have women in India who have made their mark in various fields of activities and have acquired eminence side by side with men.

But in spite of this the present day women in India, particularly in rural areas, tribal areas, and in slum areas of the cities and towns suffer from illiteracy, ill health, lack of opportunities for economic activities, political activities and social activities.

In the rural areas they still continue to suffer from various deprivations, probably due to the fact that we have not sincerely, actively and emotionally worked to raise the position and status of women in the rural, tribal and urban areas. Time has come to give serious attention to the uplift of the women in these areas. A concerted effort has to be made to bring them within the folds of:

- panchayat and municipal activities
- organisational activities
- education, social and religious activities
- economic activities

To achieve the above objectives the existing women's voluntary organisations and semi-official organisations have to be initiated, and the central and state governments have to evolve social legislation and administrative machinery to make them effective. Government efforts alone will not be enough. The efforts of the individuals and voluntary organisations have to play an important role.[2]

Women and children, who represent more than two-third (68 per cent) of the country's total population, constitute the most important target groups in the context of the present day developmental planning. Therefore, their concerns are placed on the priority list of the country's developmental agenda. Needless to say, they have the strength and support of the constitution.[3]

Though women contribute substantially to the economic resources of the family both by way of services rendered and wages earned, yet their potential is not duly recognized. There is now an increasing realisation of the fact that women play an active role and they have to be involved in developmental schemes. Gradually some measures have been adopted to involve women in developmental programmes.

Developmental policies and programmes, both in the women specific and women related sectors, put into action through various Five Year Plans, have brought forth a perceptible improvement in the socio-economic status of women in the country.

First Plan

In 1953 the Government of India set up Central Social Welfare Board (CSWB), outside the framework of government with a view to combining governmental and non-governmental resources and creating a network of agencies to deliver services in maternity and child care, health, education and training to women.

In 1954, the Central Social Welfare Board introduced the welfare extension projects and in the absence of voluntary women's organisations in rural areas promoted local women's organisations through its project implementation committees which were converted into Mahila Mandals.[4]

Second Plan

In 1958 the CSWB also introduced a socio-economic programme to promote women's economic activities. The programme was gradually extended to Mahila Mandals in the form of production units of handicrafts, dairy, poultry, piggery, sheep breeding and allied activities to expand women's employment.

Successive annual conferences of Development Commissioners later, emphasized the need to bring women into the ambit of the community development programme in a bigger way. On an experimental basis two Gram Sevikas per block were sanctioned, They were expected to work with Gram Sevikas as a team and work for women bringing to them new knowledge and information for effective utilisation of household and farm resources. Women social education organisers were appointed to provide social education to women and promote community participation.[5] The forum for promoting various activities among women, initially started as social education centres, later came to be popularly known as Mahila Mandals.

However, our planners were convinced that women needed training in household management, child development, nutrition and home crafts etc; 25 home-science wings were started in 1955 with the existing extension training centres for the training of village level women workers. The training was imparted for a period of one year to a batch of 20 trainees. The number of these training wings went up to 46 by the year 1959 and the capacity was increased from 20 to 40 to train 10,000 Gram Sevikas who were to be appointed at the rate of 2 per block. As stated earlier towards the end of the Second Five Year Plan, the Intensive Agricultural District Programme (IADP) was launched in 28 districts with assured irrigation.

Third Plan

At the beginning of the Third Five Year Plan when the major emphasis in the rural development programme again shifted to agriculture to meet the food shortages and achieve self-sufficiency in foodgrains the village level workers had to be utilized more for agricultural extension work and the women programme received a set back.

The Applied Nutrition Programme (ANP) was introduced during the Third Five Year Plan period with the objectives of imparting nutrition education to mothers through demonstration feeding, production programme and training of women functionaries. The programme was implemented through women's grassroot organisations (Mahila Mandals) and covered around 34 per cent of all community development blocks.[6]

Fourth Plan

In the Fourth Five Year Plan a special central sector scheme for rural women called—"composite programmes for women and pre-school children" was introduced with the components of nutrition, economic activity and training of associated women workers. This scheme was implemented in non-applied nutrition programme blocks.

The other two schemes namely:

(a) *Incentive Awards to Mahila Mandals*—Mahila mandals showing good performance during a year were given cash awards for undertaking certain economic projects;

(b) *Training of associate women workers were introduced*—The latter scheme was designed to provide orientation to selected women having leadership qualities in organising village women and assisting them in implementing various welfare programmes.

Fifth Plan

During the Fifth Five Year Plan, the components of demonstration feeding in nutrition programme was discontinued and a new scheme for promotion and strengthening of Mahila Mandals was introduced to promote local leadership among rural women.

- Another scheme known as the *Promotion of Voluntary Action* was initiated. The objective of this scheme was to utilize the potential of these organisations in the implementation of various programmes meant for the development of women and children;
- The concept of *minimum needs* was introduced in this plan which sought to provide elementary education, primary healthcare and nutrition, drinking water, house sites and other basic amenities to the rural poor;
- Establishment of *eight Home Science Colleges* within the agricultural universities, for providing education, research facilities and extension services to rural farm families;
- The CSWB introduced *dairy scheme* in 1973 to assist rural women to benefit from dairy development programmes undertaken by the government;
- The Board initiated a programme for *promoting Vocational Training of Women* in 1975 to increase their employability;
- In 1975-76, the Indian Council of Agricultural Research initiated a scheme to train women in simple technology;
- *Eighteen Krishi Vigyan Kendras* and seven Trainers' Training centres were established in 16 states and union territories to train farm women and girls in agricultural operations as well as in home science, home crafts and cottage industries;[7]
- Adoption of World Plan of action for the international Women's Decade: equality, development and peace, by the UN General Assembly during the year 1975-76 resulted in number of developments;
- A *new division (Bureau) for women's welfare and development* was established within the Ministry for Social Welfare entrusted with the task of coordinating,

receiving and initiating policies for women's development and service;

- A *special cell* was established within the Ministry of Labour and Employment to give greater attention to women's employment needs and problems;
- The *Equal Remuneration* Act (1976) initiated the process of removing wage disparities between men and women in the productive sector;
- A similar unit has also been established within the Ministry of Rural Reconstruction to review and supervise development programmes for rural women;
- In 1977 the planning commission appointed a working group on Employment of women;
- The Ministry of Agriculture and Rural Development appointed a working group on the development of village level organisation of rural women to review the existing programmes.

Sixth Plan

During this plan, a variety of programmes were taken up under different sectors of development to ameliorate the working conditions of women and to raise their economic and social status.

The Sixth Five-Year Plan (1980-85) for the first time in India's Development Planning included a chapter on women and development. It emphasized that 'economic' independence would accelerate the improvement of the status of women. The world conference on Agriculture Reform and Rural Development (WCARRD) in 1979 had suggested that national governments should take action to integrate women in rural development programmes.

(*a*) Three Regional Vocational training centres one each at Bangalore, Bombay and Trivandrum and a National Vocational Training Institute at Delhi with a total annual in take capacity of 600 women trainees were set up by the Directorate General of Employment and Training;

(b) Apart from these, 144 Industrial Training Institutes exclusively meant for women were functioning in different states by the end of the sixth-plan. The in take capacity in these institutions is 11,200 per annum;

(c) In the rural development sector the integrated Rural Development Programme (IRDP) accorded priority to women;

(d) A decision was also taken that minimum of 1/3 rd of the beneficiaries under Training for Rural Youth for Self Employment (TRYSEM) would be women;

(e) A new scheme namely Development of Women and Children in Rural Areas (DWCRA) was started in 1982-83 as a pilot project in 50 blocks of the country;

(f) The scheme of Krishi Vigyan Kendras introduced for bridging the gap between farmers knowledge and available technology, also covcred women;

(g) In order to encourage girls into elementary and higher education, a centrally sponsored scheme was taken up for providing financial assistance to educationally backward states for establishing non-formal education centres exclusively for girls;

(h) To boost enrollment in the primary classes early childhood education centres for children in the age group 3-6 years were set up as adjuncts to primary schools for the first time in the sixth plan;[8]

(i) The Scheduled Caste and Scheduled Tribe girls continued to receive higher rates of post metric scholarships. Other incentives include free clothing and free tuition;

(j) Separate universities for women have been established in the states of Tamilnadu and Andhra Pradesh;

(*k*) Special programmes were taken up for women in adult education centres providing education in subjects like health, nutrition, childcare and family planning;

(*l*) Under the scheme Science and Technology for women's, wide spectrum of activities were taken up;

(*m*) Added impetus was given to the training of women in instrumentation technology;

(*n*) Tribal women were also trained as rural health workers in Maharashtra;

(*o*) A number of technology demonstration-cum-training centres at selected focal points all over the country were set up by National Research Development Corporation to provide expertise and resources to women entrepreneurs in respect of new technologies relevant to their daily needs and economic enterprises;

(*p*) A major step was taken by the University Grants Commission (UGC) to provide a boost to women's participation in the field of science and technology by enhancing by 10 years of age of eligibility for women scientists;

(*q*) Priority is given to pregnant and nursing mothers belonging to weaker sections. Under ICDS special nutrition provided to pregnant women and nursing mothers;

(*r*) Prophylaxis programmes against nutritional anaemia of pregnant and lactating mothers were implemented Iron and folic acid tablets were distributed;

(*s*) The female infant mortality rate had fallen;

(*t*) A number of welfare schemes for needy women were taken up;

(*u*) Nearly 3000 women were given training in skills in modern industries and provided employment under the scheme Employment and Income Generating Training cum production centres for women;

(v) Condensed courses of education were organized by a number of voluntary organisations benefiting 1,11,000 women;

(w) All India Radio, in collaboration with different state Governments and assisted by UNICEF organized 12 radio workshops on maternity and childcare. The Song and Drama divisions of All India Radio took up programmes for women's upliftment. The Film and Television Institute of India prepared programmes highlighting women's problems and development schemes for them;

(x) Under the "Socio-Economic Programme" 3589 units were sanctioned with a coverage of 47,011 women. The scheme of 'Assistance to women in distress' covered only 9,260 women through 267 vocational courses in non-traditional trades with the aim of making these women economically independent;

(y) The Press Information Bureau took up a programme of mass education and information to promote positive social attitudes towards women and motivate people to fight social evils like dowry, child marriage, alcohol addiction, etc. A booklet entitled 'Status of Women' was published by the Directorate of Field Publicity.

Thus for creating increasing awareness of the role of women in development and the need for improvement of their status, various media units under the Ministry of Information and Broadcasting presented appealing programmes on social and economic problems and other related issues faced by women.

Seventh Plan

In the Seventh Plan the basic approach would be to inculcate confidence among women and bring about an awareness of their own potential for development, as also of their rights and privileges. The various mass communication media would be utilized extensively in this task.

Special measures would be initiated for strict enforcement of the Dowry Prohibition Act and also to prevent harassment and atrocities on women.

In Seventh Five Year Plan, an integrated multi disciplinary approach has been adopted covering employment, education, health, nutrition, application of science and technology and other related aspects in areas of interest of women. Efforts would be made to extend facilities for income generating activities and to enable women to participate actively in socio-economic development.

Major Programmes During Seventh Plan

(a) ***Education:*** At elementary stage, education has been made free for girls in all states or union territories. Priority would continue to be given to women in teacher's training programmes. Talented girls would be encouraged to pursue higher education. In order to promote technical and vocational education for girls, more women's polytechnics have been planned to set up, To boost education among the girls of the scheduled castes and tribes additional facilities shall continue to provide under the "Development of Backward Classes". Financial assistance is envisaged for construction of hostel buildings for girls at district level and for the purchase of furniture, Under the National Sports Policy, participation of women and girls in sports and games shall be encouraged. For retention of girl child in school, reduction in dropout and promotion of adult literacy, a number of special initiatives were taken;

(b) ***Health:*** The major thrust during this plan is towards the reduction of prevailing high maternal and infant mortality rates, For this purpose emphasis is placed on the expansion of Maternity and Child Health Centres (MCH). The health and family welfare services are to be made available to all women in the reproductive age group. Specifically, schemes for giving tetanus toxoid to mothers and providing proper ante-natal care will be taken up on a sizeable scale, Besides, nutrition supplements, iron and folic acid tablets would be given to mothers for bridging the calorie-vitamin and mineral deficiency gap as well as for fighting anaemia;

(c) ***Employment:*** Agriculture and Allied Sectors: Special attention would be given to improve existing skills of women and imparting to them new skills under the programmes of farmers training, fodder production, application of pesticides, budding and grafting, training in horticulture, fisheries, poultry, dairy, social forestry etc.;

(d) ***Rural Development:*** The IRDP meant for the poorest in the rural area, has been formulated for creating assets with a view to increasing the productivity and income generation ability of the beneficiaries in a specified period of time. About 20 million beneficiaries would be covered during the seventh plan. Efforts have been made under this programme to select households headed by women beneficiaries. The Scheme of Development of Women and Children in Rural Areas (DWCRA) would be strengthened and modified in order to ensure that the benefits reach the target groups;

(e) ***Industry:*** Public sector undertakings shall be persuaded to sponsor ancillary industries in collaboration with state level agencies dealing with developmental programmes for women to provide increased employment opportunities around them. Attempts would also be made to identify and target the women beneficiaries' under Entrepreneurial Development Programme (EDP) and Industrial Estates;

(f) ***Village and Small Scale Industries:*** In connection with village and small-scale industries, the scope of specific training programmes for women entrepreneurs shall be widened in order to fully familiarize them with

the technical know-how needed for setting up enterprises;

Presently, some special provisions in terms of infrastructure facilities like industrial sheds are being extended to women entrepreneurs. As this facility is not adequate, efforts would be made to set up mini-industrial estates exclusively for women on a much larger scale. Special facilities like sheds and plots at subsidized rates to units exclusively run by women and or employing female labour will be given;

The National Small Industries Corporation and other apex organisations would extend support for marketing, product design and financial support for raw material procurement. Women are expected to obtain sizeable employment under this sector;

(g) ***Khadi and Village Industries:*** During the Seventh plan the employment coverage under khadi and village industries is likely to increase from the present 3.8 million persons to 5.86 million persons. A considerable proportion of this additional employment will come to women, and the percentage share of women is expected to increase from 46 to 48 per cent during the seventh plan;

(h) ***Science and Technology:*** Programme on Science and Technology for women's would be further strengthened to identify, formulate, sponsor and implement research and development, demonstration and extension programmes, with special emphasis on providing opportunities for gainful employment or self-employment to women specially to those in rural areas;

(i) ***Social Welfare:*** Under the seventh plan, programmes of social welfare for women are meant to supplement the services available to women under other development sectors, The central Social Welfare Board shall continue to extend grants-in-aid to voluntary agencies to set up a variety of income generating units under the 'Socio-Economic Programmes' for the benefit of needy women;

Under the plan, a new scheme namely, women's Development Corporation shall be taken up for promoting employment-generating activities by supporting schemes for women's group and women from poorer sections of society;

A women's development planning and monitoring cell shall be set up for the collection of data and monitoring of plan programmes;

(j) ***Voluntary Organisations:*** These agencies have to be stimulated to extend their programmes to rural, hilly and backward areas. Besides they can also take up programmes of vocational training for adult women and girls from poorer sections on a large scale in order to enlarge and improve the avenues of employment;

(k) ***Monitoring:*** A proper monitoring mechanism will be developed to ensure optimal utilisation of facilities meant for women under different sectors and to minimize leakages. The special cells, which are being set up in the Ministries for this purpose, will be strengthened in order to ensure proper monitoring and coordination of different schemes;

(l) ***Other Measures:***

(a) Implementation of the equal Remuneration Act will be strengthened to ensure that women workers are paid wages as prescribed in the Act from time to time;

(b) Similarly, studies will be undertaken on the implementation of the Factories Act 1948, the Plantation Labour Act 1951 and Mines Act of 1952 to assess whether the interests of women are adequately protected;

(c) Emphasis will also be placed on the study and identification of factors that hinder women's employment;

(*d*) Special agencies will be set up for extending credit facilities for self-employment and home based workers;

(*e*) Relaxation of age limit for women for entry into government services and public sector undertakings will be considered;

(*f*) Avenues for creation of part time employment for women will also be explored.[9]

Some Other Developmental Programmes During Seventh Plan

(a) ***The Council for Advancement of Peoples Action and Rural Technology (CAPART):*** It is registered under the Societies Registration Act in September 1986 is headed by the Minister of Rural Development. It promotes rural technology and innovations designed to reduce the drudgery of women in several areas of household economic activities;

(b) ***Rural Sanitation Programme:*** This programme was launched in 1986. It is designed to ensure privacy for women through construction of sanitary latrines for individual households;

(c) ***Jawahar Rozgar Yojana:*** The rural wage employment programmes, NREP and RLEGP got merged into a single scheme, Jawahar Rozgar Yojana in 1989. Under this programmes, wage employment is provided in rural areas particularly on public works, which are of direct benefit to Village Community. Under JRY 30 per cent of employment opportunities are reserved for women;[10]

(d) ***Nehru Rozgar Yojana:*** This programme was launched in October 1989, It is targeted towards persons living below the poverty line in urban areas. The scheme envisages 30 per cent of beneficiaries should be women.[11]

Review of the VII Plan and the Annual Plans 1990-1992

The seventh plan continued the strategy, The National Commission on self-employed women and women in informal sector submitted a comprehensive report titled "SHRAMSHAKTI", analyzing the problems effecting large number of women in the informal sector and the steps needed to give them a better deal.[12]

A significant step taken in the seventh plan towards including women's status was identification of a number of beneficiary oriented programmes under the various sectors of development.

The number of women beneficiaries assisted under the IRDP was 34.33 lakhs in seventh plan. The percentage of women beneficiaries increased from 9.9 in 1985-86 to 25.6 in 1989-90. Under the TRYSEM 4.59 lakh women were trained for self-employment in the seventh plan. Under both the programmes the minimum percentage of women's beneficiaries has now been raised to 40 per cent.

Development of Women and Children in Rural Areas (DWCRA), launched in 1982-83 to increase rural women's access to employment, skills, training, credit and other support services, covered 187 districts in 1990-91. The programme follows a group approach. Over 28,000 women' groups were formed in the seventh plan.[13]

In 1989, out of 68.85 lakh members of dairy cooperative societies, 14 per cent were women. In Gujarat and Andhra Pradesh milk dairy women's cooperative societies were formed, Some women's cooperative societies were set up in fisheries sector also. Short-term courses for women organized in fish processing, preservation etc., Nearly 52,000 women are expected to have benefited under the special Live Stock breeding programmes, where a target of 10 per cent was earmarked for women beneficiaries.

A National Training Institute for women was set up at 'NOIDA'. A new scheme was taken up by the Ministry of Labour by providing grant-in-aid to state governments setting of women's ITI's or wings. Seats for about 21,500 women were provided under this scheme.

The scheme of non-formal education, which was introduced in the sixth plan for implementation in educationally backward states, was modified during the seventh plan to cover urban slums, hilly, tribal areas and working children. About 65,000 centres were set up by the end of 1988-89 benefiting 16 lakh girls special cells were set up in the Directorate of adult education and resource centres to plan and administer women's education programmes and to encourage their participation.

The sports authority of India conducted National Sports Festival for women. Scholarships under sports talent search scheme were awarded to women.

Women's development centres were set up in 22 universities and colleges to bring about social awareness of women's issues and focus efforts on the development of rural women.

The universal immunisation programme which aims at universal coverage of pregnant women and infants, was extended to all districts in the country. Special centres were set up to impart nutrition education to mothers through home visits by multipurpose workers.

For tackling the problem of violence against women, including domestic violence, amendments to existing laws were carried out. The legislative provisions relating to rape were amended to accord better protection to women victims.

The important role of voluntary organisations in women's development was recognized. Grants were given to them to promote and support women's development.

To provide safe accommodation at reasonable rents to working women, construction of 597 hostels, with a capacity of 38,127 seats for working women taken up. To increase women's participation in development and help them to organize themselves, awareness generation camps were conducted.

The 1991 census reported 66.189 million were main workers and 25.21 million were marginal workers. The percentage of female main workers to total main workers was 23.19 per cent. The female work participation rate was 22.69 in 1991 as compared to 19.77 in 1981.

The overwhelming majority of women are engaged in the informal sector, which not only provides low returns but is also characterized by virtual inaccessibility to credit, technology, training and other facilities.

Eighth Plan—Objectives and Strategies

The eighth plan makes a shift from development to empowerment of women. A number of measures have been taken by the Government in this direction for social and economic emancipation of women.

These measures include employment and income generating activities including self-employment with training for upgradation of skills supported by welfare and developmental measures like improvement of health, the nutritional status etc.

A major thrust in strategy for women's development will be on the formation and strengthening of grassroot level women's groups which will articulate local women's needs and play an important role in decentralized planning and implementation of programmes.

A national commission on women has recently been set up to act as a watch dog body on matters concerning women. A commissioner of women's rights will be appointed.[14]

(a) ***Employment:*** Women, who form nearly half of the population, will be recognized as a target group in the promotion of employment. Special condensed, job-oriented courses will be organized for women.

Attempts would be made to expand women's employment in the household sector providing adequate support in the areas of technology upgradation, training, credit, raw materials and marketing.

The programmes of training of women in soil conservation, dairy development, social forestry and other occupations allied to agriculture like sericulture, dairy development, horticulture and poultry will be expanded.

Vocational training of women will be a special thrust area.[15] The training programmes for women in the ITI's and other training institutions will be diversified and expanded. Part time and short-term courses will be organized as per local needs of industries, New areas with a high employment potential will be identified. Women will be encouraged in new expanding areas of technical education such as electronics, computer systems, bio-engineering communications.

Measures will be taken to reduce the element of drudgery of women through improved sanitary and environmental conditions, smokeless chullahs, biogas, solar cookers and other low cost technologies.

(b) Education: Emphasis will be laid in the eighth plan on the creation of conditions, which would enable women to participate in the educational process in a more meaningful way.

Women access to science education has to be improved and this would require careful planning to generate a pool of trained mathematics and science teachers.

Priority will be to the generation of awareness about the need for improving women's status. Mass communication and media will be effectively geared to this end. Women's colleges, Universities and women's study centres will be encouraged to take up awareness generation activities through publication of women's journals and research on women's issues.

Programmes will be designed for destitute women and women in distress by providing the necessary rehabilitation measures to make them economically self-sufficient. Special projects will be developed for the economic rehabilitation of socially disadvantage groups of women like devadasis and prostitutes. Voluntary organisations will be promoted and supported to accelerate the process of women's development. Areas will be identified where the voluntary sector is weak.

Hostel facilities for working women with creche facilities will be increased for women migrating to towns, cities and metropolitan areas for employment.

Developmental Programmes During the Eighth Plan

(a) ***Mahila Samridhi Yojana (MSY):*** The Mahila Samridhi Yojana launched on 2nd October 1993. It is one of the innovative schemes for the economic betterment of rural women. It covers wide base of 70 per cent of total women population living in villages. The objective of the scheme is to encourage thrift among rural women, Under the scheme rural women are encouraged to save by providing direct cash incentives to supplement their individual savings. This scheme would assure theme of security in times of need and enable them to exercise greater control over household resources.

(b) ***Indira Awaas Yojana:*** It was started as an important component of RLEGP (now under JRY) aiming at the construction of dwelling units, free of cost for the poorest of the poor belonging to SC's/ST's and free bonded labourers under IAY, priority is given to widows and unmarried women. IAY houses, in all cases are allotted in the name of the women members of the household or in the joint names of husband and wife.

(c) ***Panchayat Raj:*** The Constitution Act, 1992 is the momentous step in the direction of translating this concept into a reality.[16] It provides reservation to women. One-third of the total number of seats, both in reserved and unreserved categories will be reserved for women in every panchayat on rotation basis, This applies to the posts of chairperson also. This will give women a greater say in matters of local administration. It is a novel experiment to involve women in their own uplift.

(d) ***National Commission for Women:*** The National Commission for women set up in 1992 to examine laws and ensure constitutional and other safeguards concerning women,[17] to study and evaluate various economic and social initiatives taken by the Government to scrutinize individual complaints of violation of women's rights.

(e) ***Rashtriya Mahila Kosh:*** It was set up in 1993 to provide credit to at least 2 lakh poorer women in the informal sector for income generation activities through NGO's and Institutions engaged in thrift and credit promotion.

(f) ***Indira Mahila Yojana (IMY):*** The IMY was launched in August 1995 in 200 blocks of the country, It's main objective is to give a forward thrust to the education, awareness, income generation capacities and employment of women. The platform for the forward thrust is to be the self-help group at the grassroot level.

Schemes for Training for Employment

(a) ***Support to Training and Employment Projects (STEP):*** STEP seeks to empower groups of poor women in traditional sector through training and employment in dairy, handlooms, handicrafts, sericulture and fisheries sectors to improve self-employment and women's access to jobs through increased allocation and more institutions for imparting training.

(b) ***Training-cum-employment-cum-production Centres:*** Centres aim to empower women through training and employment in non-traditional sector,

(c) ***Strengthening of Support Services for Working Women:*** A National Creche Fund established for conversion of the existing Anganwadi centres into Anganwadi-cum-creches.

(d) ***Training Module for Panchayati Raj Members:*** To empower eight lakh women members of Panchayati Raj who are assuming office following reservation of one-third of women in panchayat and local bodies.

(e) ***Programmes for Child Development***

(i) Expansion of ICDS to improve the nutritional and health status of children below six years, pregnant and nursing mothers, adolescent girls.

(ii) National plan of action for the girl child: An advocacy effort for the girl child.

(f) ***Programmes for Health and Nutrition***

(i) These programmes launched during 1992-93 to ensure child survival and safe motherhood.

(ii) National plan of action on nutrition to provide nutritious food to primary school children, enactment of Infant Milk substitutes, Feeding Bottles and Infant Food Act, 1992.

(g) ***Programmes for Education***

(a) District primary education programme launched with special focus on female literacy.

(b) Total literacy campaigns for empowerment through literacy.

(c) Operation blackboard to improve school facilities, provide 50 per cent women primary school teachers and minimum literacy learning.

(d) Mahila Samakhya for Empowerment of Women

Ninth Plan—Objectives and Strategies

'Empowerment of Women' being one of the nine primary objectives of the Ninth plan, every effort will be made to create an enabling environment where women can freely exercise their rights both within and outside home, as equal partners along with men. This will be realized through early finalisation and adoption, of the 'National Policy for Empowerment of Women'.

Commitments of the Ninth Plan (1997-2002)

Objective

Empowering women as the Agents of Social Change and Development.

Strategies

- To create an enabling environment for women to exercise their rights, both within and outside home, as equal partners along with men through early finalisation and adoption of "National Policy for Empowerment of Women".
- To expedite action to legislate reservation of not less than 1/3 seats for women in the parliament and in the State Legislative Assemblies and thus ensure adequate representation of women in decision making.
- To adopt an integrated approach towards empowering women through effective convergence of existing services, resources, infrastructure and manpower in both women specific and women related sectors.
- To adopt a special strategy of "women's component plan" to ensure that not less than 30 per cent of funds/benefits flow to women from other developmental sectors.
- To organize women into self-help group and thus mark the beginning of a major process of empowering women.
- To accord high priority to reproductive child healthcare.
- To universalize the on-going supplementary feeding programme - Special Nutrition Programme (SNP) and Mid Day Meals (MDM).
- To ensure easy and equal access to education for women and girls through the commitments of the Special Action Plan of 1998.

- To initiate steps to eliminate gender bias in all educational programmes.
- To institute plans for free education for girl's up to college level, including professional courses.
- To equip women with necessary skills in the modern upcoming trades, which could keep them gainfully engaged, besides making them economically independent and self-reliant.
- To increase access to credit through setting up of a 'Development Bank for Women Entrepreneurs in Small and Tiny Sectors'.

(a) Health and Family Welfare

- The Ninth plan recognizes the special health needs of women and the girl child and the importance of enhancing easy access to primary health care. Therefore, a holistic approach with Reproductive Child Health (RCH) measures will be adopted in improving the health status of women by focusing on their age specific needs.
- To achieve the expected level of 50/1000 of IMR and 3/1000 of MMR by 2002 AD, if current trend continues, the Ninth Plan accords high priority to reproductive child health care and proposes an integrated approach with ante-natal and post-natal care and child health services.
- The other effective measures proposed in this direction include identification and management of high-risk mothers, appropriate management of anaemia, hypertension disorders and provision for emergency obstetric care.
- To reduce illegal abortions which are being performed by unqualified persons, particularly in rural areas, special efforts will be made to promote ready access to medical termination of pregnancy and intra-partum care at Primary Health Centres.

- Effective enforcement of the pre-natal Diagnostic Techniques (Regulation and Prevention of Misuse) Act, 1994 with stringent measures of punishment of both the parties.
- Under RCH care, steps for prevention and treatment of gynaecological problems, including infertility, screening and treatment of cancers especially that of breast and uterine cervix etc., will also be taken up.
- Gender-sensitive initiatives that address the sexually transmitted infections/diseases (STD's), HIV/AIDS and other sexual and reproductive health issues, will be attended to on a priority basis.

(b) Nutrition: To tackle the problems of micro-nutrient deficiencies and protein energy malnutrition (PEM), the primary focus will be on the 'at-risk groups' who are living below the poverty line and also on those who are 'nutritionally vulnerable', particularly, the women/ mothers and children.

- Special efforts will be made through the Special Action Plan of 1998 to universalize the on-going supplementary feeding programmes namely Special Nutrition Programme (SNP) for pre school children and expectant and nursing mothers and Mid-Day Meals (MDM) for school going children.
- A special package of services to prevent/control the micro-nutrient deficiencies of Vitamin A, Iron and Iodine, which are extremely important from the point of view of the health consequences on women/mothers and children.

(c) Education and Training: Education, being the most powerful instrument for empowering women, assumes special priority in the Ninth Plan.

- Towards this, special attention will be paid to the already identified low female literacy pockets and to the women and the girl children belonging to the socially disadvantaged groups viz. SC, ST's, OBC's, Minorities, Disabled etc.,

- Besides, steps will be initiated to eliminate:

  (a) Gender discrimination in the admissions;

  (b) Remove gender bias;

  (c) Remove Stereo-types in the curricula, textbooks and learning material;

  (d) Create a gender sensitive educational system;

  (e) Promote gender sensitisation of teachers on a regular basis;

  (f) Appoint more women teachers at primary level;

  (g) Reduce drop-out rates and increase enrollment and retention rates of girl children through special incentives like free supply of uniforms and text-books, mid-day meals, scholarships etc.

- The special package announced for the Girl Child on 15th August, 1997 also revolves around the very same theme of educating and empowering the girl child living below the poverty line with adequate financial support till she completes higher secondary education or gets equipped with necessary skills to earn her livelihood.

- Vocationalisation of secondary education and vocational training for women will receive high priority as one of the ultimate goals of empowering women is to make them economically independent and self-reliant.

- Efforts will be made to encourage women and girls with necessary incentives to opt for the emerging areas of technical education such as electronics, computer systems and applications, bio-engineering, bio-technology, food processing, fabric designing, etc., which have high employment potential.

- To encourage more and more girls to enter into the mainstream of higher education, Ninth plan envisages plans for free education for girls up to college level including professional courses, so as to better empower women.[18]

(d) ***Work and Employment:*** Keeping in view the ultimate objective of fulfilling the 'Right to work for every citizen', special efforts will be made to generate gainful employment through promotion/expansion of both wage and self employment opportunities for women so as to make all potential women economically independent and self-reliant.

- As in the past, there will be a special focus on women in agriculture and its allied sectors as they are in majority and form the major stock of all the agricultural operations.
- The extension services will be strengthened to cover a large number of women, keeping in mind women's role as producers.
- Efforts will also be made to introduce programmes to upgrade the skills of the displaced women to take up jobs in the new and expanding areas of employment and formulate appropriate policies and programmes to promote opportunities in traditional sectors like Khadi and Village Industries, handicrafts, handlooms, sericulture, small-scale and cottage industries and absorb those displaced women.
- Flexibility in the labour market for women will be given adequate weightage through various Structural Adjustment Programmes (SAP).
- Women in the Informal Sector, who account for more than 90 per cent, will receive special attention during the Ninth plan especially with regard to their working conditions.

- Special efforts will be made to ensure that laws relating, to both minimum and 'equal pay for equal work', for women, shall be strictly implemented.
- The Ninth plan recognizes the need for a conducive credit policy to increase the access for women to credit through appropriate institutional mechanisms like RMK, NABARD, CAPART, Women Co-operatives/SHG's and the other financial institutions.
- The Ninth plan also envisages all States/UT's to be equipped with Women's Development Corporations (WDC's) to provide both 'forward' and 'backward' linkages of credit and marketing facilities to women entrepreneurs, besides being catalysts.
- In this context, the Ninth plan also envisages to set up a 'Development Bank for Women Entrepreneurs' in the small-scale and tiny sectors.
- Efforts will also be made to gender sensitize the Trade Unions to play the role of a watch-clog with regard to protection of women's rights/interests.
- With regard to women in Services, the Ninth plan recognizes the need to initiate affirmative action to ensure at least a minimum of 30 per cent of reservation for women in services in the public sector as against the present low representation of 13.8 per cent in 1997.
- Efforts will also be made to ensure upward mobility for women in services.
- For women to join the services in a big way, support services like childcare facilities viz. creches/day care centres at the work places/educational institutions and homes for the aged and disabled will be expanded with improved facilities.

- Hostels for working-women will be expanded to promote their mobility in the employment market.

(e) ***Decision-Making:*** As the representation of women in the decision-making levels has a direct bearing on all the affirmative actions directed towards their well being and empowerment, every effort will be made to ensure that women are in adequate numbers at the decision making levels.

(f) ***Poverty Alleviation:*** As women are critical to the process of moving their families out of poverty, the present policies and programmes of poverty alleviation will be redesigned, if called for, to make them more responsive to the special needs of women in extreme poverty.

- As a first step in this direction, the Ninth plan proposes to revamp TRYSEM in its design, curriculum and method of training and thus improve the training and employment opportunities for women in poverty.
- A special mechanism will be evolved to bring forth a closer integration amongst DWCRA, IRDP and TRYSEM to extend greater access to financial assistance and training to women's groups under DWCRA.
- Efforts will be made to ensure that a minimum of 30 to 40 per cent of the benefits flow to women from all the existing poverty alleviation programmes, both rural and urban.

(g) ***Care and Protection:*** Welfare and rehabilitative services will continue to be extended for women in need of care and protection viz. the disabled/deserted/ widowed/destitute and women in difficult circumstances etc., special programmes will be designed for both social and economic rehabilitation of Devadasis, Basavis, Jogins, Sex workers, Beggars etc.,

- The plight of those young women and girls, who migrate to the cities in search of jobs and later become victims of various circumstances and social/moral danger, will receive special attention during the Ninth plan.

(h) ***Environment:*** Considering the strong impact of environmental factors on the sustenance and livelihood of women, special efforts will be made to ensure/encourage participation of women in the conservation of environment and the control of environmental degradation through programmes of social forestry, afforestation and wasteland development etc. Accordingly, necessary provisions will be made to reflect women's perspectives in the policies and programmes for the management of eco-system and natural resources.

- Emphasis will be laid on the use of science and technology to solve environment-related problems like energy and fuel conservation along with water conservation to ease women's work in and outside the home.
- Efforts will also be made for gender sensitisation of forest staff and local communities to involve wornen's groups in the planning and management of forest conservation and utilisation of forest produce.

(i) ***Science and Technology:*** Application of Science and Technology is vital for the advancement of women as it reduces household drudgery and provides better working conditions for women, particularly, in rural areas, Therefore, participation of women/women scientists in Science and Technological activities will be encouraged in the Ninth plan at ali stages.

The Ninth plan, therefore, accords high priority to research and development (R&D) for exploitation of locally available indigenous alternative sources of energy for use in the women-related household activities. To undertake these types of R&D activities, more and more girl students will be encouraged to get into science streams with attractive incentives.

(j) ***Media and Communication:*** The strategy for Media in the Ninth plan will be a combination of efforts to confront/put an end to the negative and stereotyped portrayal and depiction of women and girls, besides using all types of mass media and communication resources to change the mindset of the people and the attitudes/behavioural patterns of people through information, advocacy and analysis.

(k) ***Violence Against Women:*** To deal with the increasing problem of violence against women and the girl child within and outside the family, a comprehensive approach will be adopted through a review of all the existing women-specific legislations and remove the weak links through necessary amendments; effective implementation of the existing legislation with strong punitive measures, gender-sensitisation of the enforcement machinery, involvement of community and the voluntary organisations to act as the informants and rehabilitation of and compensation for, the victims of such violence.

- Setting-up/strengthening of Women's Cells in the approved Police Stations, family courts, Mahila courts, counselling centres, legal aid centres and nyaya panchayats will be attempted as part of the intensive efforts to curb violence against women;
- Efforts will also be made to include legal literacy in the curriculum of schools, colleges and other Training Institutes;
- The other measures include strengthening of National/State level Commissions for women, appointment of a commissioner for women's rights who would act as a Public Defender on behalf of

women; and building up of such an environment where women and girls can come forward to report to the police about the acts of violence against them, without any fear of reprisal.

(l) ***Gender Sensitisation:*** Keeping in view the Ninth plan commitment of empowering women, vigorous efforts will be made to accelerate the process of societal reorientation towards creating a gender just society. The focus in this regard will be on both men and women within the family and within the community to change their negative attitudes and eliminate all types of discrimination against women and the girl child.

(m) ***Legislative Support:*** Special efforts will be made to enforce the existing legislations effectively in safeguarding the interest of women and girls as the Ninth plan indentifies laxity in the implementation of various legislations especially the women-specific, viz. The Dowry Prohibition Act, 1961 (as amended up to 1986); Indecent Representation of Women (prevention) Act, 1986.

The findings of the recent review of all the existing legislations, both women—specific and women—related, undertaken by the National Commission for women will be examined to plug the existing loopholes through necessary amendments and exact new legislations, if necessary, to make the legislations as effective instruments in safeguarding the rights of women and the girl child and ensuring gender justice.[19]

Tenth Plan

In the context of adopting human development as the ultimate goal of all our developmental efforts, empowerment of women and development of children gains priority on the country's development agenda.

Empowerment of Women: Women as an independent target group, account for 495.74 million and represent 49 per cent of country's total population, as per the 2001 census. Empowering women as a process demands a life-cycle approach. Therefore, every stage of their life counts as a priority in the planning process.

Approach to the Tenth Plan: In the context of having a laid down National Policy, approach to the Tenth plan for empowering women will be very distinct from that of the earlier plans, as it now stands on a strong platform for action with definite goals, targets and a time-frame. Further as the process of empowering women initiated during the Ninth plan is expected to continue through and beyond the Tenth plan, there can be no better approach than translating the recently adopted National Policy for Empowerment of Women (2001) into action through:

1. Creating an environment, through positive economic and social policies for the development of women to enable them to realize their full potential;
2. Allowing the de-jure and de-facto enjoyment of all human rights and fundamental freedom by women on par with men in all spheres—political, economic, social, cultural and civil;
3. Providing equal access to participation and decision making for women in social, political and economic life of the nation;
4. Ensuring equal access to women to healthcare, quality education at all levels, career and vocational guidance, employment, equal remuneration, occupational health and safety, social security and public office etc.;
5. Strengthening legal systems aimed at the elimination of all forms of discrimination against women;
6. Changing societal attitudes and community practices by active participation and involvement of both men and women;
7. Mainstreaming a gender perspective into the development process;
8. Eliminating discrimination and all forms of violence against women and the girl child; and

9. Building and strengthening partnerships with civil society, particularly women's organisations, corporate and private sector agencies.

The operational strategy, as prescribed in the policy, directs all the Central Ministries and State Departments to draw up Time-Bound Action Plans for translating the policy into a set of concrete actions through a participatory process of consultations with all the concerned, both in the governmental and non-governmental sectors.

The process of organising women into Self-Help Groups (SHGs), started during the Ninth plan to provide them a permanent fora for articulating their needs and contributing their perspectives to development, has made tremendous progress as it brought into action more than a million SHGs all over the country. Experience has already shown that these groups have been very effective institutions at grassroot level in facilitating access to women, be it for financial or material resources or services or for information. Therefore, the Tenth plan will continue to encourage SHG mode to act as the agents of social change, development and empowerment of women.

Governmental institutions and efforts by themselves are not adequate in terms of human and financial resources to achieve empowerment/advancement of women in its various dimensions. Therefore they need to be supplemented by Civil Society Organisations (voluntary organisations). Already, a large number of such organisations have emerged throughout the country and some of them have also made significant contribution towards projecting and addressing women's issues at the grassroot levels. Services of these organisations will be encouraged, supported and availed of so that the process of empowering women becomes truly a national and people's movement.

As part of the efforts for empowering women, the Tenth plan will take note of the recommendations of the Task Force on women and children (2000) with regard to women-specific and women-related legislations and expedite action to bring forth necessary amendments and enact new legislations, if required. In this regard, special efforts during the Tenth plan will be made to consider or encourage necessary amendments in legislations relating to ownership of property and inheritance by evolving consensus on the subject and thus make them gender just, as the evolution of property rights in the patriarchal system has contributed to the subordinate status of women.

Finally, the Tenth plan will also take cognisance of the gender asymmetry in the population pyramid with 'males out-numbering females' as a whole and 'females out-numbering males' at the upper end of the age structure and calls for urgent interventions to protect the girl child, besides providing social security for the aged women.

Commitments of the Tenth Plan to Empower Women

The Approach

To continue with the major strategy of 'Empowering Women' as Agents of Social Change and Development.

Strategies

To adopt a sector-specific 3-fold strategy for empowering women, based on the prescriptions of the National Policy for Empowerment of Women. They include:

I. ***Social Empowerment:*** To create an enabling environment through various affirmative developmental policies and programmes for development of women besides providing them easy and equal access to all basic minimum services so as to enable them to realize their full potentials through:

1. Providing easy and equal access to ensure basic minimum services of primary healthcare and family welfare with a special focus on the under-served and under-privileged segments of population through Universalizing Reproductive and Child Health Services;

2. Achieving the goals set by the National Population Policy (2000) with regard to reducing Infant

Mortality Rate (IMR) to 30 per thousand and Maternal Mortality Rate (MMR) to 100 per lakh live births by 2010;

3. Supplementing healthcare and nutrition services through the Pradhan Mantri Gramodaya Yojana (PMGY) to fill the critical gaps in the existing primary healthcare infrastructure and nutrition services;
4. Tackling both macro and micro-nutrient deficiencies through nutrition supplementary feeding programmes with necessary support services like health check-ups, immunisation, health and nutrition education and nutrition awareness etc.;
5. Consolidating the progress made under female education and carrying it forward for achieving the set goal of 'Education for Women's Equality' as advocated by the National Policy on Education, 1986 (revised in 1992);
6. Providing easy and equal access to and free education for women and girls at all levels and in the field of technical and vocational education and training in upcoming and job-oriented trades;
7. Increasing enrollment/retention rates and reducing drop-out rates by expanding the support services through mid day meals, hostels and incentives like free supply of uniforms, text books, transport charges etc.;
8. Extending the existing network of regional vocational training centres to all the states and women's Industrial Training Institutes and Women's wings with General Industrial Training Institutes with residential facilities in all districts and sub-districts and provision of training in marketable trades;

9. Encouraging the media to project positive images of women and the Girl Child; change the mind-set of the people and thus promote the balanced portrayals of women and men;

10. Gender sensitizing both the administrative and enforcement machinery and ensuring that the rights and interests of women are taken care of, besides involving them in planning, implementation and monitoring of processes.

II. *Economic Empowerment:* Ensure provision of training, employment and income generation activities with both 'forward' and 'backward' linkages with the ultimate objective of making all women economically independent and self-reliant through:

1. Organising women into Self-Help Groups under various poverty alleviation programmes and offering them a range of economic options along with necessary support measures to enhance their capabilities and earning capacities with an ultimate objective of making them economically independent and self-reliant;

2. Ensuring that women in the informal sector who account for more than 90 per cent are given special attention with regard to improving their working conditions as the same continued to be very precarious without even minimum or equal wages, leave aside other legislative safeguards;

3. Making concerted efforts to ensure that the benefits of training and extension in agriculture and its allied activities of horticulture, small animal husbandry, poultry, fisheries etc., reach women in proportion to their numbers; and also issue of joint pattas for husband and wife under the Social Forestry and Joint Forest Management Programmes;

4. Ensuring that the employers fulfill their legal obligations towards their women workers in extending childcare facilities, maternity benefits, special leave, protection from occupational hazards, allowing formation of women workers associations/ unions, legal protection/aid etc.;

5. Re-training/upgrading the skills of women displaced from traditional sectors due to advancement of technology so that they can take up jobs in the new and expanding areas of employment and formulating appropriate policies and programmes to promote alternative opportunities for wage/self-employment in traditional sectors like Khadi and Village industries, handicrafts, handlooms, sericulture, small-scale and cottage industries;

6. Initiating affirmative action to ensure at least 30 per cent of reservation for women in services in the public sector as their representation in 1999 was only 14.5 per cent, along with required provisions for upward mobility;

7. Increasing access to credit for women either through the establishment of new micro-credit mechanisms of micro-financial institutions catering to women or strengthening existing arrangements in these areas along with an expansion of the limited coverage of Rashtriya Mahila Kosh.

III. ***Gender Justice:*** Eliminate all forms of gender discrimination and, thus enable women to enjoy not only de-jure but also de-facto rights and fundamental freedom on par with men in all spheres, viz. political, economic, social, civil, cultural etc., through:

- Complete eradication of female foeticide and female infanticide through effective enforcement of both the Indian Penal Code, 1860 and the Pre-Natal Diagnostic Technique Act, 1994 with most stringent measures of punishment so that a very harsh path is set for the illegal practitioners;

- Adopting measures that take into account the reproductive rights of women to enable them to exercise their reproductive choices;
- Working out strategies in close collaboration with the Ministry of Labour to ensure extension of employment opportunities and thus, remove inequalities in employment—both in work and accessibility;
- Ensuring that the value added by women in the informal sector as workers and producers is recognized through redefinition/re-interpretation of conventional concepts of work and preparation of satellite and national accounts;
- Defining the women's component plan (WCP) clearly and identifying the schemes/programmes/ projects under each Ministry/Department which should be covered under WCP and ensuring the adoption of women-related mechanisms through which funds/benefits flow to women from these sectors;
- Initiating action for enacting new women—specific legislations, amending the existing women-related legislation, if necessary, based on the review made and recommendations already available to ensure gender justice, besides, reviewing all the subordinate legislations to eliminate all gender discriminatory references;
- Expediting action to legislate reservation of not less than 1/3rd seats for women in the parliament and in the State Legislative Assemblies and thus women in proportion to their members reach decision-making bodies so that their voices are heard;
- Arresting the ever-increasing violence against women and the girl child including the adolescent

girls on top priority with the strength and support of a well-planned programme of action prepared in consultation with all the concerned, especially the enforcement authorities; implementing effectively with the strength of the Law and Order Authorities both at the centre and state levels and assessing the situation;

- Expediting standardisation of a Gender Development Index based on which the gender segregated data will be collected at national, state and district levels; compiled and analysed to assess the progress made in improving the status of women at regular intervals with an ultimate objective of achieving equality on par with men;
- Initiating/accelerating the process of societal reorientation towards creating a gender-just society.

To sum up, if gender justice is to be ensured women need to be empowered socially, economically and politically. If women are to be empowered socially, it is necessary to make every one of them literate, reach them information and generate awareness, equip them with legal literacy and help them in every way to realize their own potential. If women are to be empowered economically, it is necessary to equip them with vocational skills; provide employment and income generation, extend free channels of micro-credit, provide management skills, social security and thus allow them greater visibility. If women are to be empowered politically, the immediate need is to adopt to different forms of affirmative discriminations so that women in proportionate numbers reach critical places to ensure that their voices are heard. In fact, it is the empowerment strategy that has emerged as the most challenging task not only for those who are working for women, but also for women themselves.[20]

Women Welfare Programmes in Andhra Pradesh

Andhra Pradesh has been in forefront in implementing various developmental programmes for women in the country.

The Department of Women Development and Child Welfare has undertaken various economic and developmental programmes and relief measures for the welfare of women through implementation of different schemes.

Initially, the programmes were limited to the activities for women's welfare with four women welfare centres in Andhra State. With the formation of Andhra Pradesh on 1.11.1956, the programmes of the department were extended throughout the state and multifarious activities were undertaken for the upliftment of women belonging to economically backward classes through different schemes like providing shelter to aged women, destitutes, working women and job-oriented technical training courses etc.[21]

Programmes of the Department of Women Development and Child Welfare can be broadly classified into welfare programmes, developmental programmes, and welfare-cum-developmental programmes. Some developmental programmes are also sponsored by the Central Government.

I. Institutional Services

(a) ***State Homes:*** State Homes are meant for women discharged from correctional institutions and who are unable to protect themselves from adverse social forces and also for those who voluntarily seek shelter. They are given free lodging and boarding at the rate of Rs. 210/- per month per head.

There are 5 State Homes in the State located at Hyderabad, Mahaboobnagar, Srikakulam, Kurnool and East Godavari. Women, according to their necessity stay for 3 to 5 years. During the period, they are given training in the training-cum-production units in printing of book, binding work, screen printing, cloth weaving, mat weaving, cane and bamboo work. Marriages are also performed at government cost, as a part of rehabilitation, if any suitable persons come forward to marry.[22]

(b) ***Service Homes:*** These homes are meant for destitute women, helpless widows and deserted wives who are in the age group of 18-35 years. Rehabilitation will be made through job courses and training-cum production. During their stay with children who are below the age of 5 years are provided with free food, shelter, clothing, and medical aid. Scheduled caste women are permitted to stay for five years.

There are six Service Homes in the State located at West Godavari, Anantapur, Nellore, Krishna, Kurnool and Hyderabad.[23] Initially these homes provided training in tailoring and coaching to appear for 7th class and 10th class subsequently. Several units have been introduced like toy-making, weaving, banian and socks making, leather units and card-board units.[24] Each home is managed by a Superintendent who is assisted by Matron, two teachers, one craft instructress, part-time teachers and other ministerial staff.

(c) ***Working Women's Hostels:*** These hostels provide food, shelter and other facilities including security to the working women who are away from their families on payment of charges prescribed by the government. Those who earn monthly income of less than Rs. 3,000 are eligible for admission. There are 18 working women hostels in the state. Sanctioned strength of each hostel is 50 women.[25]

(d) ***Women Welfare Branches:*** These are the primary institutions of the Department. Children in the age group of 3-6 years are given pre-school education. For the age group of 15-35 training is given in crafts, nutrition and childcare education. There are 46 such centres in the state of which 33 are for Scheduled Castes and 13 are for Scheduled Tribes. The sanctioned strength in each centre is 30 children and 3 women with one teacher, one part-time instructress and 2 ayahs.

(e) ***Home for the Aged Women:*** These Homes provide peaceful and comfortable living for the old destitute women. The Government provides free food, shelter and clothing till death. There are two homes one at Chittoor and the another in Hyderabad with a sanctioned strength of 30 and 50 respectively. Women above 60 years of age are being given admission.

(f) ***Home for the Collegiate Girls:*** Inmates of children homes who pass X class are admitted into these institutions to pursue higher studies of their choice.

There are six homes for the collegiate girls in the state. They are at Tirupathi, Warangal, West Godavari, Hyderabad, Guntur and Vijayanagaram. The maximum period of stay is 5 years. The permissible age group is 15-25 years.

(g) ***Vocational Training Centres:*** The vocational training centres provide job-oriented technical training courses. There are seven vocational training centres in the State. They are at Srikakulam, Eluru, Karimnagar, Anantapur, Cuddapah, Warangal, and Hyderabad. Women belonging to economically backward classes having passed X class in the age group of 16-25 years are given admission in the vocational training centres. A new course for nurses training has been introduced. Free boarding and lodging is provided to 20 women and 10 are day-scholars.

(h) ***Uniform Manufacturing Centres:*** These centres provide employment oriented training to the women belonging to economically backward classes. Besides this, 10 wage workers in each centre are employed and wages are paid to them for stitching dresses and uniforms. Orders from government departments particularly schools, hospitals and public undertakings are taken. The age group is 16-35 years.

(i) ***Regional Tailoring Centres:*** In these centres, unemployed women are given job-oriented training in tailoring to appear for technical examination in tailoring and to enable them to take up craft instructress jobs or to set up their own tailoring units.

There are 3 centres in the state. They are located at Srikakulam, Prakasam and Mahaboobnagar. The sanctioned strength in each centre is 50. Women in the age group 15-35 years are admitted. A hostel is attached to each centre. The in-take capacity is 40.

(j) ***Craft Training Centres:*** In these centres, training in local crafts is imparted to the women belonging to low income group to enable them to prepare for gainful employment. There are 14 craft training centres in the state. Eligible age group is between 15-35 years.

(k) ***District Crafts including Tailoring Centres:*** These centres are for the benefit of economically backward women in the towns and villages. Training in tailoring and other crafts is imparted so as to take up self-employment scheme to supplement their family income. These centres will be shifted village to village to cover all the eligible women in the districts. There are four centres in the State. They are at Visakhapatnam, East Godavari, Krishna and Ranga Reddy districts. The centres are mobile and moved from one to another village. The sanctioned strength of each centre is 30 and the eligible group is 15-35 years.

(l) ***Women Technical Training Institute (WTTI):*** This is a state-wide institution which conducts diploma course in civil engineering architecture, computer engineering, electronics and instrumentation for girls belonging to economically backward classes. The candidates are selected by the Director of Technical Education through common entrance tests for admission into women polytechnics. The sanctioned strength is 50.

(m) ***Rescue Home:*** There is one Rescue Home at Hyderabad established under the auspices of Government for the court committed cases under the provision of suppression of Immoral Traffic Act of 1956 and the women convicted are kept there during the entire period of conviction. During the stay in these homes, efforts are made to bring change in their social and moral attitudes. During the punishment period, besides free shelter, food, clothing and medical aid, vocational training in tailoring and embroidery is imparted and for the articles prepared by them, necessary wages are paid by the institution at the time of their discharge from home. A sum of Rs. 200/- per month per adult is provided towards dietary charges. The Rescue Home is managed by a Superintendent with the help of a craft instructor and one watchman and warden.

(n) ***Integrated Child Development Scheme:*** Various nutritional studies revealed that pregnant and lactating women are facing nutritional deficiencies. In view of this, in 1975, the Government of India initiated Integrated Child Development Services (ICDS) to provide a package of nutrition, health and educational services to the mother and child. The programmes are administered through Anganwadis located in the region.[26]

The ICDS which mainly caters to children below 6 years and pregnant women and lactating mothers in the age group of 15-45 years provides a package of services which consists of (1) Supplementary nutrition, (2) Immunisation, (3) Health check-up, (4) Referral Service, (5) Nutrition and Health Education, (6) Non-formal education.[27]

Special Schemes in the World Bank Assisted ICDS Projects

The World Bank assisted project is under operation since 1.10.1990. The World Bank Project was started with a view to strengthen the existing ICDS activities in certain work areas by introducing additional components. The project covers 110 blocks, 24 tribal, 43 rural and 43 drought prone areas. The various schemes in the World Bank assisted ICDS projects are:

1. Income generating activities
2. Women's integrated learning for life
3. Adolescent Girls Scheme - 1
4. Adolescent Girls Scheme - 2
5. Nutrition rehabilitation centres.[28]

(a) ***Income Generating Activities:*** This scheme envisages activisation of Mahila Mandals at village level by involving mothers with a view to initiate income generating activities for women.[29]

(b) ***Women's Integrated Learning for Life:*** This programme aims at imparting literacy skills and knowledge of good health, hygiene, nutrition and family planning to women in the age group of 11-35 years.

(c) ***Adolescent Girls Scheme:*** To upgrade the technical skills of adolescent girls in the age groups of 11-15 years and 15-17 years respectively, Scheme I and II were initiated in World Bank assisted projects of ICDS during 1991-92.

(d) ***Nutrition Rehabilitation Centres (NRC):*** These centres are meant to provide services for combating nutritional deficiencies among "at risk" mothers and children below 3 years of age suffering from malnutrition. On the average 20 cases are admitted in each NRC every month, 80 per cent of which pertain to malnutrition while the rest are emergency cases.[30]

Mahila Samriddhi Yojana (MSY)

The MSY is a centrally sponsored scheme and launched on 2.10.1983. Through Mahila Samriddhi Yojana, every rural woman aged 18 and above can open an MSY account of money she can save. The government would contribute an incentive money to her savings. For an amount up to Rs. 300/- kept in the account for a lock-in period of one year, she would receive a governmental incentive of 25 per cent.

The Department of Women and Child Development under the Ministry of Human Resource Development gets the scheme implemented through the network of 1.32 lakh post offices of the Department of posts functioning in the rural areas. An important aspect of the programme is that of involvement of non-governmental organisations (NGOs) at all levels. NGOs will hold awareness generation camps in villages through which they would mobilize women to take up savings as a conscious choice.

Indira Mahila Yojana (IMY)

The IMY was launched in August 1995 in 200 blocks of the country. It's main objective is to give a forward thrust to the education, awareness, income-generation capacities and the empowerment of women. The platform for the forward thrust is to be the self-help group at the grassroot level.

The scheme emphasises the constitution of Indira Mahila Block Societies (IMBS) at the block level and Indira Mahila Kendras (IMK) at the Anganwadi level. At the grass-root level under every Anganwadi, there should be women's self-help groups.

Thrift Promotion

The group is also expected to have some thrift activity. The fund collected over a period can be revolved amongst the members for financial support to the expansion of their income-generation activities or also for starting of a new activity. The groups once established can also approach the State and the national level lending institutions like Rashtriya Mahila Kosh (RMK), social welfare board etc., for credit support.[31]

IMY is a strategy to co-ordinate and integrate components of all sectoral programmes by identifying programmes selected for women and to facilitate their convergence for empowerment of the women.[32]

Rashtriya Mahila Kosh (National Credit Fund for Women)

The RMK was established in 1993 by the Department of Women and Child Development, Ministry of Human Resource Development, New Delhi for the purpose of delivery of credit through women's development corporations/non-governmental organisations/self-help groups to 2 lakh poor women from both rural and urban areas whose family income does not exceed Rs. 11,000/- per annum in rural areas and Rs. 11,800/- per annum in urban areas. The interest charged is 12 per cent per annum to the ultimate borrower women and 8 per cent to the NGOs and corporations. The Women Development Corporation has been sanctioned a loan of Rs. 20 lakhs from RMK to lend through self-help group Mahila Mandals for covering 1000 women.[33]

Maternity Assistance to Pregnant Women of Agricultural Labour Families

The scheme is introduced by the State Government during the Seventh Plan period to provide assistance to pregnant women of agricultural labour families in their advanced state of pregnancy and one month after delivery.[34]

Promotion of Women Entrepreneurship

The programme is conducted by National Institute of Small Industry Extension Training (NISIET). In 1993, the programme was intended to those functionaries involved in conducting entrepreneurship development programmes for women and training activity. This programme aims to sharpen their perceptions with regard to approach and implementation of various promotional activities for women entrepreneurs.[35]

Special Scheme to Prevent Child Labour: A Special Project for Girl Child

In an effort to discourage child labour, the State Government launched a special project for girl child under which 100 girls will be adopted in each district and imparted education and vocational training courses. Andhra Pradesh continues to be the top of the list of child labour for the last 3 decades. To combat the problem there are 565 special schools (Bala Jyothi Schools) which have been extended to children who are withdrawn from child labour.[36]

In 1995, the number of schemes for liberated child labourers has been constituted. There are 105 Bala Jyothi Schemes are being constituted in the State. Various literacy programmes for women were introduced.

Rehabilitation of Girl Child Labourers: The State Government initiated a new scheme of identifying girl child labourers in the state with a view to rehabilitate them. Rs. I crore was released for the rehabilitation of girl child labourers.[37]

Girl Child Protection Scheme

This scheme was launched by the State Government during the year 1995-96. Rs. 24 crores was released for the scheme and extended to all districts. In 1996-97, the target girls were 60,000.

Promotion of Entrepreneur Skills Among Women

The National Bank for Agriculture and Rural Development, Small Scale Industries Development Bank (SIDBI) and commercial banks are encouraging women entrepreneurs by providing credit facilities.

Co-operative Development Fund (CDF)

CDF was constituted in 1992 in Hyderabad with the objective of promoting self-sufficiency of urban women through credit facilities. It promotes the thrift activity among women.

All Women Police Stations

24 all women police stations were sanctioned to each district headquarters to ensure strict implementation of laws related to women. There are 12,000 home guards functioning in the state.

In Mahila police stations, 2 sub-inspectors, 8 head constables and 16 constables tackle problems which women are either afraid or embarrassed to reveal to men. Police officers take up harassment of any kind either coming from within the family or outside along with dowry harassment cases which are fatal.

Establishment of Mahila Courts and Family Courts

A special need was felt by the State Government to focus particularly on the cases of atrocities against women which run as a counter to all developmental efforts made for women. To handle cases of atrocities more efficiently, exclusive Mahila courts have been established in the following places: (1) Hyderabad, (2) Vijayawada, (3) Visakhapatnam. These courts try out cases of bride burning, rape, outraging modesty of women.[38]

Family Courts: Seven family courts have also been established in the state headed by the District Sessions Judges at the following places: (1) Hyderabad, (2) Secunderabad, (3) Visakhapatnam, (4) Vijayawada, (5) Tirupati, (6) Warangal, (7) Kurnool. The objective of such family courts is to promote salient, speedy settlement of disputes relating to village and family affairs and other connected matters.[39] Mahila Adalats are also being organized by the National Commission for Women to provide speedy justice.

Vocational Training Courses for Adolescent Girls

The State Government introduced vocational training courses for adolescent girls in each Mahila Pranganam at district level with a target of 1000 girls to be trained per annum in the State.

Career Counselling Centres: Padmavathi Mahila University is the exclusive women's University in the country and is located at Tirupati in Chittoor District. The university has been conducting various vocational courses for women.[40]

So the State Government has taken a decision for establishment of career counselling centres for women in universities and women's colleges with Padmavathi Mahila University playing a co-ordinating role.

The Government of Andhra Pradesh is one among the few states which have already introduced a bill for setting up of a State Commission for women and the Commission will be set up soon. The State Commission is the institutional framework to strengthen policy implementation. The objectives of the commission are:

- to evolve strategies
- to recommend policy changes
- to review policy implementation for meeting economic status of women.[41]

The Committee will have full power to enquire into unfair practices against women, investigate or cause investigation into issues concerning women as a judicial court. It will also point out inadequacies and shortcomings in the law with relation to women. It will also maintain data bank relating to social, economic development of women, bring to the notice of government such issue of importance which affect a large body of women.

Women Development Corporation (WDC)

This scheme was formulated in the State during the year 1986-87. The objective of WDC is to play a catalystic role in identifying women entrepreneurs, providing technical consultancy services, facilitating availability of credits, promoting marketing of products, promoting and strengthening women's co-operatives, arranging training facilities etc.[42]

The Government of Andhra Pradesh is one among the few states which have already introduced a Bill for setting up of a State Commission for women and the Commission will be set up soon. The State Commission is the institutional framework to strengthen policy implementation. The objectives of the Commission are:

- to evolve strategies;
- to recommend policy changes;
- to review policy implementation for meeting economic status of women.

The Committee will have full power to enquire into unfair practices against women, investigate or cause investigation into issues concerning women as a judicial court. It will also point out inadequacies and shortcomings in the law with relation to women. It will also maintain data bank relating to social, economic development of women, bring to the notice of government such issue of importance which affect a large body of women. The State Commission for women Bill was passed by the State Assembly. The Commission is yet to be constituted.

Andhra Pradesh State Social Welfare Advisory Board

This board is implementing welfare programmes for the benefit of poor women, children, and the disabled through 1412 voluntary agencies. The board assists voluntary agencies in organising various schemes such as setting up of creches, providing nutrition, awareness generation, condensed courses and education, vocational training, assistance to working women's hostels, socio-economic programmes, innovative schemes and training programmes for the beneficiaries through voluntary organisations with an outlay of Rs. 350 lakh per annum for the coverage of 10,000 women and 30,000 children.[43]

Participation of NGOs in Women and Child Welfare Activities

The Department of Women Development and Child Welfare oversees processing of applications of non-governmental organisations (NGOs) and implementation of various centrally funded programmes namely RMK, National Creche Fund (NCF), Short Stay Homes, Old Age Homes for Women, National Children's Fund (NCF), Working Women's Hostels, Norwegian Assistance for Development (NORAD), Support to Training-cum-Employment Programme (STEP) etc.

The State Government is assisting active voluntary organisations working for the welfare of women and children to get 90 per cent financial assistance from the Government of India which has various sources of funding, such as Creche Fund, National Children's Fund, Women Welfare Fund, Social Welfare Fund etc.[44]

Andhra Pradesh State Financial Corporation

The Corporation has been laying great emphasis in developing self-employment opportunities and operating promotional schemes such as Mahila Udyan Nidhi scheme, National Equity Fund etc. To help various categories of entrepreneurs, the Corporation is operating 23 schemes for financial assistance and all women entrepreneurs are eligible for setting up of industries under these schemes subject to satisfying other norms of Corporation.[45]

Women Component in the Adult Literacy Programme

The target groups of total literacy campaign, post literacy campaign and continuing education are mostly weaker sections (SC and ST) including women. About 50 per cent of the target group covered under these programmes are women of all castes.

The physical targets for women beneficiaries are 44.29 lakhs in the Ninth Five Year Plan under Total Literacy Campaign and Post Literacy Campaign and 33.80 1akhs under Continuing Education.[46]

Support to Employment Programmes for Women

This is a new programme launched by the Department of Women and Child Development in the Seventh Plan 1980.

Support to the Employment programme for women or STEP consists of series of action projects intended to strengthen and improve women's work and employment in the following sectors: (1) Agriculture, (2) Small Animal Husbandry, (3) Dairying, (4) Fisheries, (5) Handlooms, (6) Handicrafts, (7) Khadi and Village Industries and (8) Sericulture etc. Series of action projects aiming at integrating women into these sectors and into mainstream of development are introduced. The action project focusses on the poorest, the most marginalized assetless women.

NGOs will be implementing agencies of the STEP action plan projects. For these programmes, the Central Government provides 90 per cent and 10 per cent by implementing agencies. The scheme provides 90 per cent assistance for income-generating activities taken up by poor women in urban and rural areas. Under each project 5000-10000 women are covered.[47]

Liberation, Rehabilitation and Economic Development of Jogin Women

The incidence of the system of Jogins/Basavis in Andhra Pradesh was first surveyed in the year 1985 when 16,287 Jogin women were identified. About 80 per cent of them were found to be the Scheduled Castes.

On the basis of the survey, various socio-economic measures have been undertaken for eradication of this practice and rehabilitation of the affected women. A special legislation called the Andhra Pradesh Devadasis Act 1988 was enacted for abolishing this system.

In order to liberate the Jogins from exploitation and to rehabilitate them, measures such as allotment of house sites and financial assistance for housing, admission of children, into schools and hostels, pensions, adult education etc., have been taken up. The objectives of the programme of rehabilitation is to secure economic independence for the Jogins so that they will not be socially exploited while simultaneously brining about social change.[48]

Andhra Pradesh Women's Co-operative Finance Corporation

This Corporation was established in the year 1975 on the eve of the International Women's Year with the twin objectives to promote equality between men and women and active involvement of women in economic development.

The Corporation has offices in all 23 districts of the State for disbursement and recovery of margin money. The Corporation has also started 20 Telugu Bala Mahila Pragati Pranganams in various crafts, small scale industry and skills. Women/girls were trained with the Corporation's own funds. Certain courses are run under the guidance of Sri Padmavathi Mahila Visvavidyalayam, Tirupati. The Corporation has constructed 15 working women's hostels.

The Corporation also runs training cum production units at Hyderabad employing women. The Corporation has also undertaken implementation of NORAD training programmes in the old city area of Hyderabad for the last 3 years. The Corporation has also undertaken the responsibility of rehabilitation of all trainees of its production units, Telugu Bala Mahila Pragati Pranganams (TBMPPs) and NORAD old city project. The Corporation also trains Anganwadi workers in its Anganwadi Training Centres.[49]

Thus Andhra Pradesh Women's Co-operative Finance Corporation caters to the needs of poor women by providing margin money, training-cum-residential facilities for rural women and constructing working women's hostels etc.

Conclusion

Women of today are surely more conscious, alert and active about their duties, rights and freedom and educational attainment. They are no more servants to their masters within the four walls of houses. On the other hand they started taking active part in almost all spheres of life. Above all they organized themselves to fight their cases which is a healthy sign of their progress.

In regard to socio-economic programmes what we find is that the policies and programmes relating to women were confined to areas like health, education and social welfare till the fifth five year plan. However as a result of much hue and cry created by women's groups during the women's year after 1975, some changes in the attitudes of governments and public at large are seen. The Sixth, Seventh, Eighth, Ninth and Tenth Plan have thus devoted a chapter on women's programmes. Besides, programmes for health, education and social welfare, these plans envisages special measures needed for employment generation for women. The equality and dignity of women shall have to be maintained at any cost to seek their full co-operation in the process of nation-building. To improve position and status of women in the society, the major responsibility lies with the public at large. There is thus a need to create a strong public opinion against the social evils mainly responsible for low status. Voluntary organisations and particularly women's associations have to be more alert and vigil in this case. The government's programmes are supposed to supplement the effort of public.

The Government of Andhra Pradesh has also implemented several developmental schemes like Mahila University, Mahila Samakhya Scheme, Podupulakshmi Scheme, Establishment of Creches, Balwadis, Women Welfare Centres, Service Homes, Vocational Training Centres, Anganwadi Centres for providing better education, nutrition and to improve the economic and social status of women and their skills. It also established Andhra Pradesh Women's Co-operative Finance Corporation to introduce different economic programmes for women.

Thus the government has given more importance to various developmental programmes during various plans to help the women. Women's participation in economic activity is of crucial importance in the context of national development.

REFERENCES

1. Empowerment of Rural Women, Deepti Aggarwal, 'Intensive Agriculture,' March-April 2001.
2. Womens' Participation in National Development, C.B.Sircar, Director, Family and Child Welfare Training Centre, Viswa Bharati, Sriniketan, *Cooperator,* August 1975.
3. Ninth Five Year Plan (1997-2002), Volume II, Thematic Issues and Sectoral Programmes, Government of India, Planning Commission, New Delhi.
4. First Five Year Plan (1951-56), Planning Commission, Government of India, New Delhi.
5. Second Five Year Plan (1956-61), Planning Commission, Government of India, New Delhi.
6. Third Five Year Plan (1961-66), Planning Commission, Government of India, New Delhi.
7. Fifth Five Year Plan (1974-79), Planning Commission, Government of India, New Delhi.
8. V.S.Mahajan, 'Women's Contribution to India's Economic and Social Development,' *Deep and Deep Publications,* New Delhi, 1989.
9. Seventh Five Year Plan (1985-90), Planning Commission, Government of India, New Delhi.
10. Anandha Raj Kumar, "Multi-Programme Approach to Women's Economic Independence," *Kurukshetra,* August 1995.
11. Ibid.
12. Seventh Five Year Plan (1985-90), Planning Commission, Government of India, New Delhi.
13. Ibid.
14. Eighth Five Year Plan (1992-97), Planning Commission, Government of India, New Delhi.
15. Ibid.
16. Anandha Raj Kumar, "Multi-Programme Approach to Women's Economic Independence," *Kurukshetra,* August 1995.
17. Dr.G.Dhawan, "Human Security and Sustainable Development," *Kurukshetra,* August 1995.

18. Ninth Five Year Plan (1997-2002), Volume II, Thematic Issues and Sectoral Programmes, Government of India, Planning Commission, New Delhi.

19. Ibid.

20. Tenth Five Year Plan (2002-2007), Government of India, Planning Commission, New Delhi.

21. Activities of Women and Children in the State of Andhra Pradesh, Department of Women Development and Child Welfare, Hyderabad, 1997, p.3.

22. Budget Management 1997-98 (Telugu) Women Development and Child Welfare, Government of Andhra Pradesh Press, Hyderabad, 1993, p.3.

23. Activities of Women and Children in the State of Andhra Pradesh, op.cit., p.4.

24. Budget Management 1997-98, op.cit., p.5.

25. Ibid., p.6.

26. Status Report, Department of Women Development and Child Welfare, 1996, Hyderabad, p.5.

27. Ibid., p.7.

28. Women Sub-Plan 1997-98, Government of Andhra Pradesh, Department of Women Development and Child Welfare, Hyderabad, 1997, p.66.

29. State Action Plan for Women A.P. 1994-2000 A.D. Department of Women and Child Development, Hyderabad, 1995, p.5.

30. Ibid., p.7.

31. Indira Misra, "Self-Employment Through IMY" in Yojana, April 1997, Vol. 41, No. 4, p 36.

32. Status Report, Women Development and Child Welfare, Hyderabad, 1996, p.5.

33. Ibid., p.6.

34. 7th Five Year Plan 1985-90 A.P. Vol.II, Department of Finance and Planning Wing, Government of Andhra Pradesh, Central Plan, 1990, p.501.

35. Promotion of Women Entrepreneurship Brochure 1993, National Institute of Small Industry Extension Training, Government of India, Hyderabad, p.2.

36. *Deccan Chroncile,* September 13, 1997, p.4.

37. *Eenadu,* October 4, 1997, p.7.

38. 'State Empowerment Policy', Government of Andhra Pradesh, Department of Women Development and Child Welfare, p.11.

39. Ibid., p.5.

40. Ibid., p.9.

41. Ibid., p.10.

42. Government of India, New Delhi, 1996. A Reference Material. Ministry of Information and Broadcasting, Government of India, 1997, p.207.

43. State Action Plan, op.cit., p.38.

44. Status Report, op.cit., p.8.

45. State Sub-Plan, op.cit., p.36.

46. Ibid., p.27.

47. Support Programmes for Women, Government of India, Brochure, New Delhi, p.3.

48. State Sub-Plan, op.cit., p.45.

49. Activities of Andhra Pradesh, Women's Co-operative Finance Corporation, A.P. Women's Co-operative Finance Corporation, Hyderabad, 1997, p. l.

3

Origin and Progress of DWCRA and Self-Help Groups

Introduction

While women were taking small loans from their group saving, it was realized that loans from savings alone would not be sufficient to emancipate them from poverty. Women require more money if they were to start some income generating activities to raise their income. The formation of groups had instilled financial discipline in the members and made them confident to handle more money. Thus the need was to have more money for the groups.

It was here that the programme of DWCRA, a sub-component of IRDP proved useful for the groups. Each group was given a revolving fund of Rs. 15,000 to start a common economic activity. It was observed that mere common economic activity was not enough to sustain the group. In most of the groups, the members took their portion of the revolving fund and carried out their economic activity. There was no group dynamics involved. Members came together only for the limited purpose of securing the DWCRA amount and once the amount was received, they tended to disintegrate. Even in the groups where the fund was revolved, there was no increase in the group amount as it was merely mechanical revolvement of funds. Groups were formed on the basis of targets given by the Government of India. Thus DWCRA remained merely a programme and could not become a vehicle of socio-economic upliftment of women.

But with the introduction of Podupulakshmi, the scenario changed. With thrift as an entry point, women came together and organized themselves into groups. They evolved their own thrift and credit management. With regular conduct of meetings it became cohesive group. The women started rotating their own funds, giving loans to members and ensuring repayment of loans. Only after the groups had carried out thrift and credit operation satisfactorily for at least one year, DWCRA amount was sanctioned to such groups. Sanction was based on objective parameters like seniority of groups, regular thrift, internal rotation of savings, regular repayment of loans, regular meetings, proper maintenance of records and other socio-developmental indicators like literacy, children education, family planning etc. This amount was released to the groups with no pre-conditions attached to it. It was left to the group members to decide as to how to use the amount. This was different from existing practice where a common economic activity was insisted upon. The two group leaders were authorized to withdraw the amount.

Women devised a novel way to use DWCRA. They put the amount in the same saving account. With this, the total funds available with the group increased and they started giving bigger loans to the members. Not all the members were given loans at a time. Only a few were selected by the group and loans were given to them to start income generating activity. The group charged interest on DWCRA amount (ranging from 12% to 24%), the same interest rate charged on the thrift amount. Moreover, interest charged ensured that the group corpus increased.

Groups were left to decide for themselves, the kind of income generating activities they would like to take up, basing on the need, skills and aptitude of the members. The groups took up various kinds of income generating activities:

> "We received DWCRA in May '96. We have purchased raw material for silk saree weaving. Each member is earning about Rs. 1000 to Rs. 1200 per month"
>
> — *Razia Sultana Group, Gudur*

> "We have merged the DWCRA fund with our group thrift fund. We are sanctioning loans to needy members. The income-generating activities taken up are: Ram Lamb rearing, crop protection, purchase of organic manure, etc."
>
> — *Mother Teresa Group, Nandikotkur*

> "DWCRA was sanctioned to our group in March '97. The amount was spent for setting up of a hotel, purchase of poultry birds and ram lamb rearing."
>
> — *Jhansi Group, Tatipadu Village, J.Bunglow Mandal*

Credit

Perhaps the most important factor for women to join the groups was availability of credit easily at low rates of interest compared to the abnormally higher rate of interest charged by the moneylenders earlier. Women require micro credit for consumption, education, health and productive purposes which was not forthcoming easily earlier. Reactions from some of the group leaders bear testimony to this:

> "Before joining the groups, we had to approach the landlord who made us to wander around him and now, loan is easily available. Rate of interest was 48-60 per cent earlier and now it is available for 24 per cent."
>
> — *Bhaghyalakshmi Group, Veldurthi Mandal*

> "Earlier some valuable ornaments and articles must be kept as surety and now we just have to sign on the promissory notes for getting loans."
>
> — *Teja Group, Orvakal Mandal*

> "Timely loans were not available earlier and now we get loans whenever we require."
>
> — *Krishna Priya Group, Midthur Mandal*

And the groups gave loans to members for various purposes right from consumption to income generating activities.

- In Krishna Priya Group of Sunkesula Village (Midthur Mandal) Lakshmi Devi was given a loan of Rs. 2,000 for health purpose. P. Chennamma was given Rs. 2,500 for purchase of pesticide and Saleema was given Rs. 2,000 for maintenance of milch animals.
- Lakshmi, a member of Jhansi group, Thatipadu village (J.Bungalow mandal) got a loan of Rs. 4,000 for Kirana business, and another member Murthiya Bee of the same group was given Rs. 2,000 for treatment of her husband.
- In Razia Sultana group of Gudur village, Alisha was given a loan of Rs. 5,000 for son's education whereas Mehroon, another member got Rs. 5,000 for her health.

Group Credit (or) Generation of Employment for Women Through DWCRA

It is being increasingly realized that women's income in the family is very important in relation to the nutritional, economic and educational upliftment of the family. Therefore a provision is made under IRDP that at least 30 per cent of beneficiaries should be women. But the mid-term review of IRDP (1987) had shown that the flow of assistance to the women members of the targeted group of households was very nominal. Hence with an objective of improving the quality of assistance to the rural women, a sharper focus was conceived through the scheme of "Development of Women and Children in Rural Areas" (DWCRA).

The scheme, DWCRA is a sub-scheme of IRDP at district level. Initially in 1982, DWCRA was launched in 50 districts in 22 states. In 1985-86, it was extended to one district each in the Union Territories. The criteria for selection of districts were general backwardness, low female literacy and high infant mortality. The programme was extended to 50 more districts in 1986-87 and 29 more in

1988-89. The government is of the view that scheme should cover all the districts by the end of the Eighth Plan.

Objectives

The main objectives of the scheme:

1. to help and promote self-employment among rural women, who are below the poverty line;
2. to organize the beneficiaries in group activity-wise and promote economic and self-reliance;
3. to organize production enhancing programmes in rural areas;
4. to generate income for the rural poor by creating avenue for production of goods and services;
5. to provide for care of the children of the working women by providing an improvement, care and food and by establishing creche/balwadis.

(a) ***Group Strategy:*** The women members of DWCRA form groups of 10-15 each for taking up economic activities suited to their skills, aptitude and local conditions. One woman from amongst the members functions as a group organizer and helps in the choice of activity, procurement of raw materials, marketing of products etc.

(b) ***Activities Covered:*** The economic activities included under this scheme are mainly cottage and household industrial activities in nature which require less technical skill and small investment. Some of these include tailoring, weaving, fibre making, food processing, bakery, poultry, matches making, leather making, leather work etc.[1]

(c) ***Selection Activity:*** The selected activity should be one for which suitable skill and training is possessed by the members of the group and raw materials and marketing facilities are available locally. The activity selected should be such that it involves all members and encourages groups cohesiveness and sense of belonging.

The scheme identifies women at the age group of 18-35 years who live below poverty line in rural areas. The identifying women are given training for 6 months and paid Rs. 200 as stipend per month. Apart from that, the organizer has to undergo a separate training. After the training is completed each beneficiary is given a loan to start their own business as self employed venture.

(d) ***Financial Pattern:*** In addition to the benefits of loan subsidy of IRDP to individual member, each group of women under DWCRA is given the lumpsum grant of Rs. 15,000 — as Revolving Fund. This amount is contributed in equal shares by Government of India, State Government and UNICEF.

(e) ***Organisational Set-up:*** The Gram Sevika at the lowest rung of the organisational set-up looks after the activities of the group at block level, assisted by the regular Mukhya Sevika and two additional Gram Sevikas. At the district level there will be one post of Assistant Project Officer (APO) who should be a woman taking charge of the programme. She is required to work under the supervision and guidance of the project Director of DRDA. At state level one Deputy Secretary or Director would be in-charge of DWCRA.[2]

(f) ***Marketing of Products:*** The interest of women in the programme can be sustained only when a proper market is arranged for their products. Some state governments have issued orders declaring the DWCRA groups are approved sources for the supply of bulk articles required by the Government Departments. The facilities offered by the various state government emporia, public sector corporations are utilized for sale and display of the DWCRA products. The Gram Shree Melas organized by CAPART are used as forums for the sale of rural products and to encourage women's groups. Supportive institutions for marketing like

District Supply and Marketing societies are being encouraged for setting up by the States. UNICEF will also provide assistance on a selective basis for necessary linkages to make the DWCRA products more marketable.

To extend the benefits of the scheme to more women in rural areas, voluntary organisations are geared up to provide assistance in the implementation of projects for providing income-generation opportunities to these women.

Supportive services like mother and child care, immunisation, provision for working conveniences, adult education etc., are provided to rural women to improve their efficiency and reduce subsequent drudgery.

Apart from direct assistance from DRDA, financial assistance up to Rs. 5 lakh has been targeted to benefit eligible voluntary agencies through the Council for Advancement of Rural Technology (CAPART). The amount would be available for projects aimed at providing income generating activities to the rural population, in particular women.

Those activities which involve training are bought under the scheme of TRYSEM. The National Institute of Rural Development (NIRD) is to act as the nodal institution for all the training activity undertaken by DWCRA.

DWCRA: Basic Problems

(a) The identification of trades is generally done without baseline surveys. Though only a few trades achieve good financial returns, they may not be relevant to the local situation or remunerative to DWCRA beneficiaries.

(b) Case studies reveal that non-traditional units have failed to achieve popularity among the rural women. The reason attributed to this crisis is lack of technical skills among rural women. The initial investment for setting up of non-traditional units is substantially high.

(c) The non-traditional items like wig-making, dress-making and cosmetics do not have sufficient marketing.[3]

(d) The women under DWCRA have not been trained in basic skills for appreciating and availing of the benefits of these viable income generating schemes.

(e) It has also been pointed out that the DWCRA products lack economic feasibility. Most products are left with no buyers in the absence of aggressive marketing.

(f) Some of the assets like machines obtained under DWCRA have failed to enter the market. The trouble would arise when schemes 'get implemented without conducting surveys to assess the reaction and acceptance levels of the target group.

(g) According to one study, the tailoring trade has faced the problem of developing an appropriate strategy for readymade garments.

(h) The major problem of dairy trade is uneven price realisation and that of mat weaving is scarcity of basic raw materials .[4]

(i) The scheme also suffers from the wrong selection of group activities by the groups.

(j) Lack of co-operative zeal among the members of the group was also observed. They generally lack management skill.

(k) The scheme suffered from inadequate availability and high cost of raw materials.

(l) The products failed to secure local demand.

(m) The products suffered from poor quality and also competition from big companies.

(n) Product diversification was an uphill task for women members whereas the market situation required it.

(o) Inadequate provision of backward and forward linkages needed for the smooth functioning of the scheme.

(p) The amount sanctioned for revolving funds remains inadequate.[5]

(q) The training period is too short to master the skill. The trainers had to wait for four to five years for starting the trades. During this period, the trainees tend to lose their grip over the skills they acquired.

(r) Conceptual clarity is lacking in many cases. In many states, training institutes are yet to be identified and set up.

(s) Lack of skill, training, staffing as per norms, low motivational levels of various functionaries, low literacy, lack of convergence with existing services, delay in release of funds from the states to DRDAs and resource constraints are some of the major problems in implementing DWCRA.[6]

(t) The scheme also suffers from many organisational difficulties.

(u) Again artificial groupings lacking in cohesion, may fail to deliver the goods. Furthermore, they are unable to agree upon and select the most suitable activity that has some chance of success.

(v) In certain cases, the assistance has proved to be a liability rather than an asset. This happens when the asset fails to generate income and the women groups have to repay loans with high interest rates.

An evaluation of DWCRA has revealed that:

(a) A low priority has been given to DWCRA by the DRDAs.

(b) Little convergence of other social services and programmes like nutrition, family welfare, immunisation, adult literacy, and

(c) Inadequate marketing outlets and infrastructural facilities.[7]

There is undue delay in the delivery of development assistance. This is mainly due to lack of functional co-ordination among the various agencies, viz., banks, DRDA and the beneficiaries. The implementing agencies generally do not take proper interest in providing any supporting facility, viz., community centres, childcare, adult education, immunisation etc.

Critical Review

The scheme of DWCRA is no doubt a promising programme aimed at providing economic liberty and bringing social awareness among the rural womenfolk and children. But the scheme suffers from certain lacunae which if removed, would result in greater success of the scheme. They are:

1. The assistance provided is too meager to start any activity and the units either be closed down or become defunct in the early stages of formation;
2. No guarantees are extended on behalf of the groups to enable them to get additional resources from the banks;
3. There is no attempt to combat the middleman's role in marketing the goods produced by the groups;
4. There is political meddling in the selection of both members of a group and the activity to be undertaken by it;
5. The Gram Sevika meant for supervision is unable to attend to the needs of the group owing to heavy burden of work;
6. There is lack of commitment among the supervisory staff in making the scheme a success which is attributed to meager payments received by them for their services; and
7. There is lack of publicity with regard to availability of the scheme and its benefits to the rural folk. If these

problems are set right, the objectives of the scheme could definitely be achieved.[8]

Strengthening DWCRA

There is need for identifying suitable and viable trades, depending on the local resources, skills and markets.

The self-employed women need to be brought close to the administrative and welfare machinery. There must be a confidence building attitude on the part of the officials. Also, frequent change in the group organizer, as is now the practice, should be completely stopped.

The ceilings for construction of multi-purpose community centres for use by DWCRA beneficiaries have also been raised to Rs. 1.90 lakh and Rs. 2.30 lakh for centres located in plain and hilly areas respectively.

The DWCRA has been laying stress on easier processing of documents to help the women meet their credit needs. Thrift and credit is an important group activity of the DWCRA scheme.

Another pilot project of Management Information Systems for DWCRA has been introduced in 19 districts. In 14 districts out of 19 planned intervention has been sought at all levels of DWCRA for better awareness education and information through mass media, mainly All India Radio.

Marketing continues to be a major problem. Therefore, supply and marketing societies should be formed at different levels to help the groups in marketing their products. It is desirable to open sale points at the block and district headquarters to promote the sale of products. A suggestion was made that State Governments should make provisions for the purchase of products made by women's groups. [9]

Conclusion

The scheme of DWCRA is aimed mainly at providing opportunities of self employment to women members of rural families below the poverty line. The benefits of the scheme have been extended to groups of women consisting of 10 to 15 members under each group. The maximum assistance sanctioned to each group is Rs. 15,000 that is Rs. 1,000 per member to take up an economic activity that suits to the talents of the group and local conditions in terms of availability of raw materials and market. The assistance sanctioned to each group needs to be shared by the Central Government, the State Government and the UNICEF in equal proportions that is Rs. 5,000 each. The assistance so provided is of recurring type and carries no interest. The group elects one of its members as group organizer who generally looks after the activities of the group. The Gram Sevika appointed specially for this purpose with the help extended by Mukhya Sevika and other two Gram Sevikas of the block, supervises the group activities. The Government also allows the groups to avail of bank credit to enable them to meet enhanced investment requirements which fulfill certain conditions. The monitoring and evaluation of the performance of the scheme is made simple by developing formats for groups, blocks and districts to obtain the required information from them. The time schedule for submission of reports and returns by groups, blocks and districts to their immediate authorities is also developed to make them accountable.

As seen in the table 3.1, the number of DWCRA and SHGs increased from I528 in 1995-96 to 21,926 by May, 2005. The number of women covered also increases from 22,920 to 2,85,038 over the same time period. Savings accumulated by the groups also increases from 82.51 lakhs in the year I995-96 to 4690.26 lakhs in the year 2005 (May). Such increased savings were good source of investment in their group's economic activities.

The table 3.1 also shows the financial assistance provided to the groups under the IRDP/SGSY scheme, Revolving Fund or Matching Grant, SHG Bank linkage and Corpus since I995-96 in Kurnool district. SHG Bank linkage

Table 3.1 Number of DWCRA Groups Since Inception in Kurnool District

Sl.No.	Particulars	Unit	1995-96	1996-97	1997-98	1998-99	1999-2000	2000-2001	2001-2002	2002-2003	2003-2004	2004-2005
1	Self-Help Groups/DWCRA											
	a. No. of Groups	No.	1528	2260	3234	4913	7850	10575	12057	18913	21082	21926
	b. Women Covered	No.	22920	33900	47536	71042	112160	150310	169576	242019	258221	285038
	c. Savings	Rs.	82.51	204.55	367.55	615.16	1010.80	1543.78	2151.45	3126.06	790.94	4690.26
2	Economic support scheme IRDP/SGSY	No.	852.01	1770.34	864.49	716.34	102.47	610.54	531.37	510.76	154.48	266.77
3	Revolving Fund/ State Matching Grant	No.	299.50	155.05	109.96	345.45	93.65	634.44	479.25	425	380.60	125.90
4	SHG Linkage	No.	0	0	0	0	0	462.32	912.37	2887.49	4474.95	5951.62
5	Corpus	Rs.	1234.02	2129.94	1342	1676.95	1206.92	3251.08	4074.44	6949.31	5800.97	11034.55

also increases from 462 lakhs in 2000-2001 to 5951 lakhs in 2004-2005.

Causes for the Failure of DWCRA Programme

The programme specifically meant for women such as DWCRA failed because of the following factors:

1. The high transaction costs;
2. Approaches of risk aversion;
3. Lending to collaterised borrowers;
4. The cultural and social distance between the formal sector bankers and the poor;
5. The exclusion of the poor from the reliable and non-exploitative sources of credit leaves them to informal sources.[10]

The Background for the Origin if SHGs

The Independent South Asia Commission for Poverty Alleviation (ISACPA, 1992)[11] argues that the centerpiece of a policy framework for poverty alleviation has to be the mobilisation of the poor in order to enable them to participate directly and effectively in the decisions that affect their lives and prospects. Excessive dependence on the state for every lead in development has curtailed initiatives of the people. Obsessive preoccupation with capital accumulation as the driving force of economic progress has resulted in neglecting the capacity of the poor themselves. Consequently, the commission favours a strategy that "mainstreams the process of social mobilisation as an essential ingredient of the growth of civil society encourages the growth of grassroots organisations for development, establishes linkages between these grassroot organisations and government and private service agencies, and without compromising the dependence of these grassroot organisations, attempts to establish a symbiotic relationship between these organisations and local government institutions" (ISACPA - 1992).[12]

Experience after experience has proved that organising the poor into self-governing communities works in relation to the myriad of their felt needs. A participatory model of micro credit initiatives implemented by NABARD in Maharashtra under their Maharashtra Rural Credit Programme (MRCP) and worldwide success story of Self Employed Women's Association (SEWA) in Gujarat and Kerala are a few illustrations in this direction.

The broad dimensions of social mobilisation are becoming increasingly known in South Asia. The main objective of social mobilisation is to induce the poor to create participatory organisations based on the direct and full participation of all members from varied socio-cultural backgrounds, irrespective of income, caste, gender or other discriminating characteristics. The social mobilisation effort for poverty alleviation must be based on entry points that are the key to poverty alleviation, redressal of the problems and obstacles identified by the poor themselves, food security, literacy and primary education, health, shelter, credit, productive infrastructure and employment.

Case for SHGs Formation

Individually, a poor person tends to be rather tentative, uncertain in his behaviour but group membership smoothes the rough edges of his behaviour pattern, making him more reliable as a borrower. A poor person feels exposed to all kinds of hazards, he requires guidance and advice from people he knows and can trust.

Membership in group gives him a feeling of protection. Thus, formation of a group would ensure the best participation of the poor in a credit programme.

The approach towards poverty alleviation should be self-help. Others should help the poor to help themselves. It is felt that individual effort is too inadequate to improve their fate. This brings about the necessity for organising them in a group by which they get the benefit of collective perception, collective decision-making and collective implementation of programmes for common benefits. The organisation holds power and provides strength, it can be an antidote to the helplessness of the poor.

The multiplier effect of investment can be vividly demonstrated in a credit programme for the rural poor through the continuous expansion of their economic base. Incomes also rise with additional investment through borrowing. The vicious cycle of low income/low savings/low investment/low income can be broken by injection of credit in the cycle. Credit/more investment/more income/more savings/more income is the result that is sought through credit intervention.

Self Help Groups are now gaining acceptance as an alternative system of credit, delivery, especially to people who are the poorest of poor. Institutions in the organized sector have come to realize that using the group mode could significantly reduce their transaction costs while at the same time strengthen monitoring of use of credit through peer pressure. The group mode enhances the rates of recovery and makes lending to poor substantially less risky as compared to the risk faced in their normal loan portfolio. Borrower selection and assessment of feasibility of the activity chosen are done with more than ordinary efficiency by the groups. With such advantages accruing to the institutions which extend credit, it is not surprising that they are increasingly inclined to support groups.

Why Self-Help Groups

Why should the individuals get into a group? What are their reasons to join such groups? Some of the reasons for such questions are:

1. ***Access to Credit:*** The poor have limited access to credit. The poorest of poor have little access to formal credit. Informal credit too is not easily available to such people because of their status. Even if it is available, it is prohibitively costly so much so that it is availed

only in life threatening situations. By joining a group people become stronger in dealing with formal institutions and accessing credit. In most of the groups, access to economic resources has been a powerful motivator;

2. ***Lender of the Last Resort:*** The formal credit structure does not recognize credit needs that are emergent, or that are necessary, if they are not for productive purposes. The emergencies that befall ones life are countless. The poorer one is, the more is the tyranny of such situations for which credit is not available. Unless a person's emergent needs are met he/she would not undertake productive effort. If a system exists that takes care of consumption credit needs, it would provide welcome relief. This is the major selling point of SHGs. Most SHGs during the initial period, give out more consumption loans. Subsequently a shift is seen towards productive loans;

3. ***Borrower Transaction Costs:*** Even where limited access to credit is possible the borrower incurs costs (other than bank charges) which are substantial. The number of visits made to the bank carry transport and incidental costs apart from wages lost during the time spent on such visits. The documentation for loans involves completion of vexatious formalities which again adds to borrower's costs. Again 'corruption costs' of paying officials in different capacities in different agencies adds to borrower's costs and his misery. If there could be a channel through which one could access credit without incurring such unconscionable costs the borrower would willingly opt for it. For most borrowers of small loans, groups meant a low transaction cost option. Dr.Puhazhendi, AGM, NABARD, has concluded that borrowers significantly reduce their transaction costs of borrowing if they access credit through SHGs;

4. ***Freedom to the Borrower:*** Formal credit has been associated with the myriad terms and conditions on use of credit in the name of ensuing security of banks interests. In rural lending for development, many stipulations have been made;

   Self-help groups offers such freedom to the entrepreneurs within limits of reason. The borrower could determine his activity, location scale of operations and choice of technology. This makes him/her more certain of his/her ability to take the risks and cope with the same;

5. ***Equality:*** The poor have always been made to feel poorer and unequal and decisions regarding his resource needs are taken by the 'wise' and 'elite'. They feel helpless before the educated and capable, running the formal and informal socio-economic systems. Only in SHGs these people are treated as equals. For the first time perhaps in their life, they enjoy such equal treatment. This sense of equality attracts people to SHGs where they can have access to resources with their 'self-worth' intact;

6. ***Confidence in Own Abilities:*** The SHGs offer a means by which they could have access to resources in their own right, without waiting on anyone, and not by another person's mercy. This gives people confidence that by saving small amounts, over a period of time they could muster resources to help each other in a big way. This gives them a feeling of being also in-charge of their own lives. They feel emboldened to conduct themselves and take a share of resources as a matter of right. This is perhaps, what Empowerment is all about. This feeling of autonomy and control over one's own life is a powerful attraction provided by SHGs;[13]

7. ***Improved Loan Recoveries:*** The peer pressure based on joint liability brings about a remarkable

improvement in loan recoveries, leading to improved loan recycling and continued access to borrowing;

8. ***Promotion of Thrift and Savings:*** Most participatory credit programmes insist on regular savings—generally a fixed small amount monthly by the members. Such compulsory saving leads towards gradual accumulation of bigger funds. Just the availability of a convenient small saving facility in their locality is likely to promote the practice of voluntary savings among the poor;

9. ***Overcoming Asymmetric Information Problems:*** The three main such problems are screening, incentive and enforcement identified under the imperfect information paradigm. The small size and familiarity of the members help SHGs to better screen the borrowers with regard to risk involved and repayment capacity. The joint liability of members creates an enforcement mechanism primarily based on peer monitoring and pressure;[14]

10. ***Take up Various Development Activities:*** SHGs being people centered organisations, can take up various development activities on participatory basis. The development activities can be in the areas of education, water supply, environmental sanitation, road access, electric power availability and even tele-communication facilities;

11. ***Help in Implementation of Income Generation Programmes:*** SHGs can help implement income generation progammes by collectively addressing entrepreneurial problems such as provisioning of inputs, improving production and marketing facilities and obtaining better terms through their collective bargaining strength;

12. In self help groups, collective action and solidarity is an important empowering mechanism.

Definition of a Self-Help Group

The definition of a self-help group was one that satisfied the following five conditions:

1. ***Purpose:*** Its express, primary purpose is to provide help and support for its members in dealing with their problems and in improving their psychological functioning and effectiveness;

2. ***Origin and Sanction:*** Its origin and sanction for existence rest with the members of the group themselves, rather than with some external agency or authority;

3. ***Source of Help:*** It relies upon its own members efforts, skills, knowledge and concern as its primary source of help, with the structure of the relationship between members being one of peers, so far as help-giving and support are concerned;

4. ***Composition:*** It is generally composed of members who share a common core of life experience and problems;

5. ***Control:*** Its structure and mode of operation are under the control of members although they may, in turn, draw upon professional guidance and various theoretical and philosophical frameworks.[15]

Self-Help Groups

The SHG is an association of people belonging to similar socio-economic characteristics residing in the same locality.

The SHG is a voluntary group "valuing personal interactions and mutual aid as a means of altering or ameliorating problems perceived as alterable, pressing and personal by most of its members."

The SHGs are voluntary associations of people formed to attain some common goals. These are groups which have similar social identity, heritage, caste or traditional occupations, and come together for a common cause and manage resources for the benefit of the group members.[16]

The SHG is a group of rural poor who have volunteered to organize themselves into a group for eradication of poverty of the members. They agree to save regularly and convert that savings into a common fund. The members of the group agree to use this common fund.

Even when group members are engaged in a similar traditional activity like basket weaving, the basis of the people's affinity is a common caste or origin.[17]

The SHGs believe in two things:

(a) The poor can transit from dependency to self-reliance much faster through social mobilisation, awareness creation than through economic interventions; and

(b) Women form the basis for social mobilisation and therefore aiming for women's empowerment is the most cost effective strategy available, even for economic development.

The SHGs aim at promoting awareness among the poor about the on-going development programmes.

SHGs are presently promoted by governments, development banks, and voluntary agencies, with focus on social and economic issues, mainly thrift and credit programmes. They are also taking up issues relating to rural industries and modernisation of agriculture.

The banks are in a better position to provide credit because of better avenue for credit absorption, and the recoveries are also better.

The group approach is cost effective so far as seeking institutional credit is concerned. The group approach can ensure wider coverage of poor families through bank credit. Also, the members of the group learn to independently approach the bank for bigger loan due to direct interaction and guidance from the banks.

Emergence of Self-Help Group for Banking with the Poor

In many third world countries, including India, despite the commendable efforts put in by the credit institutions, a large section of the poor population has still not got access to the credit from the formal banking system and depends upon conventional private sources like moneylenders, village shopkeepers etc., for their credit needs.

Besides, there is also a problem of magnitude of the borrowers, particularly in South-East Asian Countries where the demand for credit both for farm and non-farm activities from the small farmers has increased substantially. For example, by the turn of the century India may have around 200 million rural or semi-urban small borrowers. It may not be possible for any formal banking system to effectively and directly cater to the needs of so many small borrowers. Further in many countries, including India, the recycling of funds has suffered on account of the generally poor recoveries of rural loans.

(a) From the Angle of Poor

1. Due to their social, economic and educational backwardness and being unorganized they are unaware of various programmes of the facilities available from the government and banks and are generally deprived of access to such benefits.
2. They have an apprehension that the banks are not meant for poor people like them and they would not be able to get loans from the banks.
3. Lack of security to avail bank loan.
4. Documentation procedures, rigid lending policies and norms of the banks generally make the poor ineligible for bank credit.
5. The uncertainty and long delays in obtaining such loans from the banks discourage them to approach the banks.
6. In some cases, past unpleasant experience of the poor with the banks and government agencies is also a discouraging factor.

(b) From the Angle of Banks

1. General mental reservation about financing poor borrowers mainly due to the fear of bad debts.
2. Lack of security to back such loans.
3. Non-compliance of documentation and other formalities by the borrowers.
4. Non-conformity with the usual banking norms.
5. Low returns to the bank on account of lower rate of interest to be charged on such small loans in accordance with the regulations of the Central Bank or Governments.
6. Servicing large number of small loans with frequent transactions spread over a vast area is unwieldy besides involving high cost, making it inconvenient and apparently uneconomic for the banks.

The result of all this is that the vast section of poor population continues to be outside the fold of banking system despite the best efforts by all. The concept of SHGs helps resolving this situation.[18]

The Four-in-One Role of SHGs

1. ***A moneylender:*** Providing quickly small emergent loans, but without charging exploitative rate of interest.
2. ***A development bank:*** Providing small production and investment credit to the poor for their economic upliftment, but without going through the long procedures, documentation, security requirements, etc., and at lesser transaction cost.
3. ***A cooperative:*** Following participative approach of mutual cooperation and joint pressure, without the ills of selfish interest, interference of the big brothers / Government department officials etc., and with a lot of flexibility, and

4. ***A voluntary agency:*** Helping each other through their common and social upliftment among the poor people.

SHG Characteristics

Some of the basic characteristics of SHGs promoted by NGOs and banks in various parts of the country are given in Table 3.2. One of the important features observed is the homogeneity in the group in terms of social and economic status. The size of membership in each group is advocated between 10 and 20, while there is no gender specificity, majority of the groups that formed are of women. The group is expected to function in a democratic manner and the leader may be elected or selected. The basic functions envisaged are saving mobilisation, creation of common fund out of saving, availing credit from banks and loaning to members. Various purposes of loan to individuals include loans for consumption clearing outside debt, social, medical, education, business, agriculture etc., besides for common production activities.

Table 3.2 Some Basic Features of SHGs Promoted by NGOs/ Banks

1. Organisation	Homogeneity in terms of economic/socio-economic status, common identity of activities etc.
2. Nature of Target Groups	Generally poor and weaker sections of the people in rural areas and particularly women.
3. Management	Selected/elected leader leads the group. Holds meetings regularly once or twice in a month
4. Financial Instruments:	
(a) Common fund	Created out of savings, interests earned on loans, donations, etc.
(b) Savings Mobilisation	While in certain cases no fixed rate of savings, in some cases regular and fixed rate of savings and in some cases as per capacity of the members in the group.

(Contd...)

(c) Loaning	Decided by the purpose, quantum and the resources available with the SHGs. Purpose of loans for individuals include consumption, clearing outside debt, social, medical, education, business, agriculture etc., and loans for common production.
(d) Repayment period	Generally lower than prescribed by banks.
(e) Rate of interest	Varies from 12 to 20 per cent. In a few cases, the interest rates are determined by the NGOs
5. Linkage with Banks	Banks treats SHGs as borrowers.

Source: Desai and Namboodiri (2001).

Formation of SHGs

The following stages are suggested for formation of the SHGs and linking them with the banks/activity:

1. NGOs/voluntary agencies to organize small groups of 10-25 poor people, based on homogeneous socio-economic factors;
2. Through regular savings of the members, SHGs should build up their fund, to be supplemented by some contributions from the NGOs, wherever possible, as also out of the income of interest on loans and common activities;
3. NGO should train the SHG members for maintaining the accounts on savings, lending and repayments as also for finding solution to their common problems;
4. SHG should start lending operations out of the group funds to their members. Initially it will be mainly for emergent consumption, health and social needs. Subsequently small production needs can also be met depending upon the position of resources;
5. At this stage, when the groups require more funds for meeting the needs of the members for undertaking

economic activities, the banks should enter the field, interact with the groups assess its fund requirement, decide about the credibility of the group and its members, and give loans to the SHGs, for adding to the corpus funds. While the bank will charge the usual rate of interest, the group will in turn be free to charge to members any rate of interest it thinks reasonable based on the joint decision of the members. It generally varies from 12 per cent to 36 per cent. The margin in the interest rates adds to the income of the group and goes to its corpus fund;

The repayment will be made by the group, the repayments will generally be faster. There will be no collateral security. The main documents of loan will be signed by authorized group leaders. However, if required by the bank, a jointly signed document may also be obtained from all group members, if necessary, indicating some sort of mutual guarantee and responsibility for repayments;

6. Under special circumstances, in case of difficult areas where banks branch network is poor and or the banks do not have confidence in lending to SHGs or for some reason SHGs are reluctant to borrow from the banks, the banks may consider providing bulk finance to the NGO who in turn may pass on to SHGs, retaining some margin, if necessary;

7. After sometime for larger investment and production needs of the individual members, the banks may consider giving loans directly to the members on the specific recommendation of the group;

In course of time when the creditability of the group and its members is established and banks are satisfied, and also the members develop confidence to manage their affairs the NGO can slowly withdraw and move to other uncovered pockets. The banks in that case will deal directly with the SHGs and their members.

In this process of financing SHGs, banks and NGO's should take care that:

(a) Money/credit should not be made available in abundance, it should be scarce and flow should increase gradually;

(b) Savings by members should be a must before credit flows; and

(c) Group to be eligible for loan should have existed for sometime, say six months to one year, by which time it should have learnt the process of saving, loaning, repayments, accounts maintenance, mutual help and group pressure etc.[19]

Experience of Loaning Through SHGs

A case study on Kurnool experience in financing SHGs by Banks was conducted. On selective basis, banks have given loans either through SHGs or to the SHGs for poor beneficiaries. The experience has shown that recovery in the case of bank loans through SHGs were above 90 per cent as compared to the direct lending, where recovery was about 50 per cent.

Further, it was also observed that the transaction cost of the bank was reduced by about one-third when the lending was done through the SHGs.

Table 3.3 Recovery Performance

(Rs in 000)

Sl. No.	Particulars	Demand	Collection	Balance	% of recovery
	Case Branch Level				
1.	Direct Lending	3280	1395	1885	42.53
	Lending through SHGs	902	783	119	86.80
	Selected Case SHG				
2.	village level				
	Non-Group beneficiaries	66	25	41	37.88
	SHG beneficiaries	26	24	2	92.30

The transaction cost may further reduce if the loans are distributed to the SHGs as indicated above as it will require maintaining and servicing a single account.

Table 3.4 Cost of Lending Per Account

Sl. No.	*Particulars*	*SHG Members*	*Non-Self-Help Group Members*
1.	Salary and allowances and travel expenses	83	135
2.	Establishment expenses	8	8
3.	Other expenses	14	14
	Total	105	157

The reasons for better repayments in case of loan to or through SHGs are:

1. Quick easy and realistic appraisal of the loan activity and the borrower by the group;
2. Flexibility of lending procedures and norms and quick availability of loans;
3. Effective follow up on the part of group members leading to proper utilisation of loan; and
4. Group pressure and social stigma as also fear of expulsion from the group and deprivation of future benefits etc.

Based on the conditions prevailing in many less developed countries in regard to the credit availability to the poor it is apparent that the banks can play a crucial role in the process of economic upliftment of the poor by accepting concept of SHGs for providing credit to the poor and vulnerable sections of the society.

The general impression that the poor are not bankable is ill founded. They are very much bankable. If properly organized and given the proper set up, they can save, they are good borrowers and their repayment rates are far better than those of the other better off borrowers.

Need for Gender Centred Development

Poor women's voice is seldom heard in the corridors of power. Plans and policies are invariably made at high levels where women's representation is, often, glaringly absent. Unless poor women have access to decisions that effect and influence their lives, policies, and programmes will continuously fail to integrate poor women into the mainstream of development. This has already become evident from numerous examples in South Asia region, for instance, institutional credit programmes in most countries still pursue a gender bias against poor women and the need for collateral security makes the situation worse. Women are on the frontlines of household and community efforts to escape poverty or cope with its impact. But, they often lack power in participating in decision making within the family, in the community, or in national and international arenas. Gender equality must be a part of every country's strategy for eradicating poverty, both as an end and as a means to ensure success. Without gender equality, poverty eradication will not be achieved and any resources invested in other areas will be wasted.

Hirway (1984)[20] holds that a gender centred development approach that keeps gender equity at the centre of the development process is needed and not at the margin to be addressed by adhoc piecemeal programmes. That is, the development strategy should address the problem of exclusion and marginalisation of rural women while working for their higher incomes and higher welfare.

The low social status of women in the rural society stems from the insignificant economic status ascribed to them in the rural economy resulting in their continued economic dependence on the male members of the household. One major contributing factor to this state of affairs is poor access to financial support from formal institutional sources.

However, from early nineties, financial institutions and Government of India are recognizing the informal groups or SHGs promoted by government agencies or NGO's, as a potent tool for empowerment of rural women. This has facilitated provision of institutional loans to women in rural areas. The announcement in the Union Budget 1998-99 to link two lakh informal groups with the banks and provide them financial support during the subsequent five years has given an impetus to the process of group formation among the poor in the rural areas. Efforts made by National Bank for Agriculture and Rural Development (NABARD) for implementing the linkage programme of the SHGs with the formal credit institutions have provided further fillip for this approach (NABARD, 1999).[21]

Women's Movement

Throughout history women have collectively struggled against direct and indirect barriers to their self-development and their full social, political and economic participation. The history of the women's movement is usually dated to the social reform movements of the 19th century and when campaigns for the betterment of the conditions of women's lives were taken up, initially by men. By the end of the century women had begun to organize themselves. Gradually they took up a number of causes such as education, conditions of women's work and so on. The women's organisations started struggle for women's rights in the early part of the twentieth century. At present women movement focuses its attention on equality and empowerment. The activism within the women movement has influenced policy and planning of the government for development and empowerment.

Women's movements in general are directed by objectives like to promote better understanding of the process of social, technological and environmental changes, to contribute to the pursuit of human rights and to develop alternative concept, approach and strategies to bring out necessary changes for bettering the life of women with autonomy, freedom and full rights of citizens.

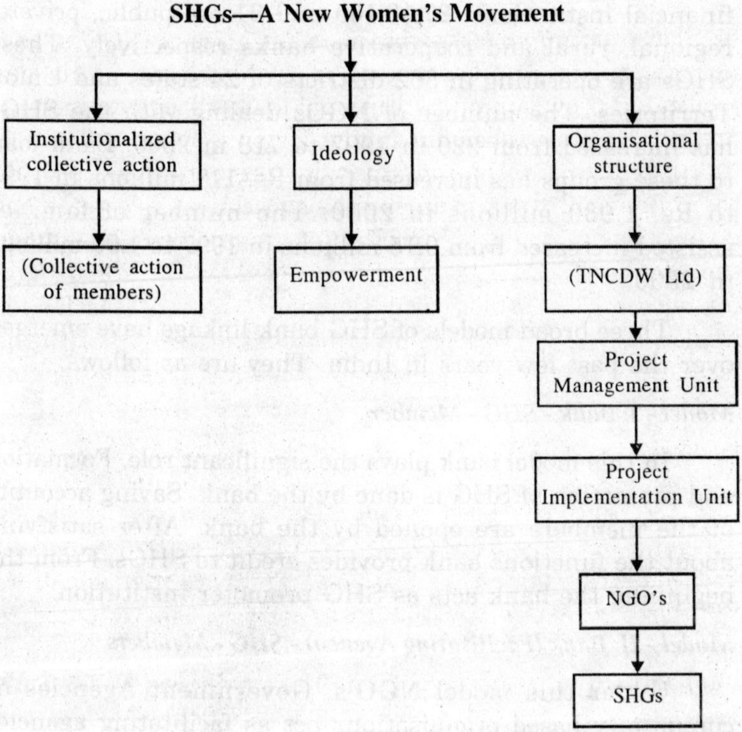

Progress of SHGs

It is probably the world's largest and most successful micro-finance programme for the rural poor outstanding for its emphasis on self-reliance and local autonomy of the very poor. NABARD proposes to reach 100 million of India's rural poor with savings and credit by 2008.

NABARD has brought out a publication on some basic data on SHGs (NABARD, 1999-2000). According to this, the number of SHGs availing credit has increased from 3,841 in 1997 to 81,780 in 2000. The total number of SHGs linked to the banks stand at 1,14,755 in March 2000. Eighty five per cent of them are women groups. The number of financial institutions extending credit to SHGs has increased from 120 in 1997 to 266 in 2000. Out of the 266 financial institutions, 27,13,165 and 61 are public, private, regional, rural and cooperative banks respectively. These SHGs are operating in 362 districts of 24 states and Union Territories. The number of NGOs dealing with the SHGs has increased from 220 in 1997 to 718 in 2000. Bank loan to these groups has increased from Rs. 118 millions in 1997 to Rs. 1,930 millions in 2000. The number of families assisted increased from 0.15 millions in 1997 to 1.90 millions in 2000.

Three broad models of SHG bank linkage have emerged over the past few years in India. They are as follows:

Model - I: Bank - SHG - Member

In this model bank plays the significant role. Formation and promotion of SHG is done by the bank. Saving accounts of the members are opened by the bank. After satisfying about the functions bank provides credit to SHGs. From the beginning the bank acts as SHG promoter institution.

Model - II: Bank (Facilitating Agency) - SHG - Members

Under this model NGO's, Government Agencies or community based organisations act as facilitating agencies from SHGs. The groups are developed, nurtured and trained by these agencies. Bank observes the operations of the SHGs and after satisfying the functions helps them to open savings accounts and provides credit directly to the SHGs. Seventy per cent of the SHGs are linked under this model. The State Government agencies like DRDA and DWDA play active role in linkage of this model. Cooperatives have a greater role to play. They should take laudable efforts in linkage exercises.

Model - III: Bank - NGO - MFI - SHG - Members

This model is totally different from other two models. Under this model SHGs are nurtured, promoted and even financed by NGO's. NGO's act as facilitator and micro finance intermediaries (MFI's). After sometime, when the SHGs have fully developed and stabilized, banks are being approached by the NGO's for loans for on lending to SHGs. Very important development in this model is that NGO's have also been found to federate the SHGs and gradually equip the SHG federations to take on this role. Sixteen per cent of the SHGs are linked during the year 1999-2000.

Disbursement under Model I remains more or less the same. 13 per cent in 1997 and 14 per cent in 2000. The major change that has taken place is with regard to Models II and III where as the share of Model II has gradually increased from 45 in 1997 to 70 per cent in 2000; that of Model III has been continuously declining from 42 in 1997 to 16 per cent in 2000. Lending institutions are thus becoming more comfortable in dealing with grassroots SHGs which is a positive development.

Average credit per SHG extended under Models I, II, III are Rs. 25,056, Rs. 20,415 and Rs. 16,190 respectively. Models II and III together account for 85.7 per cent of the SHGs and 82.4 per cent of disbursement indicating a substantial involvement of the NGO's in the credit business of the SHGs.

Three sets of Financial institutions namely commercial banks, Regional Rural Banks (RRB's) and cooperatives account for 55, 41 and 4 per cent of the SHGs and 66, 30 and 4 per cent of credit per SHG by these institutions are Rs. 24,765, Rs. 14,734 and Rs. 19,091 respectively. The cooperative sectors involvement in SHG is quite negligible except in the eastern region (especially in West Bengal) where it accounts for 21 per cent of credit. Unless the State Governments change the laws, it is difficult for them to lend to the SHGs outside the framework of Primary Agricultural Cooperative Societies (PACS's).

The linkage with the cooperative credit system is proverbially poor. As such need of the hour is to make an earnest effort to bring about effective linkage with the cooperatives.

The programme of linking SHGs with cooperative banks have to be geared up. So far cooperative banks have covered only 14 states and one union territory. As on 31.3.2000 cooperatives have linked 4028 SHGs. The intermediation of the SHGs between the banks and the rural poor would cut down the transaction costs for both banks and the rural clients. Further it would help evolving supplementary credit strategies for meeting the credit needs of the poor by combining the flexibility, sensitivity and responsiveness of the informal credit system, with the strength of technical and administrative capabilities and financial resources of the formal financial institutions. Mutual trust and confidence between the bankers and the rural poor too can be built up. The internationally accepted successful banking experiment of Bangladesh Grameena Bank can be viewed as a useful model and the tool of social engineering.[22]

In order to supplement the efforts of voluntary organisations informing SHGs in rural areas, the International Fund for Agricultural Development is providing financial assistance to recognized institutions to set-up SHGs to engage in agricultural and allied activities.[23]

NABARD and SHGs

The National Bank for Agriculture and Rural Development (NABARD) launched a pilot project in 1992 for linking SHGs with formal lending institutions to promote the habit of thrift. NABARD provided refinance to banks for on lending to SHGs. Similar projects have been functioning in countries like Bangladesh, Malaysia, Korea, Philippines and Indonesia.

Beginning with 255 SHGs launched by the bank in 1992-93, the figure reached 620 in 1993-94 and 2122 by 1994-95. As on March 1998, the total number of SHG's linked to banks were 14,317 with group savings aggregating to about Rs 80 million. The programme had benefited nearly 1,50,000 rural families. Till March 31st 2001, loans aggregating Rs. 766.20 crore have been sanctioned to state governments for projects being implemented by SHGs and NGOs.

The poor communities requires continuous support. Presently NGO's working with SHGs meet most of their costs of operations through assistance available from government agencies/apex donor agencies including international organisations. But the SHGs cannot afford to depend on such external assistance on a permanent basis.[24]

What is however of concern is the skewed growth of the SHG. This is mainly because of presence of large number of NGO's here. Sixty one per cent of the NGO's operate in the Southern region where 74 per cent of NGO's linked SHGs function. The poorer regions like North-Eastern, Eastern and Central, which are credit starved areas, account for only 0.2, 4.1 and 6.9 per cent of SHG credit respectively.

In the Eastern region 64 out of 82 NGO's (78 per cent) are in Orissa alone, indicating a further skewness within a region. In the southern region Andhra Pradesh accounts for 60 per cent of the SHGs and 57.3 per cent of the SHG credit. In the central region, Uttar Pradesh accounts for 82 per cent of the SHGs.

In 2001, national conference on SHGs and SGSY was organized at NIRD and we present the data from the proceedings of the conference regarding the progress of SHGs and activities under SGSY in different regions and states in India. States which had good head—start with SHGs particularly Southern states have shown better performance as is evident from the data set given in Table 3.5.

Besides the availability of NGO's. the ability, integrity, experience and finally their acceptability by the financial institutions are the other factors that help the SHGs in getting credit. Whereas in the western and southern regions, the average number of SHGs per NGO having availed bank credit is 92 and 66 respectively, in other regions these figures are below 30. Among the states, Andhra Pradesh, Gujarat, Maharashtra, Karnataka, Bihar, Tamil Nadu and Uttar Pradesh far better with 145, 109, 76, 62, 59, 55 and

53 credit linked SHGs per NGO respectively. Among these Bihar, Maharashtra, Uttar Pradesh and Gujarat have 8, 18, 23 and 25 NGO's which have been accepted by the financial institutions (Rajaram Das Gupta, 2001).[25]

Table 3.5 SHGs in India

Sl. No.	*State/Region*	*No. of SHG*	*No. of SHGs started economic activities*	*Total Women members (both SHG & Ind., swarozgaris)*	*Percentage of funds utilized to total funds*
	Northern Region				
1.	Chattisgarh	11528	1624 (14.1)	5909 (38.71)	20.16
2.	H.P	1764	638 (36.16)	5008 (49.89)	67.45
3.	J&K	NR	NR	0	45.89
4.	M.P	34369	1425 (4.14)	11618 (28.22)	77.75
5.	U.P	37466	227 (0.60)	28865 (23.26)	57.48
6.	Uttaranchal	2004	-	4 (5.8)	3.34
7.	Haryana	1974	67 (3.39)	8297 (48.89)	81.50
8.	Punjab	1223	176 (14.39)	4512 (37.91)	131.99
	Eastern Region				
1.	Orissa	18076	1169 (6.46)	2134 (24.7)	94.18
2.	West Bengal	6911	844 (12.21)	11006 (70.70)	7.51
3.	Bihar	9640	3426 (35.53)	28508 (26.06)	47.37
4.	Jharkhand	3962	814 (20.54)	10353 (34.37)	46.74
	Western Region				
1.	Goa	38589	0	7 (30.43)	5.07
2.	Gujarat	9219	805 (8.73)	8803 (30.10)	90.71
3.	Maharashtra	36004	1477 (4.10)	33696 (38.52)	82.03
4.	Rajasthan	3326	32 (0.96)	17888 (40.19)	77.25
	Southern Region				
1.	A.P	219007	2985 (1.36)	40784 (69.39)	73.41
2.	Karnataka	13403	1441 (10.75)	17174 (59.16)	58.62
3.	Kerala	17944	508 (2.83)	11390 (68.32)	151.71
4.	Tamil Nadu	43985	4712 (10.71)	73384 (87.99)	120.94

(Contd...)

	North-Eastern Region				
1.	Arunachal Pradesh	42	42(100.00)	348 (45.72)	28.5
2.	Assam	6341	799 (12.60)	3997 (39.90)	56.48
3.	Manipur	0	N R		0
4.	Maghalaya	346	33 (9.53)	753 (95.43)	0
5.	Mizoram	102	43 (42.15)	728(100.00)	52.70
6.	Nagaland	86	86(100.00)	1376(100.00)	17.38
7.	Tripura	237	160 (67.51)	5191 (52.70)	43.75
8	Sikkim	103	5 (4.850)	1873 (23.43)	82.17

Source: National Conference on Self-Help Groups Movement in the Country and Swarnajayanthi Gram Swarojgar Yojana, June 23-24, 2001

Background Material: National Institute of Rural Development, Rajendra Nagar, Hyderabad - 500 030

Note: Values in parenthesis are percentages.

Further, the NABARD is making an exercise of bringing variety of institutions in the formal and non-formal sector and groom them to take up the role of Self-Help Groups promoting Institutions. NABARD is expected to associate about 4000 NGOs and other agencies in the task by the year 2008. It is also expected that about 1000 federations or cooperatives of SHGs will have to be involved to take up financial intermediation.

Strengthening SHGs

There is need for promoting interactions between the SHGs and government officials. This is necessary to acquire a more realistic understanding of the harsh realities. The SHGs should be free from the influence of vested interest.

Also experience has shown that women Self-Help groups are more effective and have better chances of survival.

Banks do guide the SHGs and this involves some costs. These cannot be borne by banks on a permanent basis. The participating families have to meet their costs.

After sometime, the families try to withdraw some portion of their accumulated capital. As bank finance is linked to pooled savings, such withdrawals go against the interest of the groups. Hence the repayment pattern of the SHG needs more stress than the amount of savings.

Rural Development Strategies in developing countries ought to assign an important role to SHGs in order to successfully implement pro-poor development schemes.

Summing Up

Rural poverty is mostly concentrated in South Asia and that too on the Indian sub-continent. Rural women are doubly disadvantaged segments are by passed by the development process and remain excluded from the benefits under various schemes of development with an account on poverty reduction. The emergence and progress of the SHG movement is expected to bring about greater social mobilisation through economic empowerment and capacity building. The stakeholders, government, NGO's and other community based institutions are facilitating their promotion and stabilisation. The SHGs are linked with financial institutions for financial assistance and they are showing signs of consolidation and expansion though their spread is characterized by geographical skewness.

REFERENCES

1. C. Thangamuthu and N. Manimekalai, 'Generation of Employment for Women Through DWCRA,' *Journal of Rural Development,* Vol. 8(4) pp. 431-438 (1989) NIRD, Hyderabad.

2. Dr. Satyanarayana Reddy and Dr. C. Renuka, 'A Boon for Rural Women,' *Yojana,* December 15, 1994.

3. A.P. Reddy, Y. Suresh Reddy and P. Mohan Reddy: 'Women and Rural Development—A Study of DWCRA in Cuddapah District,' *Kurukshetra,* Sep 1994, p. 21.

4. N. Prem Kumar and A. Rahul Kumar, 'DWCRA: A Case Study' *Yojana,* March 31, 1992, p. 28.

5. D.S. Dhillon and B.S. Hansra, 'On Making DWCRA Effective' *Kurukshetra,* Sep-1991, pp. 25-26.

6. C.S. Singhal, 'DWCRA: Problems and Prospects,' *Social Welfare*, July-August, 1992.
7. Mahipal, 'Planning for Women's Progress under Panchayati Raj,' *Yojana*, Feb 28, 1994, p. 24.
8. Dr. Satyanarayan Reddy and Dr. C. Renuka, 'DWCRA—A Boon for Rural Women', *Yojana*, Dec-15, 1994.
9. Archana Sood, 'Development of Rural Women—Perception and Outcome', *Kurukshetra*, September 1994, p. 17.
10. N.Manimekalai and G. Rajeswari, 'Empowerment of Women Through Self-Help Groups, *Margin, Vol.* 32, No. 4 (July-September. 2000).
11. IS ACPA (1992): Independent South Asian Commission for Poverty Alleviation.
12. Ibid.
13. N. Srinivasan, 'Why Self-Help Groups—Borrower's Point of View', *National Bank News Review*, January-March 1996. pp. 18-19.
14. K.R. Lakshmikantan, 'Self-Help Groups in the Life of the Rural Poor—A Pilibhit Case Study,' *Women's Link*, April-June 2000 pp. 9-10.
15. Leon H. Levy, 'Self-Help Groups: Types and Psychological Process,' *Journal of Applied Behavioural Sciences*, pp. 311-312.
16. S. Krishnan, 'Poorest of the Poor are Now Bankable', *The Economic Times*, October 28, 1996.
17. Moin Qazi, 'Self Help Groups: A Novel Approach to Rural Development' *State Bank of India Monthly Review*, September 1997, p. 461.
18. Subhash C. Wadhwa, 'Self-Help Groups for Reaching the Poor' *Financing Agriculture*, Vol. 27 (1-3) 1995.
19. Ibid.
20. Hirway Indira (1984), Programmes for Poverty Eradication: A Critique of Target Group Approach, Sardar Patel Institute for Economic and Social Research (Mimeo).
21. NABARD (1999), Banking with the Poor: Financing Self-Help Groups, CGM, NABARD, Hyderabad.

22. Dr. B.B. Barik and Dr. P.P Vannan, 'Promoting Self Help Groups—As Sub System of Credit Cooperatives,' *The Cooperator,* January 2001.

23. R. Maria Inigo and K. Kanagaraj, 'Development of Rural Women' *Southern Economist,* February 15, 1998, p. 3.

24. Dr. I Satyasundaram, 'Challenges and Opportunities,' *Social Welfare,* July 2001.

25. Rajaram Das Gupta (2001), 'Working and Impact of Rural Self-Help Groups and Other Forms of Micro Financing,' *Indian Journal of Agricultural Economics,* Vol. 56, No. 3.

4

Characteristics and Performance of Sample DWCRA and SHGs in the Study Area—Kurnool District

INTRODUCTION

Women in the unorganized sectors are suffering in several ways. Their economic status is very low. They do not have access to crucial input like credit. Empowerment of women has therefore assumed importance. Organisation of the poor is crucial for their upliftment.

Despite the vast institutional credit network, the attempt to serve the weaker sections particularly the poor could yield only limited success. As a result in recent years Self-Help Groups are emerging as an alternative strategy to institutional credit.[1]

The World Bank Report (1991) has observed that "women are central to the success of poverty alleviation efforts in the short and medium as in the long run."

The goals of poverty reduction and empowerment of women can be effectively achieved if poor women could organize into groups—for community participation as well as for the assertion of their rights in various services related to their economic and social well being.[2]

The effective management and development of women's resources like their abilities, interest, skills and other potentialities are of paramount importance for the mobilisation and development of human resource. Yet, many women do not assert themselves owing to social inhibitions and disabilities.[3]

Lack of entrepreneurial ability and marketable skills restricted women to the traditional sectors which did not yield enough income so as to enable them to cross the poverty line.

SHGs are of a recent phenomenon and are emerging in several fields of rural and urban development. They are not only fighting against income poverty but also human and environmental poverty and are engaged in social and community mobilisation processes (Chamber, 1994).[4] Deep rooted social evils and customs like child marriages, castism and untouchability are also taken up by SHGs. Since the SHGs are mostly formed by the economically deprived, socially excluded, politically marginalized, culturally isolated segments of rural society, they encounter a multiplicity of hurdles on the path of their activities. In this chapter, it is proposed to deal with some of the structural characteristics as well as functions being performed by the SHGs that figure in our study.

We start with a brief outline of the SHGs movement in Andhra Pradesh as a prelude to our sample study.

Progress of Women SHG Movement in Andhra Pradesh: Groups Formed and Assisted

Of the total women Self Help Groups in the country, the State of Andhra Pradesh accounts for nearly 30 per cent (Commission of the Rural Development's Report, 1998).[5] Within Andhra Pradesh, 17 districts are having more than 10,000 women groups, (Table 4.1) only 5 districts are having less than 10,000 women Self Help Groups. East Godavari has a phenomenally larger number of 40,059 women Self Help Groups. In terms of coverage, 14 per cent of women population of the state are members of women SHGs. While 84 per cent of the groups are promoted by DRDA, 16 per cent are promoted under other governmental organisations and by non-governmental organisations. DRDA has promoted 80 per cent of groups in Telangana, 75 per cent in Rayalaseema and 90 per cent in coastal districts. The details of number of members organized (Social Categorywise) are depicted in Table 4.1. Of the 3,12,624 groups in the state, 49 per cent of groups have been assisted with revolving fund/ matching grant as per their eligibility. 54 per cent of groups have been assisted with revolving fund/matching grant in Telangana, 57 per cent in Rayalaseema and 44 per cent in coastal districts (Table 4.1).

The formation of DWCRA groups, which commenced in 1982-83, has gradually picked up and reached its peak in the year 1999-2000. The considerable increase in the number, during 1998-99 and 1999-2000 can be related to the intensified social mobilisation activities through campaign mode adopted by the State Government under the aegis of Janmabhoomi. Special mention should be made about the Mahila Janmabhoomi conducted in the year 1999 in which a large number of groups were formed to cover each and every habitation (CRD's report, 1999).[6]

An analysis of women Self Help Groups by caste reveals a skewed pattern of distribution. The proportion of groups formed with weaker sections (SC, ST & BC) is higher than their population proportion. The SC groups constitute 25 per cent. The ST and BC groups form 8 per cent and 27 per cent of the total groups respectively. It means that there is a built-in mechanism in groups' formation process for benefiting weaker sections. While the Government of India guidelines stipulated a coverage of 50 per cent to the SC's and ST's, the performance in Andhra Pradesh has been 33 per cent.

Self Help Groups (SHG) Linkage with the Bank: Kurnool Experience

While DWCRA fund is coming to the groups, what was needed by the groups was direct finance by the banks. The Government sponsored schemes have their own limitations primarily because of two reasons:

Table 4.1 Agency-wise Groups Formed and Assisted as on March 2000

(Rs. 000's)

Sl. No.	Name of the District	Groups Category			Promoted by			Assistance to groups		
		Total	DWCRA	Other SHG	DRDA	Other Govt. Org.	Vol. Org.	Revolving Fund	Matching Grant	Total
1	2	3	4	5	6	7	8	9	10	11
1.	Adilabad	9543	6755	2788	7710	1370	463	4939	1816	6755
2.	Kammam	9132	3818	5314	9132	0	0	3818	0	3818
3.	Mahaboobnagar	14737	9367	5370	9937	3000	1800	6679	2688	9367
4.	Karimnagar	20142	5574	14568	18092	0	2050	5708	1593	7301
5.	Ranga Reddy	10246	4634	5612	9936	82	228	4634	508	5142
6.	Nalgonda	13341	5766	7575	11210	900	1231	3583	2183	5766
7.	Warangal	14500	5503	8997	9500	400	4600	5503	2828	8331
8.	Nizamabad	8031	5243	2788	3932	1311	2788	3800	1443	5243
9.	Medak	15495	9930	5565	12838	1800	857	6255	3675	9930
	Sub Total of Telangana	**115167**	**56590**	**58577**	**92287**	**8863**	**14017**	**44919**	**16734**	**61653**

(Contd...)

1	2	3	4	5	6	7	8	9	10	11
10.	Chittoor	11502	6064	5438	6700	2786	2016	4258	1806	6064
11.	Kurnool	11836	5269	6567	8836	0	3000	3919	1315	5234
12.	Cuddapah	3949	3949	0	3949	0	0	3949	0	3949
13.	Anantapur	20263	9958	10305	16304	2416	1543	5807	5893	11700
	Sub Total of Rayalaseema	**47550**	**25240**	**22310**	**35789**	**5202**	**6559**	**17933**	**9014**	**26947**
14.	East Godavari	40059	18173	21886	38284	1775	0	6073	12100	18173
15.	Srikakulam	10841	5159	5682	9481	600	760	3162	1997	5159
16.	Visakhapatnam	10787	3349	7438	10547	240	0	3349	365	3714
17.	Guntur	14738	3723	11015	12908	607	1223	5859	2688	8547
18.	Nellore	12526	7301	5225	12526	0	0	5708	1593	7301
19.	West Godavari	11150	5309	5841	10000	1000	150	4634	508	5142
20.	Krishna	18200	6536	11664	16685	640	875	5309	1227	6536
21.	Prakasam	21854	7375	14479	15854	4500	1500	6833	542	7375
22.	Viziayanagaram	9752	3988	5764	9041	0	711	3371	617	3988
	Sub Total of Andhra	**149907**	**60913**	**88994**	**135326**	**9360**	**5219**	**44298**	**21637**	**65935**
	Grand Total	**312624**	**142743**	**169881**	**263402**	**23427**	**25795**	**107150**	**47385**	**154535**

Table 4.2 Statistics of Agency-wise Groups Formed and Assisted as on March 2000 in Andhra Pradesh and Region-wise

Sl. No.	*Name of the item*	*Andhra Pradesh*			*Andhra*		
		Mean	*Standard deviation*	*Coefficient of variation*	*Mean*	*Standard deviation*	*Coefficient of variation*
1.	Revolving Fund	4843.1818	1159.5497	23.9418	4922.0000	1354.7477	27.5243
2.	Matching Grant	2153.8636	2600.9121	120.7556	2404.1111	3720.1230	154.7400
3.	Total Assistance	6997.0455	3271.3124	46.7527	7326.1111	4379.3537	59.7773

Sl. No.	*Name of the item*	*Telangana*			*Rayalaseema*		
		Mean	*Standard deviation*	*Coefficient of variation*	*Mean*	*Standard deviation*	*Coefficient of variation*
1.	Revolving Fund	4924.3333	1146.3366	23.2790	4483.2500	895.7032	19.9788
2.	Matching Grant	1859.3333	1148.6827	61.7792	2253.5000	2543.3089	112.8603
3.	Total Assistance	6783.6667	2077.5487	30.6257	6736.7500	3421.3180	50.7858

1. The groups can get DWCRA fund only once and one time assistance does not ensure that the groups could really overcome economic poverty; and
2. Number of groups which can be covered under the above scheme are limited because of scarce resources of the Government.

What was required was linking of some of the groups with the banks directly, which would ensure flow of regular credit to the groups forever, enabling them to undertake their economic activity.

NABARD launched a pilot project for linking SHGs with the banks in 1992, as it was realized that banking with the poor through the self help groups, is the only way of making available, the credit to the unreached and uncared so far, that to in adequate quantity, at the right time with the minimum documentation.

Banks were reluctant to lend to DWCRA and Podupulakshmi groups. Primarily because these were organized by the Government and bankers were sceptical of any Government Programmes, based on previous experiences. Also improper functioning of some of DWCRA groups formed earlier, spread the notion amongst bankers that DWCRA and Podupulakshmi groups are not SHGs as prescribed by NABARD and hence they should not be financed.

Another difficulty which was experienced was that many of the groups were 30 member groups whereas NABARD guidelines prescribed, financing for groups below 20 members. In case more than 20 members were there, the groups should be registered. And finally, most of the branch managers never visited any groups and hence were not aware of the characteristics of these groups.

To overcome all these drawbacks, series of workshops and orientation camps were organized for branch managers to sensitize them about SHGs.

During July, 1997, divisional level meetings were organized in which group leaders/branch managers/MDO's/AG's/VDO(w)/NGO's participated. All the important partners in the programme were brought together. Training on various aspects of SHGs and their financing was followed by face-to-face interaction of the group leaders with branch managers. It helped in two ways:

1. Bankers interacted with the group leaders directly for the first time. They saw the records maintained by the groups and could judge whether the groups were satisfying all the norms for SHGs or not. It also removed their misconception that groups were formed only to garner government funds.

2. When groups came into contact with the bankers, they understood their strength and weaknesses, came to know the banker's psychology and what the banker looks in a group. The groups tried to rectify the defects if any, in their groups.

Thus, a modest beginning was made when Andhra Bank financed two groups on October 30th 1997 in Kolimigundla mandal. Other banks started following and by the end of March 1998, 214 groups had been benefited from this. It had a dramatic effect. Direct loans from the banks, without any subsidy component from the Government, called for strict financial discipline on the part of the groups. Only few members had to avail loans in the beginning and the remaining members got loans only when the members who had availed loans in the beginning repaid.

These groups became trend setters for the remaining groups. The other groups realized that they could also have bank credit provided they are improved. Thus there was an incentive for better functioning of the groups. The most welcome feature is that the bankers are themselves coming forward to finance the SHGs. The confidence of the women has gone up tremendously as they were no longer dependent on the subsidy doles by the Government and they had gained the capacity to access bank loans directly.[7]

Networking of the Groups

Though SHGs are able to tap DWCRA, IRDP and even direct bank loans, the capacity of individual groups to access various resources as well as to participate in various programmes is limited. In various group level, village level and mandal level training programmes and meetings, the women groups expressed the desire to get networked into various federations. The village level federations were the first to emerge. They faced common problems and discovered that their strength would go up, if they joined hands together instead of each group going in its own way. The groups in the village network elected a Board of Directors having representatives from all the groups in the village network. The village networks evolved their own thrift and credit management mechanism. The groups pooled a portion of their savings into the network. Any external assistance received from the Government and the Banks also pooled in the network. Individual SHGs could take loans from these networks. In fact, the whole process of networking marks one stage forward from self help to mutual help. The groups could help each other by transfer of surplus funds from one group to another through these networks.

41 such village level networks have emerged till March 1998. The groups in 17 such networks were provided matching grant to the extent of their savings from IRDP infrastructure by DRDA. The groups have pooled all the amount plus a fixed portion of their savings into the network and are giving loans to the individual groups out of this amount. The interest earned by the network is being used for maintenance of records and other miscellaneous expenditure incurred by the networks. The community based organisations are acting as catalysts to support and strengthen these networks and federations. A large number of training and capacity building programmes were organized for the network leaders and members.

With the organisation of mandal level conventions, once in every 3 months, mandal level federations have also emerged in 21 mandals. The village network leaders are members of the mandal federation. Thus, a 3-tier structure is emerging.

Individual women forming themselves into SHGs, the SHGs in a village getting networked into a village federation, and finally the village networks getting federated at the mandal level.

These village level and mandal networks have emerged as grassroot level people's institutions, which are dynamic, vibrant and viable. They are coming forward to participate in various Government Programmes meant for them.

The Government of Andhra Pradesh is setting up a "Women's Fund" to support working capital needs of such networks or federations.

The ultimate objective is to develop these people's organisations and strengthen their capacity so that they can have access to all the Government Programmes.

Rules, Regulations and Working Norms

Each SHG formulates its own rules and working norms with certain common features as recommended by the promoting agency. They are:

1. Membership within the range of 10-15;
2. Participatory Management;
3. Regular savings and utilisation of savings for meeting the credit needs of its members;
4. Fixed interest rate for savings and loans issued by the group;
5. Each group consists of two elected leaders; and
6. File the details and keep Joint Bank account.

All the groups are following most of these rules and norms in actual practice.

Size of Sample SHGs

It may be recapitulated that I have chosen a sample of 150 women SHGs spread over the three divisions of the districts. Their structure in terms of membership is small. They are supposed to be cohesive and homogeneous in terms of certain characteristics (D.K. Ghosh, 1995).[8] "Small is beautiful", is a well known thing and this is more true in the case of social groups than purely economic organisations. For the sake of analysis, we have classified the sample SHGs into 4 categories namely those that are below 10 members,' between 11 and 15 members, between 16-20 and 21 and above members. All these particulars are furnished in Table 4.3.

It may be noticed from the statistics incorporated in Table 4.3, the size of the SHGs is centering between 11 and 15 members. Thus the size structure is quite uneven.

Table 4.3 Size of the SHGs: Division-wise

Size of the Group		*Kurnool Division-I*	*Nandyal Division-II*	*Adoni Division-III*	*Total*
	Count	5	2	4	11
Below 10	% within size of the group	45.5	18.2	36.4	100.0
Members	% within the division	10.0	4.0	8.0	7.3
	% of Total	3.3	1.3	2.7	7.3
	Count	35	38	38	111
11-15	% within size of the group	31.5	34.2	34.2	100.0
Members	% within the division	70.0	76.0	76.0	74.0
	% of Total	23.3	25.3	25.3	74.0
	Count	9	10	8	27
16-20	% within size of the group	33.3	37.0	29.6	100
Members	% within the division	18.0	20.0	16.0	18.0
	% of Total	6.0	6.7	5.3	18
	Count	1	0	0	1
21 and above	% within size of the group	100.0	0	0	100
Members	% within the division	2.0	0	0	0.7
	% of Total	0.7	0	0	0.7

Source: Field Data.

Chart 4.1 Size of SHGs—Kurnool District

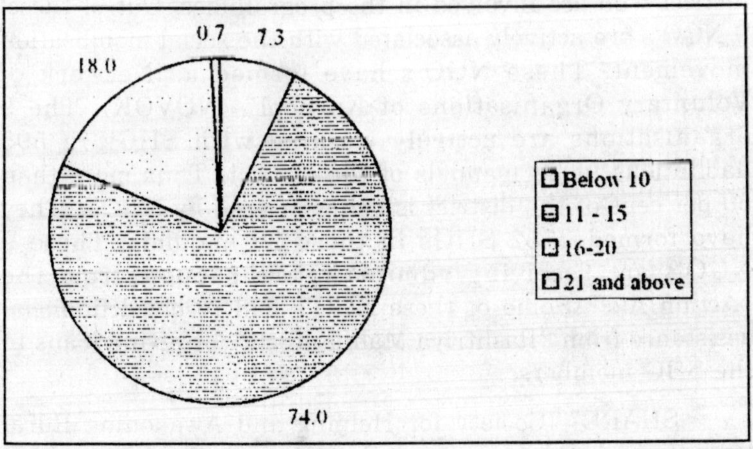

Facilitating Agencies

Women from the weaker sections of society cannot automatically come together and form themselves into groups, because of the resistance of male members within and outside the household. An outside facilitating agency is necessary for their group formation and for nurturing it at the beginning (Sakuntala Narasimham, 1999).[9] Moreover formal arrangements made through banks and co-operative institutions have failed to provide resources to them. While the appeal of economic programmes will be to attract women's groups for an economic and remunerative activity, the main objective is to organize women in groups to monitor the social development indicators intensively (Strategy Paper, Andhra Pradesh, 2001).[10] The public intervention is necessitated through the agency of DRDA which is concerned with the implementation of poverty alleviation programmes at the district level. The situation has prompted the Non-Governmental Organisations (NGO's) to organize women Self Help Groups (SHGs) to provide them credit and to encourage the habit of thrift among them (M.S. Kallur, 2001).[11]

The NGO Network in the District

There are 22 Non-Government Organisations in the district who are involved in the programmes. Out of these, 9 NGO's are actively associated with the social mobilisation movement. These NGO's have formed a "Network of Voluntary Organisations of Kurnool" (NOVOK). The 9 organisations are actively working with SHGs in 595 habitations in 29 mandals of the district. Thus more than 50 per cent of the district is being covered by NGO's. They have formed 3782 SHGs in these 29 mandals. These 9 NGO's are receiving administrative support from the "Action Aid". Some of these NGO's had received financial assistance from "Rashtriya Mahila Kosh" for giving loans to the SHG members.

"SHARE" (Society for Helping and Awakening Rural Poor through Education), a voluntary organisation working in the district has established a "Grameena Bank" on the lines of "Bangladesh Grameena Bank" model at Veldurthy, one of the mandal headquarters. After identifying the village in which to work, the organisation identifies the rural poor women and organizes one week awareness camp. The women are then organized into groups of five members each and they are sanctioned loans by the bank.

Initially, an amount of Rs. 4000 is given to the member and the members are expected to purchase assets within 15 days of the sanction of the amount. The organisation is working in 4 mandals. The most interesting feature is that the recovery rate is almost 100 per cent with no defaulters. Though the SHARE model is different from the model adopted by district administration, it brings out one important point clearly, namely, the "poor are bankable".

The UNDP Assistance

While the district administration launched the social mobilisation movement in February 1995, the United Nations Development Programme (UNDP) launched the Poverty Alleviation Project in 3 districts of (Mahaboobnagar, Kurnool and Anantapur) of Andhra Pradesh in May 1995.

The project was also based on the same strategy adopted by the district administration of Kurnool, namely, social mobilisation.

Social mobilisation is the critical element, centre-piece and fulcrum around which the UNDP programme revolves. The basic premise and conviction on which the programme is firmly based is "The willingness within the people to help themselves". This innate potential is being harnessed by providing social guidance through the triad of Social Organisation, skill development and capital formation.

Initially, the programme was taken up in 41 mandals of Kurnool district and then in 1996, the mandals were reduced to 32 (6 intensive and 26 non-intensive). Currently, the programme is being implemented in 7 mandals of Kurnool district.

The programme proposes to involve local voluntary organisations and the Government Machinery in the execution of poverty alleviation schemes. Aimed at the communities existing below the poverty lines, it is hoped that these schemes will achieve:

(a) Social Organisation;

(b) Skill Development;

(c) Financial independence and sustainability in the target communities.

The project is entrusting to a team of National Project Professionals consisting of:

(a) A National Project Coordinator;

(b) 5 project professionals and Administrative support personnel consisting of a Statistician and 5 social organizers.

The team is supported in its work by 18 Partner Voluntary Organisations (PVO's). The PVO's have assigned 22 Community Coordinators and 122 Community Volunteer's on a full time basis for the implementation of the project.

In Kurnool, there are 4 PVO's having 9 community coordinators and 40 community volunteers. In the 7 mandals where the programme is in implementation, 743 SHGs have been formed with 15,424 members with a thrift of Rs. 86 lakhs. The project aims to achieve the following objectives:

1. Stabilizing and strengthening the already formed. SHGs or organisation of the groups and bringing the leftover poor into the mainstream of development;
2. Bringing conceptual clarity;
3. Consolidation and strengthening of the work already done;
4. Self-management and sustainability of the self help groups;

5. Increase resource base, asset creation, and income generation.

To achieve the above objectives, the vital inputs required to build the capacity and upgrade the skills of the project, are provided through trainings, workshops, seminars, exposure visits, etc.

The ultimate objective of the programme is to develop grassroot level people's institutions which would take on the problem of poverty, in all its dimensions.

Thus, the strategy adopted by Kurnool district administration and the UNDP assisted project was one and the same, namely social mobilisation. While the district administration started the movement in February 1995, the UNDP project was introduced in May 1995. While the UNDP confined itself to 7 intensive mandals, the district administration was making an attempt to replicate the model throughout the district.

Table 4.4 Number of Mandals Covered by Different Organisations

Sl.No.	*Name of the Organisation*	*Mandals*	*Percentage*
1.	Districts as a whole	54	100
2.	Only District Administrative Support	25	46
3.	District Administrative Support and NGO's other than UNDP Mandals	22	41
4.	UNDP operated Mandals	7	13

Graph 4.2 Number of Mandals Covered by Different Organisations

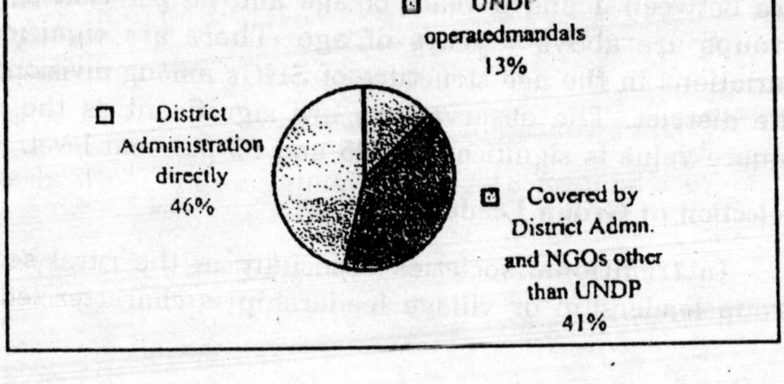

It may be noted from Table 4.5 that DRDA had promoted 56.7 per cent, while the NGO's have facilitated 33 per cent, UNDP facilitated 9 per cent and the others 1.3 per cent of SHGs in our sample. There are however significant variations in the contribution of facilitating agencies among divisions of the district and the observations are significant as the chi-square value is significant at 95 and 99 per cent level.

Graph 4.3 Facilitating Agencies in Sample Divisions

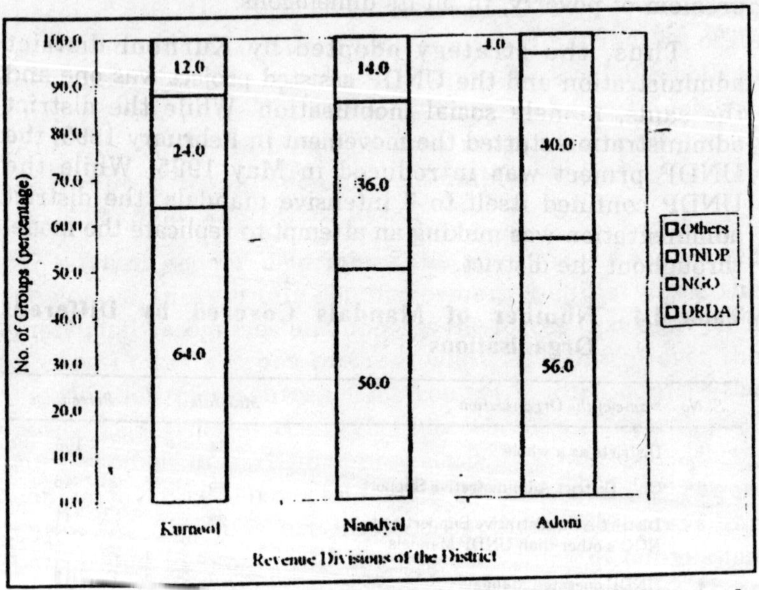

As may be seen from Table 4.6, 19 per cent of sample SHGs are below 3 years of age, 59 per cent of the groups are between 4 and 6 years of age and 23 per cent of the groups are above 7 years of age. There are significant variations in the age structure of SHGs among divisions of the district. The observations are significant as the chi-square value is significant at 95 and 99 per cent level.

Selection of Group Leader

In traditional societies especially in the rural sector group leadership or village leadership is characterized by

Table 4.6 Age of Self-help Groups in Sample Mandals

(in percentage)

Age of Self-help Groups (Years)		*Kurnool Division-I*	*Nandyal Division-II*	*Adoni Division-III*	*Total*
	Count	10	9	9	28
0-3	% within age of SHG	35.7	32.1	32.1	100
	% within the Division	20.0	18.0	18.0	18.7
	% of Total	6.7	6.0	6.0	18.7
	Count	28	31	29	88
4-6	% within age of SHG	31.8	35.2	32.9	100
	% within the Division	56.0	62.0	58.0	58.7
	% of Total	18.7	20.7	19.3	58.7
	Count	12	10	12	34
and	% within age of SHG	35.3	29.4	35.3	100
above	% within the Division	24.0	20.0	24	22.7
	% of Total	8.0	6.7	8.0	22.7

Chi-square value 0.543**

Source: Field Data

* 95% (0.95) level of significance

* 99% (0.99) level of significance

Graph 4.4 Age of Self-help Groups in Sample Mandals

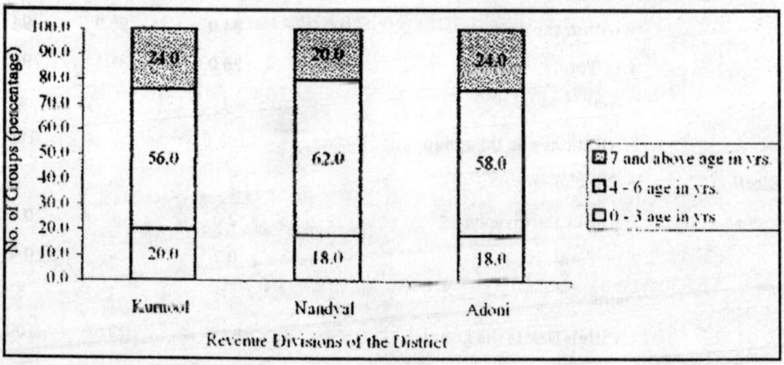

land ownership. In spite of several advances made in the industrial and tertiary sectors, the survival strategies are built around land ownership and management. The poor are usually landless and depend on the non-agricultural activity or belong to category of agricultural labourers who are mostly dependent on wages. Only in recent times, self-employment schemes are promoted to provide a means of livelihood to the rural poor. Women by tradition are secluded from being active on the economic front. They have remained cloistered and confined within the four walls of the home and dismissed as "The Second Sex" (Mukta Mittal, 1995).[13] The emergence of internal leadership among the rural poor women is a challenging and difficult task. But given a conducive and favourable environment, prepared by the facilitating agency leadership emerges. We have attempted to capture the process of leadership emergence in terms of election and unanimous choice by the group. The results were shown in Table 4.7.

Table 4.7 Selection of the Group Leader in Three Divisions of the District

Selection of the Group Leader		*Kurnool Division-I*	*Nandyal Division-II*	*Adoni Division-III*	*Total*
Unanimous	Count	50	42	49	141
	% within how is the group leader chosen	35.5	29.8	34.8	100
	% within the division	100.0	84.0	98.0	94
	% of Total	33.3	28.0	32.7	94
Election	Count	-	1	-	1
	% within how is the group leader chosen	-	100.0	-	100
	% within the division	-	2.0	-	0.7
	% of Total	-	0.7	-	0.7
Nomination	Count	-	7	1	8
	% within how is the group leader chosen	-	87.5	12.5	100
	% within the division	-	14.0	2.0	5.3
	% of Total	-	4.7	0.6	5.3

Chi-square value: 12.698**

Source: Field Data

* 0.95 level of significance

* 0.99 level of significance

A glance of the statistics of Table 4.7 reveals that unanimity in the choice of group leader prevails in 94 per cent of the groups and election and nomination are confined to 1 per cent.

Usually the group leaders play a major role in identifying the members and forming the group. They also play a major role in keeping all the members together for its smooth functioning. There are two leaders in each group. One is a first leader and the other is a second leader. In the absence of first leader, second leader will look after the group activities. The observations are significant as the chi-square value is significant at 95 and 99 per cent level.

Group Meetings

Group meetings represent group dynamics in action. They indicate a social and psychological setting which demonstrates their collective strength, to the men-folk and organisational ability. They provide a forum for the members of the groups, to initiate discussion, interact with one another and learn from each other, not only regarding business affairs but also personal concerns. Regular group meeting set a perfect stage for introducing further discipline into groups affairs. They facilitate SMART governance (Vision 2020).[14] It may be worthwhile to expand the term SMART; Simple, Moral, Accountable, Responsive and Transparent governance. The meetings enable the members to resolve some of the pending issues such as collection of deposits, disbursal of loans and also find solutions to pressing social issues like child marriages, atrocities on women in and around their neighbourhood. We present a birds eye view of group meetings in Table 4.8 and 4.9.

Two types of meetings are generally conducted by each SHG and they include:

1. Meeting for money transactions; and
2. Monthly meetings to discuss general issues pertaining to the group. Usually all the members used to attend

Table 4.8 Group Meetings in a Month in Sample Mandals

Number of Group Meetings Conducted		*Kurnool Division-I*	*Nandyal Division-II*	*Adoni Division-III*	*Total*
	Count	18	24	15	57
1 (Once)	% within number of meetings conducted in a month	31.6	42.1	26.3	100.0
	% within the Division	36	48.0	30.0	38.0
	% of Total	12	16.0	10.0	38.0
	Count	22	25	31	78
2 (Twice)	% within number of meetings conducted in a month	31.5	42.1	26.3	100.0
	% within the Division	44.0	50.0	62	52
	% of Total	14.7	16.6	20.6	52
	Count	7	1	2	10
3 (Thrice)	% within number of meetings conducted in a month	70.0	10.0	20.0	100.0
	% within the Division	14.0	2.0	4.0	6.7
	% of Total	4.7	0.7	1.3	6.7
	Count	3	-	2	5
More than 3 times	% within number of meetings conducted in a month	60.0	-	40.0	100.0
	% within the Division	6.0	-	4.0	3.3
	% of Total	2.0	-	1.3	3.3

both the meetings. Participation of members in meeting, intended for money transactions is made compulsory. If a member does not attend the meeting despite being intimated, he will be fined to the extent of Rs. 5. If the group members are not educated, the local Anganwadi teacher is generally entrusted to record these activities including money transactions, for which a token honorarium is paid. As far as the monthly meetings are concerned, all the groups record the minutes of monthly meetings.

It may be noticed that the frequency of meetings is comparatively higher, that is twice in a month. It is 32 per

Table 4.9 Average Attendance of the Members at Group Meetings in Sample Mandals of Three Divisions

Average Attendance at Group Meetings		*Kurnool Division-I*	*Nandyal Division-II*	*Adoni Division-III*	*Total*
	Count	1	1	2	4
25%	% within average attendance	25.0	25.0	50.0	100.0
	within name of the Division	2.0	2.0	4.0	2.7
	% of Total	0.7	0.7	1.3	2.7
25-50%	Count	2	1	2	5
	% within average attendance	40.0	20.0	40.0	100.0
	% within name of the Division	4.0	2.0	4.0	3.3
	% of Total	1.3	0.7	1.3	3.3
50-75%	Count	6	5	8	19.0
	% within average attendance	31.6	26.3	42.1	100.0
	% within name of the Division	12.0	10.0	16.0	12.7
	% of Total	4.0	3.3	5.3	12.7
>75%	Count	41	43	38	122
	% within average attendance	33.6	35.2	31.1	100
	% within name of the Division	82.0	86.0	76.0	81.3
	% of Total	27.3	28.7	25.3	81.3

Chi-square value: 2.9165** *Source:* Field Data

* 95% level of significance (95%) * 99% level of significance (99%)

cent of the groups in Kurnool Division, 42 per cent of the groups in Nandyal division and 26 per cent of the groups in Adoni Division. Here again we perceive a positive correlation between the frequency of the meetings and the level of development of the groups concerned. However the groups which are conducting meetings more than 3 times or weekly once are in less in percentage, in the three divisions, that is 6 per cent of the groups in Kurnool Division and 4 per cent of the groups in Adoni Division. There are no groups in Nandyal Division which conduct meetings once in a week.

It may be clear from the Table 4.9 that more than 75 per cent of attendance is recorded in case of 82 per cent of the groups in the district. Less than 25 per cent and 25-50 per cent of attendance is recorded in very less percentage of groups in the district. They are 2.7 and 3.3 per cent. Therefore, attendance to the meetings is the indicator of group discipline. It is also clear that women members in the group, are so active and interesting to have timely discussion of their economic, and social problems and also they are trying their level best to increase their standards of living in the community. There is a positive relationship between the level of attendance at group meetings and the solvation of various social and economic problems of their communities. The observations are significant as the chi-square value is significant at 0.95 and 0.99 level.

SHG Member Beneficiaries under IRDP

IRDP is the most important poverty alleviation programme that has been launched in the country in the early 1980's to directly attack extreme poverty in the rural sector. It is not a programme confined to India alone. It is in operation in most countries of Asia and Africa. There is a specialized institution called Centre on Integrated Rural Development for Asia and the Pacific (CIRDAP), which renders technical assistance and advice to the member countries of its coverage. (CIRDAP - RDR, 1999).[15] Under IRDP assistance in the form of loan, subsidy is given under various schemes to help the poor to cross the poverty line. The IRDP scheme has been in operation in all the districts of Andhra Pradesh and it has been renamed by integrating all other allied programmes as Swarna Jayanti Gram Swarozgar Yojana (SGSY). In case of our samples 38 per cent, 35 per cent, 58 per cent of groups in three divisions of the district have received assistance under the IRDP programme.

Occupational Status of Group Leaders

Our sample groups are homogeneous. It is felt that an analysis of the occupational pattern of group leaders is representative of the groups as a whole and therefore, we have studied the occupational pattern of group leaders.

Table 4.10 Primary Occupation of the Group Leaders in Three Divisions of the District

Agriculture

	Kurnool	*Nandyal*	*Adoni*	
	Division-I	*Division-II*	*Division-III*	*Total*
Count	18	20	25	63
Percentage	36.0	40.0	50.0	42.0

Petty Business

	Kurnool	*Nandyal*	*Adoni*	
	Division-I	*Division-II*	*Division-III*	*Total*
Count	15	18	20	53
Percentage	30.0	36.0	40.0	35.3

Household Industry

	Kurnool	*Nandyal*	*Adoni*	
	Division-I	*Division-II*	*Division-III*	*Total*
Count	17	12	5	34
Percentage	34.0	24.0	10.0	22.7

The primary occupation of group leaders in the three divisions represented in the above tables. 50 per cent of group leaders' primary occupation in Adoni division is agriculture. After this Nandyal and Kurnool divisions follows.

40 per cent of group leader's primary occupation in Adoni division is petty business. This division is followed by Nandyal and Kurnool divisions.

Primary occupation of 34 per cent of the group leaders of Kurnool division are engaging in household industry. This division is followed by Nandyal and Adoni divisions.

The above three primary occupations of the group leaders in the three divisions can be represented through a pie diagram.

Graph 4.5 Primary Occupation of the Group Leaders in Kurnool District

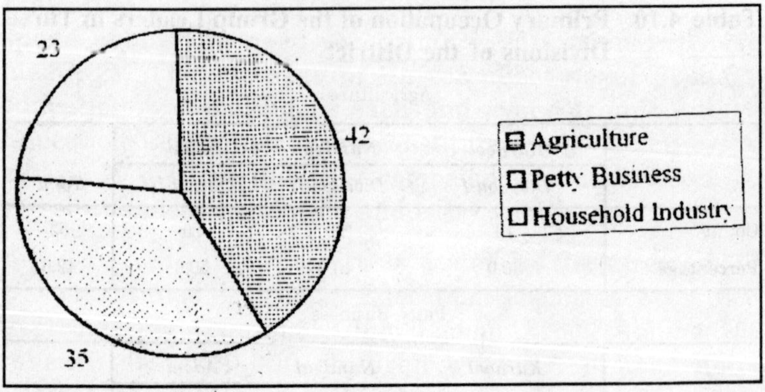

Household Assets

Lack of assets is an effect as well as a cause of poverty in terms of income opportunities, consumption and capability building of people and their own institutions. People without assets tend to be consumption - poor because they relay mainly on selling their labour in poorly paid markets. They have nothing to sell or mortgage in hard times, and are economically dependent and politically weak.[16] Our sample groups are composed of the asset poor. Their asset base is very slender. We have classified their asset structure under four categories viz., land, house, gold and others. The raw data is converted into value terms and the details of the asset status presented into 5 categories are shown in Table 4.11.

Households with assets worth Rs. 50,000 and below, constitute 82 per cent within our sample mandals. Households with assets status ranging between Rs. 50,001 - 1,00,000 account for 12.7 per cent. Households with assets worth Rs. 1,00,000 and above constitute 5.3 per cent. The observations are significant as the chi-square value is significant at 95 and 99 per cent level.

Distribution of SHGs by Financial Transactions

Promotion of thrift among the poorest of the poor is the most formidable task especially in a rural society driven

Table 4.11 Value of Household Assets

Value of Household assets		*Kurnool Division-I*	*Nandyal Division-II*	*Adoni Division-III*	*Total*
No Assets	Count	15	10	12	37
	within value of household assets	40.5	27.1	32.4	100.0
	% a within the Division	30.0	20.0	24.0	24.7
	% of Total	10.0	6.7	8.0	24.7
Below	Count	12	18	11	41
25,000	% within value of household assets	29.3	43.9	26.8	100
	% within the Division	24.0	36.0	22.0	27.3
	% of Total	8.0	12.0	7.3	27.3
25,000	Count	15	12	18.0	45
50,000	% within value of household assets	33.3	26.7	40.0	100.0
	% within the Division	30.0	24.0	36.0	30.0
	% of Total	10.0	8.0	12.0	30.0
50,001 -	Count	6	6	7	19
1,00,000	% within value of household assets	31.6	31.6	36.8	100.0
	% within the Division	12.0	12.0	14.0	12.7
	% of Total	4.0	4.0	4.7	12.7
More than	Count	2	4	2	8
1,00,000	% within value of household assets	25.0	50.0	25.0	100.0
	% within the Division	4.0	8.0	4.0	5.3
	% of Total	1.3	2.7	1.3	5.3

Chi-square value 5.53**

* 0.95 (95%) value of significance

* 0.99 (99%) value of significance

by the culture of poverty and indebtedness. Even now the ordinary agriculturist is supposed to be born in debt, lives in debt dies in debt and bequeaths debt. Suicides by farmers in Andhra Pradesh especially by those who are engaged in the production of cotton are not uncommon and they are attracting national attention (The Hindu, 2002).[17] Often the deaths of the poorest of the poor on account of economic distress do not get reported in the press. Nobody from the dominant sections of rural society bothers about such occurrences. The vulnerable are forced to make arrangements for their burial. Under these circumstances, group formation by the ultra poor is inevitable, to promote thrift and thereby increasing their savings to overcome from the bondage of moneylenders and traders (Sakuntala Narasimhan, 1999).[18] In Table 4.12, we present a few aspects of savings and credit mobilisation by sample SHGs.

As stated earlier, promotion of thrift and the habit of saving is the co-ordinal principle of group formation in the context of overcoming persistent poverty of the ultra poor, in the rural sector. Since the income generating opportunities are limited, the capacity to undertake thrift programmes is also limited. However they are motivated and induced to save meagre amounts regularly and pool up these savings to be deposited in the account of the group in the nearby bank. In this process they are further driven by a changed attitude to overcome the habits of wasteful expenditure and effect the savings in the process.

The data in the Table 4.12 reveals that 86,80 and 82 per cent of SHGs are able to save less than Rs.50 per month in the three divisions of the district. Similarly 12, 18 and 18 per cent of SHGs are able to save Rs.51-100 per month. But the capacity to save Rs.100 and more is very poor, that is 2, 2 and 0 per cent in case of Kurnool, Nandyal and Adoni Divisions. To reduce the percentage of poverty among these groups, savings should also be utilized for income generating activities.

The accumulated deposits of SHGs in the category of less than Rs. 10,000 are 12, 10 and 16 per cent in respect of three divisions respectively. The deposits in the category of 20,001-30,000 are more in case of three divisions of districts. They are 40, 44 and 38 per cent respectively. It indicates that savings are encouraging in the districts.

Table 4.12 Distribution of SHGs by Financial Transactions

Sl. No.	*Item*	*Kurnool Division-I*		*Nandyal Division-II*		*Adoni Division-III*	
		Number	*Per cent*	*Number*	*Per cent*	*Number*	*Per cent*
1.	Amount collected per month (in Rs)						
	(a) Less than 50	43	86.0	40	80	41	82
	(b) Rs 51-100	6	12.0	9	18	9	18
	(c) Rs 100 and more	1	2.0	1	2	0	0
2.	Deposits (in Rs)						
	(a) Up to 10,000	6	12.0	5	10.0	8	16.0
	(b) 10,001 - 20,000	14	28.0	21	42.0	16	32.0
	(c) 20,001 - 30, 000	20	40.0	22	44.0	19	38.0
	(d) More than 30,000	10	20.0	2	4.0	7	14.0
3.	Revolving Fund (in Rs)						
	(a) Nil	2	4.0	5	10.0	8	16.0
	(b) Less than 15,000	26	52.0	21	42.0	19	38.0
	(c) 15,000	19	38.0	20	40.0	20	40.0
	(d) More than 15,000	3	6.0	4	8.0	3	6.0
4.	Bank Loan (in Rs)						
	(a) Up to 10,000	6	12.0	3	6.0	2	4.0
	(b) 10,001 - 30,000	18	36.0	21	42.0	19	38.0
	(c) 30,001 - 50,000	19	38.0	18	36.0	21	42.0
	(d) More than 50,000	7	14.0	8	16.0	8	16.0

Chi-square value: 17.962**

Source: Field data.

* 95% level of significance

* 99% level of significance

There are a few SHGs in each division which have yet to receive revolving fund. In its term, the bank concerned gets refinance of the revolving fund from the apex institution namely the NABARD (NABARD, 2001).[19] In respect of 52, 42, 38 per cent of SHGs the revolving fund (RF) received is less than Rs. 15,000. 38, 40 and 40 per cent of SHGs have received revolving fund of Rs. 15,000. Similarly the number of groups which have received revolving fund of more than Rs. 15,000 are less in percentage. They are 6, 8 and 6 per cent of the total in three divisions of the district. In respect of 4, 10 and 16 per cent of SHGs no revolving fund is received so far in the three divisions of the district. However this per cent is higher in case of third division. So, third division shall be given priority in sanctioning the revolving fund to SHGs in the district. However, there is a positive relationship between the level of development and the flow of revolving fund to SHGs.

As SHGs have been linked to the Banks, they are approaching banks for bank loans to supplement their investment in income generating activities. 12, 6 and 4 per cent of SHGs have obtained bank loan up to Rs. 10,000. 36, 42 and 38 per cent of SHGs obtained loan above Rs. 10,000 and below 30,000. In the same way 38, 36 and 42 per cent of SHGs obtained loan amount between Rs. 30,001 - 50,000. The number of groups who get loan amount more than Rs. 50,000 are less in percentage. They are 14, 16 and 16 per cent of the SHGs in three divisions of the district. It is clear from the Table 4.12 that a higher proportion of the groups in the district have obtained loans above Rs. 10,000 and below Rs. 50,000. With regard to development and flow of Revolving Fund to SHGs, there is a positive relationship.

Transaction Costs

In the case of the loans borrowed from the lending agencies the payment of interest is involved. In addition to interest costs there are transaction costs which are variously classified and computed. These costs are common to both borrowers and lenders. (K.G.Karmakar, 1999)[20] In the case of SHGs, visits to banks and the offices of the government and NGO's and other service organisations are undertaken by the leaders of the group. Time and cost of journey, food and other incidental expenses are involved in going round these offices. We have tried to capture only one aspect of transaction costs in terms of frequency of visits made in a month on an average by the leaders/active members of the group and set forth these particulars in Table 4.13.

Table 4.13 Visits to Banks and other Offices in a Month

Sl. No.	*Time of Visits to Offices*	*Kurnool Division-I*	*Nandyal Division-II*	*Adoni Division-III*	*Total*
1.	Count	10	25	39	74
	% within average attendance to the offices	13.5	33.8	52.7	100.0
	% within the Division	20.0	50.0	78	49.3
	% of Total	6.7	16.6	26.0	49.3
2.	Count	38	23	7	68
	% within average attendance to the offices	55.9	33.8	10.3	100.0
	% within the Division	76.0	46.0	14.0	45.3
	% of Total	25.3	15.3	4.7	45.3
3.	Count	2	1	3	6
	% within average attendance to the offices	33.3	16.7	50	100.0
	% within the Division	4.0	2.0	6.0	4.0
	% of Total	1.3	0.7	2.0	4.0
	Count	0	1	1	2
More than 3	% within average attendance to the offices	-	50.0	50.0	100.0
	% within the Division	-	2.0	2.0	1.3
	% of Total	-	0.7	0.6	1.3

Chi-square value: 22.866**

Source: Field Data

* 95% level of significance

* 99% level of significance

It is clear from the Table 4.13 that 20, 50 and 78 per cent of the representatives of the sample SHGs in three divisions make a single visit to the offices with which they have to transact business. The frequency of visits is twice to the extent of 76, 46 and 14 per cent of the leaders of the sample SHGs in three divisions of the districts. The frequency of visits is thrice to the extent of 4, 2 and 6 per cent of the leaders of the sample SHGs in the district.

Similarly the frequency of visits that is more than 3 times is to the extent of 2, 2 and 1.3 per cent of the leaders of the sample SHGs in the district. However the larger percentage that is 94.6 per cent of the leaders of the sample SHGs in the district are attending offices monthly once and twice. Only 6 and 2 per cent of the leaders of the sample SHGs in the district are attending Government offices 3 times or more than three times in a month.

Allocation of Credit

Credit allocation among the members of the group is usually done at the periodical meetings held at the place of their convenience. It is decided after a prolonged discussion and ascertaining complete information from each and every member of the group. This process is in sharp contrast to the existence of information asymmetry that characterizes credit transaction under the formal institutional credit delivery system. This information asymmetry is one of the reasons for unsatisfactory coverage of the poor by the formal sector agencies and the persistence of NPA's (Non-Performing Assets) at a very high level (NABARD, 2000).[21] There is a need to reach the unreached by institutional agencies in order to provide access to credit while substantially reducing transaction costs for both financial institutions and clients (Zeller and Sharma, 1998).[22] Self Help Groups approach is the most suitable mechanism for achieving cost efficiency and thereby promoting the strength of lenders and borrowers alike. We present the findings of our study regarding access to credit, allocation of credit and the rate of interest charged by SHG in Table 4.14.

The Table 4.14 reveals that credit access is nil for 4, 2 and 6 per cent of SHG in three divisions of the district. 56, 38 and 42 per cent of groups in the three divisions of the district have credit access above Rs. 10,000 and below Rs. 20,000. 24, 30 and 24 per cent of SHGs in the three divisions have credit access up to Rs. 40,000. A less percentage of groups that is 6, 14 and 8 per cent of the groups have credit access more than 40,000. It is clear from

Table 4.14 Allocation of Credit and Rate of Interest

Sl. No.	Credit and Interest Rate	Kurnool Division - I		Nandyal Division - II		Adoni Division - III	
		Number	Percentage	Number	Percentage	Number	Percentage
1.	Credit Access						
	(a) Nil	2	4.0	1	2.0	3	6.0
	(b) Less than Rs 10,000	5	10.0	8	16.0	10	20.0
	(c) Rs 10,001 - Rs 20,000	28	56.0	19	38.0	21	42.0
	(d) Rs 20,001 - Rs 40,000	12	24.0	15	30.0	12	24.0
	(e) More than 40,000	3	6.0	7	14.0	4	8.0
2.	Allocation of Amount						
	(a) Equally	45	90.0	40	80.0	38	76.0
	(b) Repaying capacity	1	2.0	-	-	1	2.0
	(c) Economic backwardness	4	8.0	10	20.0	11	22.0
3.	Interest Rate						
	(a) 0-8.5%	-	-	-	-	-	-
	(b) 8.6 - 15%	22	44.0	21	42.0	30	60.0
	(c) More than 15%	28	56.0	29	58.0	20	40.0

Chi-square value: 15.587**
Source: Field Data
* 95% level of significance
* 99% level of significance

this table that credit accessibility shall be increased in the district to reduce the poverty and to increase the income generation activities and thereby their living standards.

Whatever credit that is accessed from the banking institutions is to be shared between the members on the basis of consensus at the meetings. In 90, 80 and 76 per cent of SHGs in the three divisions of the district, credit is allocated equally among members. In the three divisions equality occupies a predominant place. From this, these groups can also be able to achieve social justice in the community. However repayment capacity is a negligible proportion in the allocation of credit in the three divisions of the districts. The same is the case with regard to economic backwardness except in the case of Adoni Division. In Kurnool Division, a very negligible proportion of groups (8 per cent) is allocating credit on the basis of economic backwardness. Similarly Nandyal Division and Adoni division are allocating credit to 20 and 22 per cent of the SHG on the basis of economic backwardness. Thus in the allocation of credit the equality is given more weightage than the repayment capacity and economic backwardness.

Rural credit markets are characterized by segmentation and fragmentation and therefore there is persistence of dichotomy in the credit market as it is in the case of most other markets in the rural sector (Von Pischke Ekal, 1983).[23]

On the basis of our fieldwork, we notice the persistence of segmentation in the credit market even among SHGs. We notice from the data set of Table 4.16 that the credit allocations are made at 2 ranges of rates of interest. They are 8.6 - 15 per cent and more than 15 per cent.

Though it is based on and related to the local credit market, the divergence in the rates of interest is conspicuous and significant across the groups and sample mandals. 44, 42 and 60 per cent of SHGs provide credit to their members in the range of 8.6 - 15 per cent rate of interest in the three divisions of the district. In Adoni division a higher percentage of SHGs are providing credit in this range of interest. 56, 58 and 40 per cent of the SHGs are providing credit to their members in the range of interest that is more than 15 per cent in the three divisions of the district. In Kurnool and Nandyal divisions more than half of the group are extending credit in this range of interest rate. The intention of the groups in keeping higher interest rates is to increase their financial resources.

Financial Functions of SHGs

Self Help Groups, especially DWCRA groups undertake a wide variety of functions. We outline a few of the functions pertaining to financial and credit aspects in this part of the chapter.

Historically, the rural poor have been deprived of the access to institutional credit because they are mostly asset poor and could not offer the type of collateral needed by the formal financial institutions. Therefore, they have been compelled to borrow from the informal agencies of credit with whom they had a linkage in terms of factor and product market. The interpenetration of credit of other markets in most cases worked to the disadvantage of the poor (Kaushik Basu, 1984).[24] Markets become interlocked through price and non-price links, given that the social power is vested in the dominant rural forward classes and that the dominant party often combines multiple functions, thus enjoying a superior status simultaneously in a number of markets and perpetuating the status quo (M.H. Khan - 1981).[25]

SHGs are mostly informal groups where members pool savings and relent in the group on a rotational basis. One of the distinctive features of SHGs is that they are formed outside the aegis of bureaucracy and political parties with limited scope for the latter's intervention (Bhatt: 1989) and its risks, costs and benefits are shared among its members on an equitable basis (Verhagen, 1987). In this sense, SHGs are people's organisations which are free from politicisation and bureaucratisation and are fully participatory and give ample opportunity to their members to take part in all the activities of the group including decision-making. Another important feature of SHGs is that they evolve and function on the basis of felt needs of the people largely by making use of local resources. Functioning of a group mainly with the help of locals also ensures the sustainability of group (Sukhpal Singh, 1995).[26] The SHGs have also been able to provide primitive banking services to its members that are cost effective, flexible and without defaults. Based on local requirements, SHGs have evolved their own characteristics of functioning. The common characteristics of SHGs can be summarized as follows:

1. Group members usually create a common fund by contributing their small savings on a regular basis;
2. Groups evolve flexible systems of working (sometimes with the holp of NGO's) and manage pooled resources in a democratic way;
3. Loan requests are considered by groups in periodic meetings and competing claims on limited resources are settled by consensus;
4. Loans are given mainly on trust with minimum documentation and without any security;
5. The loan amounts are small, frequent for short duration and are mainly for unconventional purposes;
6. The rate of interest vary from group to group and the purpose of loan. It is higher than that of banks but lower than that of moneylenders;
7. At periodic meetings, besides collecting money, social and economic issues are also discussed;
8. Defaults are rare due to group pressure and ultimate knowledge of the end use of credit.

Summing Up

Self-Help Group movement is taking deep roots in rural Andhra Pradesh. There is a spectacular growth of SHGs in all the districts though there are significant differences across districts in terms of group formation and assistance rendered. DRDA is in the forofront of organising women into self help groups, popularly called DWCRA groups and arranging for financial assistance to the groups for various activities, mainly leading to generation of income. NGO's and banks of all kinds are playing an important role in facilitating and assisting in formation and functioning of women SHGs. Most of the SHGs consist of 10-15 members. Small size of membership has its inherent advantage in bringing about group homogeneity, cohesiveness and democratic governance. Due to the failures and pit falls of individual beneficiary oriented poverty alleviation programmes, group lending and peer monitoring are emphasized by multilateral funding agencies, financial and banking institutions and even by governments. People participatory approach is emphasized in all spheres of poverty eradication. That is why the number of SHGs is bouncing and most of them are in the formative stage and come into existence with great expectations of receiving some benefit or the other.

Selection of group leaders is unanimous in a vast majority of cases and election-nomination are not desired except in a few cases. Group meetings are held once or twice in a month in the vast majority of cases. In very few groups, meetings were held weekly or fortnightly. Transaction costs in terms of visits to offices by leaders of SHGs are also inversely related to the level of development of the district. The group leaders have taken the advantage of IRDP, SGSY schemes and the incidence of benefits is positively related to the incidence of poverty. The primary occupation of the SHG leaders significantly differs between the sample mandals. So also is the status of the household assets of SHG leaders located in the sample mandals of our study. These characteristics are governing their economy and society.

In some cases it is found that the amount accumulated by the groups amounted to several hundred thousands and have formed women's bank with the help of promoting institutions on the lines of celebrated grameena bank of Bangladesh. Initially, the members will start income generating activities, with the help of bank finance, however, gradually they will become self reliant in financing and future growth. If all goes well the groups will have self-sustainable self-employment opportunities.

We have examined the nature and functioning of self help groups in the sample mandals. Analysis of structure of several self help groups showed that they were mostly a homogeneous group in terms of their socio-economic background, which contributed to the cohesiveness and solidarity of the group.[27] I found that the money contributed by the members of Self-Help Groups was pooled together and used as revolving fund, and regular loans were given to its members on priority basis decided by the members themselves. Now the members get loan at a lesser interest and they are free from the clutches of moneylenders.

REFERENCES

1. Self Help Groups, An Alternative to Institutional Credit to the Poor: A Case Study in Andhra Pradesh, K.P. Kumaran, *Journal of Rural Development,* Vol. 16 (3), pp. 515-530 (1997) NIRD, Hyderabad.
2. Empowering Strategies for Rural Women in India, Meenaxi Anand Choudhary, *Kurukshetra,* March 1996. p.21.
3. Uma Joshi, 'Rural Women: A More Purposeful Role,' *Kurukshetra,* August 1997, p.94.
4. Chambers, Robert (1994). "Poverty and Livelihood: Whose Reality Counts?" Overview Paper II, UNDP Stockholm, Round Table, "Change: Social Conflict or Harmony?" 22-24 July.
5. Government of Andhra Pradesh (1998), Annual Report of the Commission of the Rural Development, Hyderabad.
6. Government of Andhra Pradesh (1999), Annual Report of the Commission of the Rural Development, Hyderabad.
7. Ajay Jain, Poverty Alleviation Through Social Mobilisation, The Kurnool Strategy.
8. Ghosh D.K (1995), Group Cohesiveness in DWCRA Groups: An Application of Sociometric Approach, *Kurukshetra,* May-June.
9. Sakuntala Narasimhan (1999), Empowering Women: An Alternative Strategy from Rural India, *Sage Publications,* New Delhi.
10. Government of Andhra Pradesh (2001), Strategy Paper, II.
11. CIRDAP (1999), Rural Development Report, Dhaka.
12. Rajaram Dasgupta (2001), 'Working and Impact of Rural Self Help Groups and Other Forms of Micro Financing,' *Indian Journal of Agriculture Economics,* Vol. 56, No. 3.

13. Mukta Mittal (1995), Women Power in India, *Anmol Publications Pvt. Ltd.*, New Delhi.

14. Government of Andhra Pradesh, Vision - 2020, Hyderabad.

15. CIRDAP (1999), Rural Development Report, Dhaka.

16. IFAD (2001), Rural Poverty Report, Oxford, New York.

17. *The Hindu* (2002), April 27, Chennai.

18. Ibid.

19. NABARD (2000) Annual Report, Mumbai.

20. K.G. Karmakar (1999), Rural Credit and Self Help Groups, Micro Finance Needs and Concepts in India, *Sage*, New Delhi.

21. NABARD (2001), Annual Report, Mumbai.

22. Zeller, Manfred and Manohar Sharma (1998), Rural Finance and Poverty Alleviation, Food Policy Report, International Food Policy Research Institute, Washington DC, USA.

23. Von Pischke, J.D. et al., (1983), Rural Financial Markets in Developing Countries: Their Use and Abuse, John Hopkins University, Baltimore, USA.

24. Kaushik Dasu (1984), The Development Economy: A Critique of Contemporary Theory, *Oxford University Press*, Delhi.

25. Mohammad Haan Khan (1981), Underdevelopment and Agrarian Structure in Pakistan, A Westview Replica Edition. Westview Press, USA.

26. Sukhpal Singh, *Journal of Rural Reconstruction*, Volume 32 July-Dec; 1999 No. 2. Self Help Groups of the Rural Poor in India—An Analysis.

27. K.P. Kumaran, Self Help Groups: An Alternative to Institutional Credit to the Poor: A Case Study in Andhra Pradesh, *Journal of Rural Development*, Vol. 16(3), pp. 515-530 (1997) NIRD, Hyderabad (India).

5

Income and Employment Generation and Capacity Building

INTRODUCTION

Women constitute half of the human population and the rural women in India constitute nearly 77 per cent of the total female population. They contribute significantly to agriculture and allied activities etc., and also artisanal activities, apart from the household activities.[1]

It is being increasingly realized that women's income in a family is very essential and important in relation to the nutritional, economic and educational upliftment of the family. Therefore, a provision is made under IRDP that at least 30 per cent of the beneficiaries should be women. But the mid-term review of IRDP (1987) had shown that the flow of assistance to the women members of the targeted group of households was very nominal. Hence with an objective of improving the assistance to the rural women, a sharper focus was conceived through the scheme of 'Development of Women and Children in Rural Areas' (DWCRA) in 1982-83. This was launched in 50 districts. This was an attempt to involve women more intensively in economic activities (NABARD, 1999).[2] The focus of DWCRA was on economic activities of rural women to be taken up in groups. The purpose of the group was also to enable women to take a larger amount of loan, so that by pooling their individual loans they could start a viable non-farm activity. DWCRA was successful to a large extent in Andhra

Pradesh, (Dev, 1999).[3] On the model of the DWCRA groups, Self Help Groups have been promoted all over the country to fight against rural poverty. The formation of DWCRA groups and SHGs itself is a replication of the Grameena Bank model of Bangladesh which has several success stories of empowering women (Karmakar, 1999).[4] Self Help Groups enable the rural poor to aim for economic empowerment and a right to live with dignity.

To improve the economic situation of women during the early development decade much emphasis was put on developing skills.

Money earned by women, is not only means to her survival and that of her family but also a certain amount of dignity and independence for her. In this respect one had to be watchful in upgrading the skills of employed women.[5]

Self Help group model of Self-Employment generation seems to be a workable model. However, there will be need for utmost care in promotion of self-help groups. The government should adopt absolutely participatory approach towards identification and strengthening of Self-Help Groups. As far as possible, heterogeneous groups should be discouraged as they will have high probability to break away later. The major focus should be laid on homogeneous groups (in terms of common interest and socio-economic status) as they will be more promising in future from the point of view of sustainability of efforts. In this chapter, it is proposed to deal with some selected aspects of income generating and capacity building activities as well as asset formation by the sample SHGs.

Economic Activities Undertaken by Groups

Economic deprivation is an all pervasive phenomenon among the ultra poor, who constitute the bulk of the membership of the SHGs. Hither to, a wide variety of welfare generative programmes have been administered based on the welfarist approach for the rural poor. Realizing the inadequacies of the welfarist approach, empowerment approaches have been evolved at different levels as it leads to the participation of stakeholders both at the level of selection, execution and monitoring of projects (World Bank 2000-2001).[6] Although it is widely accepted that economic betterment is a necessary but not a sufficient condition (Sakuntala Narsimhan, 1999).[7] It should necessarily precede social mobilisation and community awareness as means of overcoming extreme poverty. We have classified the economic activities undertaken by the members of SHG into 5 broad categories. Here again, the activities undertaken by the members of each SHG differ. However, for the purpose of our convenience whatever is the major activity of the sample group, is considered to be the activity of all the members of that group. There is an element of simplicity and arbitrariness underlying this assumption. This has been necessitated because of our constraint, physical as well as financial in the course of our field investigation to establish contact with all the members of a particular group. Under this compulsion and on the basis of aforesaid assumption we have classified the activities undertaken by the SHGs into the following categories as shown in Table 5.1.

As the shortage of capital is a common concern amongst the poor, petty business and trade are undertaken by 36, 30 and 24 per cent of SHGs in three divisions of the districts. Milch animals and dairying is undertaken by 25 and 21 per cent of SHGs in the district. We notice that petty trade, milch animals, dairying, account 76 per cent of the SHGs in the district. Sheep rearing, handicrafts and other activities are undertaken by 16, 4 and 4 per cent of SHGs in the three divisions of districts. Thus, there is a significant difference in the activity pattern of the SHGs of our sample mandals in the district. The observations are significant as the chi-square value is significant at 1 and 5 per cent level.

PROBLEMS FACED BY THE GROUPS

Group promotion is a starting point and groups have to build motivation for undertaking viable activities among

Table 5.1 Activity Undertaken by the Group

(In percentage)

Sl. No.		*Group Activities*	*Kurnool Division-I*	*Nandyal Division-II*	*Adoni Division-III*	*Total*
1.	Petty	Count	18	15	12	45
	Business	% within activity undertaken by the group	40.0	33.3	26.7	100.0
		% within the Division	36.0	30.0	24.0	30.0
		% of Total	12.0	10.0	8.0	30.0
2.	Cattle	Count	12	10	16	38
	Milch animals)	% within activity undertaken by the group	31.6	26.3	42.1	100.0
		% within the Division	24.0	20.0	32.0	25.3
		% of Total	8.0	6.6	10.7	25.3
	Dairying	Count	10	9	12	31
		% within activity undertaken by the group	32.2	29.0	38.7	100.0
		% within the Division	20.0	18.0	24.0	20.7
		% of Total	6.7	6.0	8.0	20.7
3.	Sheep-rearing	Count	6	10	8	24
		% within activity undertaken by the group	125.0	41.7	33.3	100.0
		% within the Division	12.0	20.0	16.0	16
		% of Total	4.0	6.7	5.3	16
4.	Handicrafts	Count	3	2	1	6
		% within activity undertaken by the group	50.0	33.3	16.7	100.0
		% within the Division	6.0	4.0	2.0	4.0
		% of Total	2.0	1.3	0.7	4.0
5.	Others	Count	1	4	1	6
		% within activity undertaken by the group	16.7	66.7	16.6	100.0
		% within the Division	2.0	8.0	2.0	4.0
		of Total	0.7	2.6	0.7	4.0

Chi-square value = 8.16

Significant at 0.05 level (5%)

Significant at 0.01 level (I%)

Graph 5.1 Activity Undertaken by the Group

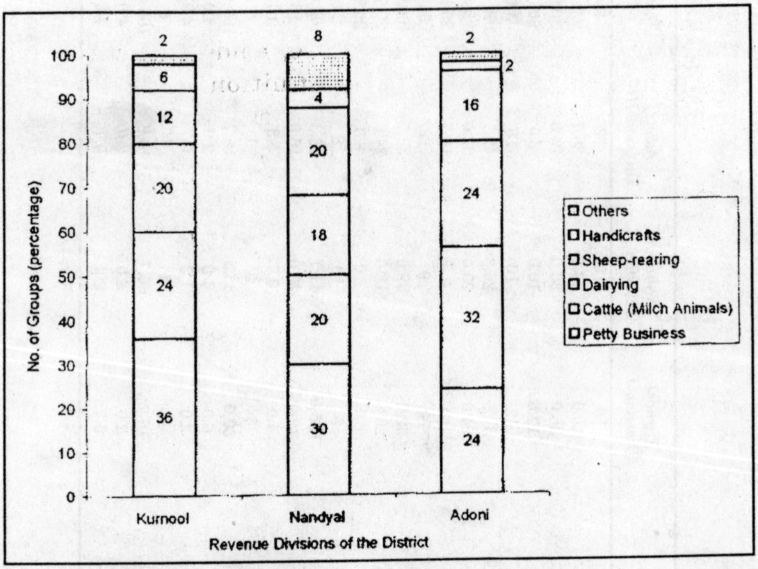

the members. When the group comprises the poor and the disadvantaged, the group is beginning from a position of handicap. The agencies which are in the business of promoting the groups, have to ensure that the members are able to examine the realities around them and take appropriate steps for making the best use of the opportunities, which the group offers to them. We find that our sample SHGs encounter a wide variety of operational problems partly due to inadequate preparation for undertaking income generating activities and by expectations of supporting services, linkages and inputs from the agencies of the Government, financial institutions and NGO's (NABARD, 2000).[8] We have classified the problems under the four categories as mentioned in Table 5.2.

Apparently 10, 16 and 18 per cent of the sample SHGs do not encounter any problems. However, the members of the groups are facing certain problems in conducting their activities from the members of their households such as husband and mother-in-law. But they are not considered here. 24, 30 and 26 per cent of SHGs are facing the problem of shortage of raw materials and other inputs in the district. Financial problems relate to the chronic deficit of the household economy of the members of the SHGs due to limited opportunities of productive employment, and therefore generation of income for consumption and production. This problem is more pronounced in the first division. 50, 40 and 36 per cent of the SHGs are facing

Table 5.2 Problems Faced by the Group

Problems Faced by the Group		*Kurnool Division-I*	*Nandyal Division-II*	*Adoni Division-III*	*Total*
No Problems	Count	5	8	9	22
	% within problems faced by the Group in making the products	22.7	36.4	40.9	100
	% within the Division	10.0	16.0	18.0	14.6
	% of Total	3.3	5.3	6.0	14.6
Collection of Raw Materials	Count	12	15	13	40
	% within problems faced by the Group in making the products	30.0	37.5	32.5	100
	% within the Division	24.0	30.0	26.0	26.7
	% of Total	8.0	10.0	8.7	26.7
Problems from Government Organisations	Count	8	7	10	25
	% within problems faced by the group in making the products	32.0	28.0	40.0	100.0
	% within the Division	16.0	14.0	20.0	16.7
	% of Total	5.3	4 7	6.7	16.7
Financial Problems	Count	25	20	18	63
	% within problems faced by the group in making the products	39.7	31.7	28.6	100
	% within the Division	50.0	40.0	36.0	42.0
	% of Total	16.7	13.3	12.0	42.0

Chi-square value: 3.53

* 0.01 level of significance

* 0.05 level of significance

financial problems in the district. Next to financial problems, the problems faced by the groups is inadequacy of services rendered by the Government departments and service providing agencies. 16, 14 and 20 per cent of the groups are facing problems from Government departments as shown in the Table 5.2.

Graph 5.2 Problems Faced by the Group

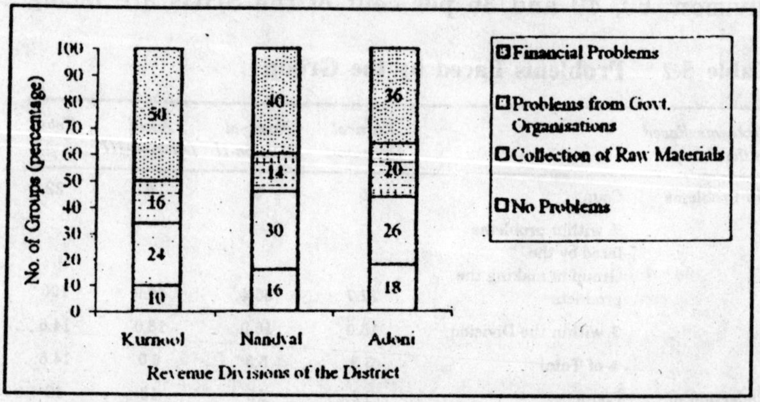

Of all these problems financial problem is more pronounced than the other. Whatever financial assistance is given by the Government, Bank or any financial institution, this has to be distributed among 10-15 members of the group. Therefore each member is getting a very less amount due to which they are facing the problem of inadequate resources to invest in their economic activities. Thus poor investment leads to poor incomes and employment. Thus, the operational problems of sample SHGs exhibit divergence. The observations are significant as the chi-square value is significant at 0.01 and 0.05 level.

PROBLEMS OF MARKETING THE PRODUCT

Problems of marketing the product that is produced are ever present for all business units—small, medium and big, national or multinational organisations. Management information systems and marketing surveys are not possible or relevant for tiny units like the SHGs (Shylendra, H.S. 1999).[9] We represent our findings relating to the sale of products-services produced by the sample SHGs in Table 5.3.

Table 5.3 Marketing Problems

Sl. No.	*Marketing Problems*		*Kurnool Division-I*	*Nandyal Division-II*	*Adoni Division-III*	*Total*
1.	No Problems	Count	2	1	1	4
		% within problems regarding sale of output	50.0	25.0	25.0	100.0
		% within name of the division	4.0	2.0	2.0	2.7
		% of the Total	1.3	0.6	0.6	2.7
2..	Lack of propaganda and poor quality	Count	18	8	6	32
		% within problems regarding sale of output	56.3	25.0	18.7	100
		% within name of the division	36.0	16.0	12.0	21.3
		% of the Total	12.0	5.3	4.0	21.3
3.	Lack of good price	Count	15	19	17	51
		% within problems regarding sale of output	29.4	37.2	33.3	100
		% within name of the division	30.0	38.0	34.0	34.0
		% of the Total	10.0	12.7	11.3	34.0
4.	Information gaps and problems	Count	15	22	26	63
		% within problems regarding sale of output	23.8	34.9	41.3	100
		% within name of the division	30.0	44.0	52.0	42.0
		of the Total	10.0	14.7	17.3	42.0

Source: Field Data.

Direct access to transport and markets is also crucial if women are to maintain control over the products of their labour. Where women are not permitted in the market place, male family members who sell their goods receive the cash or agents skin off the profit for example, in silk

Graph 5.3 Marketing Problems

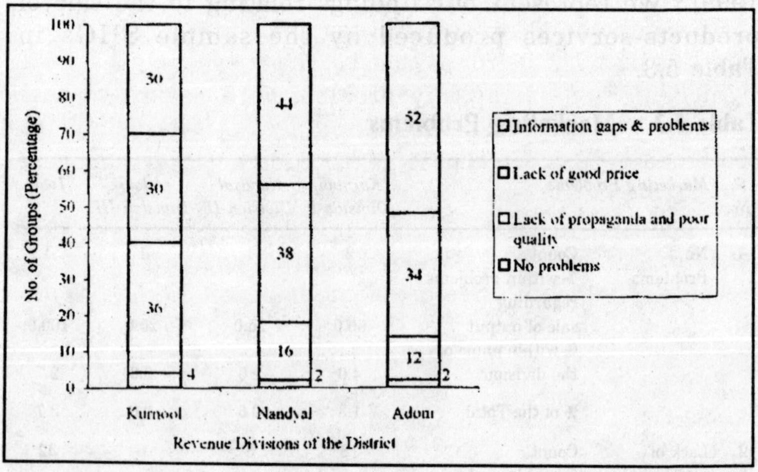

weaving industry in Banaras, cloth produced at home and sold by the husband to intermediaries, leaves the women with "no control nor a separate share of the earnings."[10] Women in some areas have adapted to the requirements of female seclusion by trading out of their homes with children as intermediaries or by organising their own markets. In the north-eastern hill areas of India, women sell various items of dress, furnishings and food products as well as their own weaving, from parched stalls in the urban women's market and in smaller rural women's markets throughout the state of Manipur.

Situated as they are in remote and isolated rural pockets, they do not have adequate market information for their inputs as well as output. Communication channels are mostly informal and distorted, despite the rapid advances in mass communication and information technology in the urban sector. Improved communications can also play a part in reducing informational asymmetries. The village pay-phones, used by the Grameena Bank in Bangladesh were found to lower transaction costs and to enhance the empowerment and status of women (Von Braun et al., 1999).[11] We do not have good communication network in our sample mandals. Information gaps and information problems are encountered by 44, 52 and 42 per cent of SHGs respectively in three divisions of the district. There are less number of groups that is 2.7 per cent in the district which are not facing any problem with regard to their economic activities. The problem of lack of propaganda and poor quality is more, that is 36 per cent of SHGs in Kurnool Division than in other two divisions (16 per cent and 12 per cent). The problem of remunerative price to their products is faced by the 30, 38 and 34 per cent of SHG respectively in the three divisions. It is a common problem in case of three divisions in the district. Of all the marketing problems faced by the SHGs in the district, the problem of lack of information is most prominent. In this way, the nature and character of marketing problems faced by SHGs differ significantly.

METHOD OF TACKLING PROBLEMS OR REMEDIES

Since the Self-Help Groups are in the early stages and yet to graduate to the stage of maturity, they have to rely on the support of outward agencies which have facilitated their promotion. This tendency is not conducive to their autonomy and may need to a dependency culture which is supposed to be overcome by group strength. However, problem tackling and decision-making are not that simple especially under conditions of transition from a traditional to a modern set up. There are a variety of ways and means of tackling the operational problems of SHG Ventures. We have classified them under four broad categories and the details are shown in Table 5.4.

Group efforts are fostered to solve the issues and to tackle the problems of their activity from time to time on the basis of collective wisdom and group discussion. This is the true spirit of democracy in action. 36, 38 and 48 per cent of SHGs resolve their problems by themselves in the three divisions of the district. NGOs generally nurture the groups promoted by them by helping them mostly by way of advice and technical assistance which are not generally forthcoming from governmental agencies. The rapport established by the functionaries and field workers of NGOs have gone a long way in fostering self confidence and capability to face the challenges of day-to-day business activities (Sakuntala Narasimhan, 1999).[12] In our sample mandals, the NGOs operating are of recent origin and do not possess so much of experience in enabling the SHGs to overcome their problems.

Table 5.4 Methods of Tackling Problems

(in percentage)

Sl. No.	Methods of Tackling Problems		Kurnool Division-I	Nandyal Division-II	Adoni Division-III	Total
1.	NGOs	Count	10	13	12	35
		% within the division	20.0	26.0	24.0	23.3
		% of the Total	6.7	8.7	8.0	23.3
2.	By Themselves	Count	18	19	15	52
		% within the division	36.0	38.0	30.0	35.0
		% of the Total	12.0	12.7	10.0	35.0
3	By Govt. Agencies	Count	9	8	7	24
		% within the division	18.0	16.0	14.0	16.0
		% of the Total	6.0	5.3	4.7	16.0
4.	By taking Help of well-wishers or elders	Count	13	10	16	39
		% within the division	26.0	20.0	32.0	26.0
		% of the Total	8.7	6.7	10.7	26.0

Chi-square value = 2.58

Source: Field Data

Significant at 0.05 level (5%)

Significant at 0.01 level (1%)

However, they have assisted 20, 26 and 24 per cent of SHGs in the three divisions in their income generating activities. Governmental departments operate in a dichotomous way and their operations are not generally people oriented.[13] In spite of the advent of mandal setup in district administration as early as 1985 bureaucratic tendencies persist and the attitudes of departmental functionaries are yet to undergo a change in favour of the

Graph 5.4 Methods of Tackling Problems

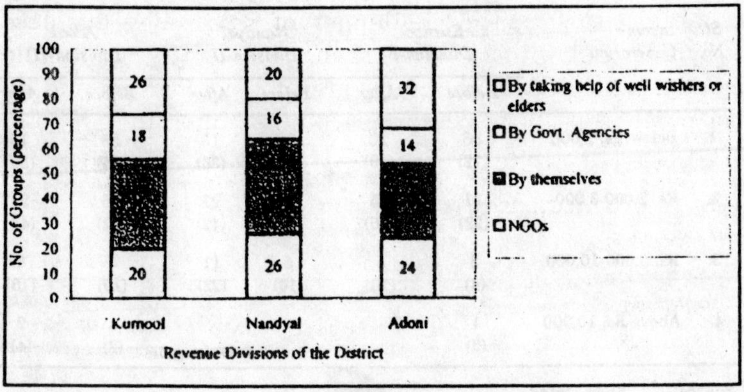

rural poor which is wanted to create prosperous Andhra Pradesh (Vision, 2020).[14] In the sample mandals government agencies have helped 18, 16 and 14 per cent of SHGs respectively in three divisions. Elders of the village society by tradition and custom play an important role in influencing the activities that are undertaken by the groups by offering their advice. 26, 20 and 32 per cent of groups in the district have been assisted by the elders of the villagers in tackling their problems. The observations are significant as the chi-square value is significant at 1 and 5 per cent level.

INCOME GENERATION AND DECISION-MAKING WITHIN THE HOUSEHOLD

Generation of income by the members of the group is the central purpose of most group formations especially those under DWCRA. We have stated the activities undertaken by the groups earlier and in this context, we propose to outline the income effect of group activity.

The entire analysis in this session proceeds on the assumption of other things being equal. In other words, we attribute the net increase in the income of the household is due to activity undertaken by the group member. We have presented the average income level under four broad categories as shown in Table 5.5.

Table 5.5 Income Generation

(Monthly Income)

Sl. No.	*Income Generation*	*Kurnool Division-I*		*Nandyal Division-II*		*Adoni Division-III*	
		Before	*After*	*Before*	*After*	*Before*	*After*
1	Below Rs. 2,000	36 (72)	20 (40)	32 (64)	18 (36)	28 (56)	15 (30)
2.	Rs. 2,000-3,000	11 (22)	25 (50)	13 (26)	21 (42)	16 (32)	24 (48)
3.	Rs. 5,000-10,000	2 (4)	5 (10)	5 (10)	11 (22)	5 (10)	9 (18)
4.	Above Rs. 10,000	1 (2)	-	-	-	1 (2)	2 (4)

Source: Field Data.

A glance at Table 5.5 shows that the average income earned by the women has increased and so the status of women improved in terms of income. There has been an improvement in the average household income of the groups in all the three divisions as the proportion of SHGs below

Graph 5.5 Income Generation

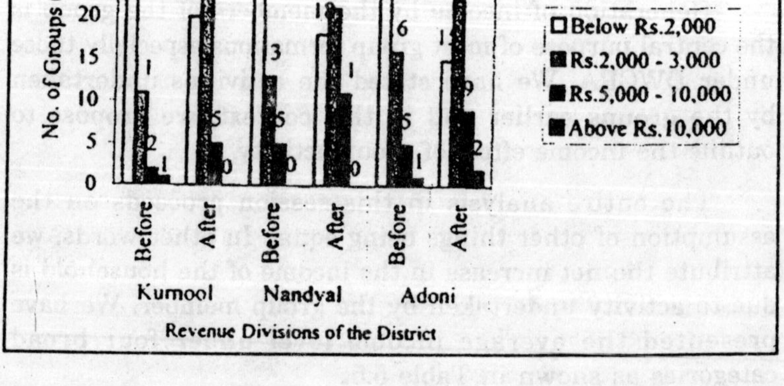

Rs. 2,000 is reduced by 32, 28 and 13 percentage points. In the range of income of Rs. 2,000 - 5,000 also there has been an improvement in the incomes of group and thereby the number of groups in this range of income increased by 28, 16 and 16 per cent in the three divisions of the district. Similarly, in the income range of Rs. 5,000 - 10,000 the improvement is not so considerable. The number of groups increased in this range of income are 6, 12 and 8 per cent. However the improvement in the income of groups in the range of Rs. 10,000 and above is very marginal. On the whole, the income effect may be considered to be positive. All the beneficiaries who were found to live below poverty line prior to the implementation of DWCRA have now crossed the poverty line.

Decision-making within the household, and among others is a function of the share of women's income in the total household income. Studies reveal that women's income contribution to household income and their economic status in terms of decision-making are positively related in most countries of South Asia (CIRDAP, 1998). We set out the situation with regard to decision-making within the household by the members of the sample SHG in Table 5.6.

Table 5.6 Household Decision-Making in Asset Transactions

Sl. No.	*Decision-Making*		*Kurnool Division-I*	*Nandyal Division-II*	*Adoni Division-III*	*Total*
1	Improved	Count	45	42	38	125
		% within the division	90.0	84.0	76.0	83.3
		% of the Total	30	28	25.3	83.3
2	Status quo	Count	5	8	12	25
		% within the division	10	16.0	24.0	16.6
		% of the Total	3.3	5.3	8.0	16.6

Chi-square value = 3.72
Source: Field Data
Significant at 0.05 level (5%)
Significant at 0.01 level (1%)

As expected we noticed an improvement in the position of SHG women with regard to decision making to the extent of 90, 84 and 76 per cent respectively. The rest of the cases which are negligible the status-quo continues. However the improvement is less in case of Adoni division compared to others. The observations are significant as the chi-square value is significant at 0.05 and 0.01 level.

Graph 5.6 Household Decision-Making in Asset Transactions

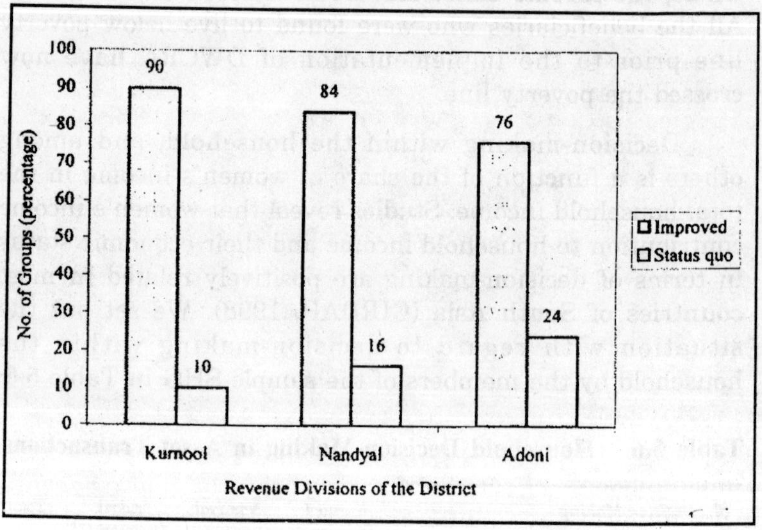

EMPLOYMENT GENERATION BY SECTORS AND GENDER

Employment generation is the process mechanism through which household income is enhanced. Low income is only a symptom but not the cause of poverty. But it is the lack of employment opportunity that is at the root of the problem of poverty (HDR, 1997).[15] It is customary to measure rural employment on the basis of number of days, instead of man-days in a particular year. The usual status measure is followed here. It might appear to be somewhat of an over estimate of stock of employment. We have adopted the usual status approach, which considers days of employment but not man-days. It means that a person is employed for some part of the day, it is treated as employment and counted in the number of days of employment (RDR, 1994).[16] We have followed the usual status concept in the estimation of employment level in our study.

Table 5.7 Employment Generation

Sl. No.	*Classification (No. of days)*	*Kurnool Division-I*		*Nandyal Division-II*		*Adoni Division-III*	
		Before 2000	*After 2000*	*Before 2000*	*After 2000*	*Before 2000*	*After 2000*
1.	Below 100	16 (32)	11 (22)	20 (40)	18 (36)	30 (60)	28 (56)
2.	101-200	18 (36)	19 (38)	12 (24)	12 (24)	14 (28)	12 (24)
3.	201-300	11 (22)	12 (24)	8 (16)	9 (18)	6 (12)	6 (12)
4.	More than 300	5 (10)	8 (16)	10 (20)	11 (22)	0	4 (8)

Note: Figures in parentheses indicate percentages to total.
Source: Field Data.

It is clear from the Table 5.7 that there is an improvement in the employment status of women in all the sample mandals of the district. However, the improvement is not uniform due to different resource endowments of the areas and human capital endowments of women members of SHGs in different locations. There is a reduction in the proportion of SHG groups found working below 100 days by 10, 4, and 4 per cent in the three divisions of the district. However, the incidence of unemployment and underemployment is found in the sample mandals of the three divisions in the district both before and after the advent of the SHGs. High incidence of unemployment is the driving force for the migration or exodous of the rural poor (Sakuntala Narasimhan, 1999).[17] There is a marginal decline in the proportion of SHGs in the employment range of 101-200 days and 201-300 days. In the last category of employment range more than 300 days, there is an improvement to the tune of 4, 2 and 8 per cent in the sample mandals of the three divisions we therefore find an overall improvement though of a marginal character in the employment status of women.

We have classified the activities in which our samples are employed into three categories namely those who are engaged in agriculture, agricultural allied activities, and non-agricultural activities in the rural sector. We have naturally excluded migrants from the rural sector who are employed in the urban sector. Our's is an exercise in comparative statistics relating to employment status of men, women and children in four categories of activities in the district. We start with SHGs engaged in agriculture who mostly belong to small and marginal farmers.

Table 5.8 indicates that there is a decline in the days of employment on an average in the lowest employment range by 29 per cent in the three divisions of the district. There has been an increase in the days of employment on an average in the range of 101-200 days by 23 per cent in the district. However the increase in the days of employment on an average in the range of 201-365 days is marginal that is 7 per cent. If continuous credit support is given to the rural women, income generation activity will be encouraged and generation of employment will also be more.

We notice the incidence of child labour in all the three divisions of the district though its proportion varies. There is an increase in the first incidence of child labour over time in the two divisions of the district in the first range of employment. The incidence of child labour under the second employment range disappeared in case of Kurnool and Adoni division. However a little incidence of child labour was found in the second division. In the third range of employment there is a modest decline in the first division and no child labour was found in the second and third divisions.

Table 5.8 Employment Generation by Gender and Age in Agriculture

Sl.	Number of	Kurnool Division-I						Nandyal Division-II						Adoni Division-III					
		Before			After			Before			After			Before			After		
No.	Days	M	W	C	M	W	C	M	W	C	M	W	C	M	W	C	M	W	C
1	0-100	31	50	28	33	33	50	45	50	50	47	35	46	50	50	47	42	38	50
		(62)	(100)	(56)	(66)	(66)	(100)	(90)	(100)	(100)	(94)	(70)	(92)	(100)	(100)	(94)	(84)	(76)	(100)
2.	101 -200	13	-	14	15	13	-	2	-	-	1	11	4	-	-	3	6	10	-
		(26)		(28)	(30)	(26)		(4)			(2)	(22)	(8)			(6)	(12)	(20)	
3.	201-365	6	-	8	2	4	-	3	-	-	2	4	-	-	-	-	2	2	-
		(12)		(16)	(4)	(8)		(6)			(4)	(8)					(4)	(4)	

Note: Figures in parentheses indicates the respective percentage.
Source: Field Data.
M = Men; W = Women; C = Children.

Table 5.9 Employment Generation by Gender and Age in Allied Activities

Sl.	Number of	Kurnool Division-I						Nandyal Division-II						Adoni Division-III					
		Before			After			Before			After			Before			After		
No.	Days	M	W	C	M	W	C	M	W	C	M	W	C	M	W	C	M	W	C
1.	0-100	44 (88)	47 (94)	43 (86)	44 (88)	41 (82)	48 (96)	45 (90)	50 (100)	39 (78)	45 (90)	38 (76)	50 (100)	49 (98)	50 (100)	50 (100)	48 (96)	42 (84)	50 (100)
2.	101-200	4 (8)	2 (4)	3 (6)	6 (12)	5 (10)	2 (4)	4 (8)	-	8 (16)	5 (10)	11 (22)	-	1 (2)	-	-	2 (4)	7 (14)	-
3.	201-365	2 (4)	1 (2)	4 (8)	-	4 (8)	-	1 (2)	-	3 (6)	-	1 (2)	-	-	-	-	-	1 (2)	-

Note: Figures in parentheses indicates the respective percentage

Source: Field Data.

M = Men; W = Women, C = Children.

However, women and children from small and marginal farmers are constrained to resort to the employment owing to economic compulsion. It is clear from the table that higher proportion of population is concentrating in the first range of employment than the others. It means higher level of underemployment is present in district.

In the agriculture and allied activities, there is a decline in the days of employment on an average in the lowest employment range in the three divisions of the district. However the employment status of women in the second and third employment range has improved in all the three divisions of the district. The incidence of child labour was more in the first division in the three employment ranges when compared to other two divisions in the district. However in second and third range of employment, no child labour was found in the Kurnool and Nandyal divisions of the district. The incidence of employment in second range (101-200 days) is very low and in third range (201-365 days), the employment is very negligible.

It is clear from Table 5.10 *(see on next page)* that in the non-agricultural sector, in respect of women, there is an improvement in the status of employment in the first employment range in the three divisions of the district. In the second range of employment, there is an improvement in the status of employment of women in the three divisions. In the third range of employment, there is a little improvement in the status of employment of women in the first division and no improvement in the second and third divisions. Incidence of child employment is reduced in all the divisions of the district.

No child labour is found in the second and third employment ranges in the Nandyal and Adoni divisions. As the government has opened child labour schools, the percentage of child labour has declined.

ASSET STATUS

Assets are defined and classified in several ways. An asset is anything that can be used, without being used up,

Table 5.10 Employment Generation by Gender and Age in Non-Agricultural Activities

Sl.	Number of	*Kurnool Division-I*						*Nandyal Division-II*						*Adoni Division-III*					
		Before			*After*			*Before*			*After*			*Before*			*After*		
No.	*Days*	*M*	*W*	*C*	*M*	*W*	*C*	*M*	*W*	*C*	*M*	*W*	*C*	*M*	*W*	*C*	*M*	*W*	C
1	0-100	48 (96)	50 (100)	46 (92)	43 (86)	42 (84)	50 (100)	50 (100)	50 (100)	46 (92)	45 (90)	47 (94)	50 (100)	46 (92)	49 (98)	48 (96)	45 (90)	44 (88)	50 (100)
2	101-200	1 (2)		3 (6)	6 (12)	7 (14)	-	-	-	4 (8)	3 (6)	3 (6)	-	3 (6)	1 (2)	2 (4)	3 (6)	6 (12)	-
3.	201 -365	1 (2)	-	1 (2)	1 (2)	1 (2)	-	-	-	-	2 (4)	-	-	1 (2)	-	-	2 (4)	-	-

Note: Figures in parentheses indicates the respective percentage.
Source: Field Data.
M = Men; W = Women; C = Children.

to increase regular return above receipts from labour, whether hired or self-employed and thus enhance producers income or consumer's welfare. Typical assets are land, wells, cattle, tools, shares, skills, health and roads.[18] In this context we are not concerned with community assets such as roads and other peripheral infrastructure, human endowments such as education, skills, health and financial assets such as shares. Because some of these assets are non-existent in the context of the rural poor.

The poor are hard pressed to gain assets. Much income and work are committed to basic consumer needs (and social obligations). Inheritances are small and rare. The poor readily lose assets. In hard times, they must often sell or mortgage them, to avoid even deeper transient poverty.[19]

Many of the poor have access to land without having ownership rights. Tenancy is common. Tenancy does not provide collateral or a secure hedge against risk, and access to the land from one year to the next is often uncertain (WDR, 1990).[20]

We have classified the assets of our sample groups into five categories. We have computed average for each group under each category and these details are presented in Table 5.11.

As expected the land asset is quite negligible. 84, 76 and 88 per cent of the sample SHGs were found to possess land worth 20,000 and below before joining the SHGs. In the subsequent period there is a little change in the proportion of SHGs under this category in two divisions of the district. However there is a modest improvement in the Nandyal division. The remaining SHGs which are quite negligible are distributed over Rs. 20,000 and above value of landed property in all the divisions in the district. Similarly more or less the same picture is replicated in case of rural housing of our samples. 96, 80 and 96 per cent of sample SHGs in the three divisions possess houses whose value is below Rs. 20,000. As vigorous efforts have been

Table 5.11 Asset Formation

(Monthly Income)

Sl. No.	*Item*	*Kurnool Division-I* *Before*	*Kurnool Division-I* *After*	*Nandyal Division-II* *Before*	*Nandyal Division-II* *After*	*Adoni Division-III* *Before*	*Adoni Division-III* *After*
1	Land						
	(a) Below Rs. 20,000	42 (84)	40 (80)	38 (76)	40 (80)	44 (88)	41 (82)
	(b) Rs. 20,001 - 50,000	7 (14)	8 (16)	6 (12)	7 (14)	5 (10)	6 (12)
	(c) Rs. 50,001 - 1,00,000	1 (2)	1 (2)	4 (8)	2 (4)	1 (2)	3 (6)
	(d) Above Rs. 1,00,000	-	1 (2)	2 (4)	1 (2)	-	-
2	House						
	(a) Below Rs. 20,000	48 (96)	45 (90)	40 (80)	39 (78)	48 (96)	38 (76)
	(b) Rs. 20,001 - 50,000	1 (2)	3 (6)	8 (16)	9 (18)	1 (2)	11 (22)
	(c) Rs. 50,001 - 1,00,000	1 (2)	2 (4)	2 (4)	2 (4)	1 (2)	1 (2)
3	Gold						
	(a) Below Rs. 20,000	50 (100)	49 (98)	50 (100)	50 (100)	50 (100)	50 (100)
	(b) Rs. 20,001 - 50,000	-	1 (2)	-	-	-	-
	(c) Rs. 50,001 - 1,00,000	-	-	-	-	-	-
4	Household Articles						
	(a) Below Rs. 20,000	49 (98)	43 (86)	50 (100)	42 (84)	48 (96)	47 (94)
	(b) Rs. 20,001 - 50,000	1 (2)	7 (14)	-	6 (12)	2 (4)	3 (6)
	(c) Rs. 50,001 - 1,00,000	-	-	-	1 (2)	-	-
	(d) Above Rs. 1,00,000	-	-	-	1 (2)	-	-
5.	Other Assets						
	(a) Below Rs. 10,000	46 (92)	42 (84)	48 (96)	37 (74)	39 (78)	36 (72)
	(b) Rs. 10,001 - 20,000	2 (4)	7 (14)	1 (2)	10 (20)	6 (12)	11 (22)
	(c) Rs. 20,001 - 50,000	2 (4)	1 (2)	-	1 (2)	4 (8)	3 (6)
	(d) Above Rs. 50,000	-	-	1 (2)	2 (4)	1 (2)	-

Source: Field Data.

made by the state to improve rural housing under the different Five Year Plans; the housing status of the rural poor has shown a modest improvement in all divisions of the district in the subsequent period.

The possession of gold by rural households is a part and parcel of social status and an acceptable means of collateral for credit access. But since gold is the most liquid of all the non-financial assets of rural households, Its stock is insignificant. A majority of households are found possessing gold worth less than Rs. 20,000 both before and after group formation. No group is possessing gold worth more than Rs. 20,000 in all the three divisions of the district.

Household articles such as utensils, transistors, furniture, electrical equipment are generally possessed and a greater proportion of the SHGs are found to be possessing articles worth Rs. 20,000 and below. Other assets are of negligible value. 84, 74 and 72 per cent of SHGs are found to possess other assets worth below Rs. 10,000 in all three divisions of the district. 14, 20 and 22 per cent of SHGs are found to possess other assets worth Rs. 10,001 - 20,000. A very negligible proportion of SHGs are found to possess other assets in the other two categories. Thus just as in other categories of assets there is a poor asset base with uneven distribution. Because of the poverty trap asset deprivation is a pervasive phenomenon. Alcoholism among the men folk adds fuel to the fire of poverty and therefore, assetlessness is a striking feature of our samples as in the case of the ST, SC women groups (Sakuntala Narasimhan, 1999).[21]

CAPACITY BUILDING

The manner in which a group comes into existence, the efforts made by the promoting agency in training and building the capacities of the group members for self management, internal norms of functioning developed by the group which enhance democracy, transparency, accountability, equity and gender sensitivity. How the group resolves conflicts, the nature of leadership, are some of the crucial factors which determine the path of a group, is likely to transverse in the future—whether it will evolve as a highly matured and self-reliant group or whether it will disintegrate at the earliest appearance of a problem. On many occasions, groups are formed only to meet some targets. Some other times, groups are formed in a hurry in order to corner a readily available benefit. Many groups are constituted artificially just for the sake of a programme without giving importance to allowing the existing latent leadership impulses to emerge naturally. The promoting agencies also are deficient in the kind of skills and patience required to deal with communities to sensitise them about the issues involved and prepare them for the group formation (Rai and Tandan, 1999).[22]

As the Self Help Groups are organized by different agencies under different circumstances, there is a need to bring about a clear understanding of the concept and build the capacities of the poor to manage their own institutions on a sustainable basis. Therefore, capacity building has been realized as an important tool to strengthen the groups. All the DRDAs have initiated the process of training and capacity building to the officials incharge of this programme through various institutions such as NIRD, CAPART, NABARD, NGOs and other institutions having the expertise. The capacity building exercise is gradually extended to the field level functionaries, volunteers and through them to the ultimate stakeholders. The frequency of training programmes for the volunteers in the districts ranges from monthly, quarterly, half yearly to yearly intervals. Training programmes are designed to impart skills not only to group leaders but also to all members of groups on topics like the role and responsibilities of leaders and members, management norms for strengthening the groups book-keeping systems and leadership. The duration of the training also ranges from one day to five days. The training methodology consists of classroom discussions, field studies, role-plays, exposure visits, sharing of experiences etc. Audio-visual aids, charts and simulation exercises are some of the techniques used in the training. The content of the training programmes covers diverse topics like basic orientation to book-keeping, functional literacy, group dynamics, health, hygiene and accessing government services (Government of Andhra Pradesh).[23]

Training programmes are conducted by all the promoting agencies either independently or jointly at the mandal, divisional or district level in order to inculcate self-confidence and impart the skills of the trade to the stakeholders. The relationship between training and development is well established in the literature (G.Pracharopoulas and M.Woodhall, 1986).[24] In Table 5.12, we present a few details of the training undergone by the stakeholders and their perception of the benefit of training.

It is clear from the Table 5.12 that 74, 64 and 60 per cent of SHG members have undergone training with regard

Table 5.12 Capacity Building

Sl. No.	*Particulars*	*Kurnool Division-I*	*Nandyal Division II*	*Adoni Division-III*
1.	Undergone Training			
	(a) 1 to 5 persons	37 (74)	32 (64)	30 (60)
	(b) 6 to 10 persons	5 (10)	12 (24)	8 (16)
	(c) 11 to 15 persons	3 (6)	4 (8)	10 (20)
	(d) 16 to 20 persons	2 (4)	2 (4)	2 (4)
	(e) None	3 (6)	-	-
2.	Improvement of Skill			
	(a) Yes	44 (88)	46 (92)	48 (96)
	(b) No	6 (12)	4 (8)	2 (4)

Source: Field Data.

to operational aspects of their economic activity in the first category of 1-5 persons. However the number of groups who have undergone training in the other categories like 6-10, 11-15, 16-20 are less. It means in majority of groups 1-5 persons have undergone training. The perception of the stakeholders regarding the benefit of training is positive. 88, 92 and 96 per cent of SHGs are of the opinion that there is a definite improvement in the skill of the member after undergoing training.

FINDINGS

It was found in the present study that after joining SHG groups, the involvement of women in income generation activities has increased. They stated that after receiving assistance from banks, NGOs, Government (RF), they are now able to undertake income generation activities on a wider scale and more efficiently. This might be clear from the following statements made by members interviewed:

1. Before joining the SHG groups, women who were engaged in small trading could not run their business smoothly due to lack of capital. Sometimes they had to take loans from local moneylenders at very high interest rates. Because of this, they could not earn desirable profits and often incurred loss. But now they have adequate capital for their business ventures. Now they also earn profits and can even save money after repayment of loan instalments and can spend on household necessities;

2. In the case of poultry rearing, sheep rearing, milch animals, many women were already involved in this activity before joining the group approach, but on a small scale at the family level. Now they engage in this activity commercially as they receive training, credit, input support, supervision and marketing support from NGOs. Mortality rate of poultry birds, sheeps, other animals has reduced, so they can also earn more profits than before;

3. Rural women traditionally cultivate vegetables in their homestead land for household consumption and sell the surplus. After receiving training and credit from NGOs, they have started vegetable cultivation on a commercial basis;
4. Due to their involvement in income generating activities many women have switched over from traditional to non-traditional activities and are now simultaneously engaged in multiple income generating activities throughout the year;
5. Over half of the women who receive credit from the banks/NGOs still involve their male counterparts for utilizing it in different income generating activities. Moreover, the rural culture restricts women's access to large-scale income generating activities;
6. Women have used their incomes for a wide variety of uses including purchasing assets, making repairs on their living units, meeting household food and non-food expenses, meeting children's educational demands and saving for daughter's marriage, etc. But they have yet to reach a stage where they can take independent decisions regarding the using of their incomes. However, survey findings have suggested that whereas previously women had no say in the income accrued from their NGOs loans, when those loans were used by their husbands, now their husbands often consult them about how to spend this income;
7. Nevertheless women are able to develop a savings behaviour due to their involvement with income generating activities.

Although it cannot be stated that women have become completely empowered as yet, at least now they have begun to acquire positive self-perceptions of their own personal interests. These self-perceptions will allow them to assert themselves and demand for their rights in their struggle towards socio-economic empowerment.

It is true that the involvement in income generation activities is reducing women's economic dependence on their husbands and other male kin for personal and household expenditures. At the same time their contributions to household asset purchase and investment and savings also increase overtime. Women have also reported an improvement in their relationship with their husbands, primarily because they provide them with capital for investment purposes.

Summing Up

Large number of rural women are severely affected by poverty. In this regard we think income generating activities play an important role towards resolving this deep rooted problem in the economy of India.

Rural women's involvement in income generating activities is usually tend to be home-based and small in response to restrictions on mobility, time, access to capital and credit. Overcoming economic deprivation and distress by the provision of opportunities for gainful employment is the surest means of facilitating economic emancipation and tackling income poverty.

In terms of asset ownership, it is clear that the longer a women remains involved in income generating activities and the more employment opportunities she has, the more scope she will have to purchase large assets such as cow, land as well as other productive and non-productive assets. Nevertheless women are able to develop a savings behaviour due to their involvement with income generating activities. Survey findings have revealed that women are able to assert some kind of control over these assets as well as on the use of savings.

It is true that managerial and financial problems of women have been identified as the most pervasive and fundamental constraints in the growth of income generating activities.

We have noticed a positive impact on women's employment in all divisions though of varying degrees and therefore, an increase in the share of women's income in the household income which is not explicitly brought out but is implied, and therefore an improved status of women in household decision-making. The asset status is generally very thin and small and there is an uneven distribution. Thus the majority of the women involved in income generation activities increase their mobility and ability to make purchases and major household decisions, their ownership of productive assets, their legal and political awareness and participation in public campaigns and protests. While the magnitudes of their incomes may be relatively small, the effect of women's empowerment is substantial.

Capacity building in terms of training programmes is widely covered. Naturally the same psychological tendency and attitude is noticed regarding the benefits of training received by the stakeholders. Empowering women with economically productive work will enhance their contribution to rural development.

REFERENCES

1. N.Manimekalai and G.Rajeswari, 'Empowerment of Women Through Self Help Groups,' *Margin* Vol. 32, No. 4, (July- Sept. 2000).
2. NABARD (1999), Annual Report, Mumbai.
3. Dev, S. Mahendra (1999), "State Interventions and Women's Employment," in T.S.Papola and Alakh N.Sharma (Eds) (1999), "Gender and Employment in India," *Vikas Publishing House Pvt. Ltd,* New Delhi, pp. 373-41 l.
4. Karmakar, K.G. (1999), "Rural Credit and Self Help Groups, Micro Finance Needs and Concepts in India," *Sage Publications,* New Delhi.
5. Ms.Jessie B.Tellis, Nayak (1982), "Outline for a Course on Women and Girls in Education and Income Generation for Women, Non-Formal Approaches," Indian Social Institute, New Delhi.
6. The World Bank (2000-2001), World Development Report, *Oxford,* New York.

7. Sakuntala Narasimhan (1999), Empowering Women: An Alternative Strategy from Rural India, *Sage Publications,* New Delhi.

8. NABARD (2000), *Annual Report,* Mumbai.

9. Shylendra, H.S. (1999), Promoting Women's Self Help Groups, Lessons from an Action Research Project of IRMA, Anand, India, Working Paper No. 121.

10. Government of India, Report of the Committee on the Status of Women in India, Ministry of Education and Social Welfare, New Delhi, 1974.

11. Von Braun, J. Bayes, F. and Akhter, R. (1999), Village Pay Phones and Poverty Reduction, ZEF Discussion Papers on Development Policy No. 18, Center for Development Research, University of Berlin.

12. Sakuntala Narasimhan (1999), "Empowering Women: An Alternative Strategy from Rural India," *Sage Publications,* New Delhi.

13. UNDP (2000), Human Development Report, *Oxford,* New York.

14. Government of Andhra Pradesh (1999), *Vision-2020,* Hyderabad, India.

15. UNDP (1997), Human Development Report. *Oxford,* New York.

16. NIRD (1994), Rural Development Report; Rural Employment, Hyderabad, Andhra Pradesh.

17. Sakuntala Narasimhan (1999), "Empowering Women: An Alternative Strategy from Rural India," *Sage Publications,* New Delhi.

18. IFAD (2001), "Rural Poverty Report, The Challenge of Ending Rural Poverty," *Oxford*, New York.

19. Ibid.

20. The World Bank (1990), World Development Report, *Oxford,* New York.

21. Sakuntala Narasimhan (1999), Empowering Women: An Alternative Strategy from Rural India, *Sage Publications,* New Delhi.

22 Rai and Tandon (1999), "Voluntary Development Organisation and Socio-economic Development," Indian Economic Association, 82nd Conference Volume, Amritsar.

23. Government of Andhra Pradesh, Guidelines for Swarnajayanthi Gram Swarozgar Yojana, Panchayati Raj and Rural Development Department, Hyderabad.

24. George Pracharopoulas and Moureen Woodhall (1986), Education for Development, An Analysis of Investment Choices, *Oxford,* New York.

6

Poverty Alleviation Through Social Mobilisation—the Kurnool Strategy

INTRODUCTION

Social development is an important pre-requisite for economic development, which is mainly achieved through modern system of education. In the Indian villages particularly among women, the literacy rate is one of the lowest. Illiteracy leads to traditional beliefs and values which adversely affect rational thinking and personality development. In a recent study conducted in the state of Andhra Pradesh, it was found that one of the important functions of Self Help Groups is to promote social development among its members. This is attempted through motivation and awareness creation. Informal education through folk media played a major role in achieving this objective. It helped to undertake social reform activities by eliminating social evils like untouchability, bonded labour, alcoholism apart from exploitation of agricultural labourers by landlords (Kumaran, 1994).[1]

Participation of rural women is intended not just to enable a large number of them to involve in the process of development, but also to enable them to share the benefits of public programmes and thereby raise their living standards. Creating equal access to and control over resources and products of their labour, attacking patriarchial structures in family and community, creating adequate opportunities and institutions for rural women's participation are some of the main concerns to be tackled when we consider the issue of empowering rural women.

People's participation in development is an educational process aimed at creating a sense of awareness, involvement, a belongingness and possession or ownership. The participatory approach is assumed to develop self-confidence, competence and managerial capacity. It enables women to discover their innate potential, increase their aspiration level and mobilize their resources for productive purposes.[2]

Mere identification of women as a target group and doing out benefits for them does not solve the problems of rural women. To ensure that rural women's interests are articulated in planning and their needs are met, there is a need for encouraging grassroots organisation and work through them to emancipate women in all angles, social, political and economic. To the extent that discrimination, exploitation and oppression are reduced over a period of time, one can interpret this as reduction in inequalities (Mukherji, 1984).[3] From a state of powerlessness that manifests itself in a feeling of 'I cannot' empowerment contains an element of collective self-confidence that results in a feeling of 'we can'. With reference to awareness, empowerment has deeper meanings, not just an understanding of situation but an ability to act (IDS, Jaipur, 1991).[4]

In most South Asian countries, the status of women is low and their socio-economic conditions are much more depressed than that of men. In India, while the constitutional and legal status of women is equal to that of men in all respects, the reality is that they suffer in all spheres of social and economic life. Poverty, in fact is one of the aspects of their deprived condition. Low earning, lower wages, low level of skills, limited access to the factors of production, low literacy, malnutrition, poor standard of health, greater exposure to domestic violence and vulnerability to sexual crimes are some of the other dimensions of their low status.

Women need to be viewed not as beneficiaries but as active participants in the process of development and change. Her capacity to work, her knowledge and her skills are often the only resources to call upon for survival in poor households. Thus women become the critical actors in the process of moving their families out of poverty. It is a general fact that money earned by poor women is more likely to be spent on basic needs of life, children and family than earning generated by men. This realisation would bring women as the focus of development efforts.[5]

Strategies for empowering women must focus beyond economic restructuring, to include restructuring of social relations which constrain and restrain women. Rural SC/ST women who form a subset of the rural poor population, lack not only money incomes and skills but also more vitally self-assurance and motivation. Information and awareness ensure that exploitation can be fought and reduced, and in that sense, awareness is empowerment.[6] The participatory approach to development of the poor is increasingly emphasized in the literature (Amartya Sen, 1995)[7] feels that "What is important is not so much what people receive, as how much involvement they have, and what part they play in the process of growth itself." Francine Fournier (1997) aptly points out that the poor will have to learn to break their silence, to give up their dependence on the middlemen, and to assert that they belong to the centre and not to margins. In other words, a true civil society will come only when the large constituency of the poor is empowered.[8]

APPROACHES TO DEVELOPMENT OF THE POOR

There are three sets of approaches to the development of the poor, the welfarist approach, the service delivery approach and the empowerment approach.

The welfarist approach proceeds on the assumption that the poor need compassion and care as are resourceless, resources either in cash or kind need to be transferred to them (A.C. Pigou, 1960).[9] The welfarist approach has a crucial role in times of general distress, natural calamities, civil strife, communal disturbance, epidemics and social upheavals. The approach by definition, does not take cognizance of the structural causes of poverty and under development nor does it deal with the processes and policies responsible for their perpetuation (IFAD, 1996).[10]

The service delivery approach moves a step ahead. In this approach, it is accepted that if human capabilities are built, the causes of poverty could be circumvented. Once these capabilities are built, the underlying assumption is that the process of development can start or where such a process is on, it is accelerated. It is a significant leap from the welfarist approach.

The empowerment approach is built upon the service delivery approach. It intends to cause development by empowering the people. The empowerment approach believes that structures, processes and policies that cause and perpetuate poverty and hinder development are best challenged by empowering the people themselves (SAARC, 1992, Haq Mahbubul, 1997, Holcombe, 1995).[11] Empowerment approach builds capacity, capability and willingness to take decisions by organising the community, by raising their consciousness, and by providing services. An enabling environment is created by challenging those elements in the system that are exploitative and by seeking changes in policies which are anti development.[12] (Amitava Mukherjee, 1999).

REPLICATION OF THE GRAMEENA BANK MODEL

Mohammad Yunus, the founder of the Grameena Bank of Bangladesh is the pioneer of the empowerment approach in the context of the poor rural women of Bangladesh (Holcombe, 1995).[13] The successful experience of the Grameena Bank in relation to poverty stricken women is replicated in most countries of Asia especially in Indonesia and Thailand. Even in India the RRB's are based on the Grameena Bank model (Karmakar, 1999).[14] The essence of

Grameena Bank Project is social development, credit is used as a catalyst in the process. All members of the Grameena Bank have agreed upon certain obligations called the 16 decisions which embraces areas such as:

1. The four principles of Grameena Bank—discipline, unity, courage and hard work. We shall follow and advance in all walks of our lives;
2. We shall bring prosperity to our families;
3. We shall repair our houses and work towards constructing new houses as soon as possible;
4. We shall grow vegetables all the year round. We shall eat plenty of them and sell the surplus;
5. During the planting season, we shall plant as many seedlings as possible;
6. We shall plan to keep our families small. We shall minimize our expenditure. We shall look after our health;
7. We shall educate our children and ensure that they can earn enough to pay for their education;
8. We shall keep our children and the environment clean;
9. We shall build and use pit latrines;
10. We shall drink tubewell water. If it is not available, we shall boil water or use alum;
11. We shall not take any dowry in our son's weddings neither shall we give any dowry in our daughter's weddings. We shall keep the center free from the curse of dowry. We shall not practice child marriage;
12. We shall not inflict any injustice on anyone, neither shall we allow anyone to do so;
13. For higher income, we shall collectively undertake bigger investments;
14. We shall always be ready to help each other. If anyone is in difficulty, we shall help;

15. If we come to know of any breach of discipline in any center, we shall go these and restore discipline;

16. We shall introduce physical exercise in all our centers. We shall take part in all social activities collectively.

All these 16 decisions are covered by the variety of activities and functions undertaken by the SHGs. Most of them are guided by consideration of self interest and they contribute to public interest at large. Some of these activities are already covered in earlier chapters. The rest of them which have a social bearing are covered in the present chapter mostly based on our perceptions of the functioning of sample groups and the qualitative as well as quantitative data from the field survey.

ROLE OF SHGs IN WOMEN DEVELOPMENT ISSUES

Women's development is a part of a Society's overall effort at improving its human resource potential. However, no human resource development is possible without a corresponding improvement in the status of half of its population. In India women work as wives, mothers, agricultural labourers, wage earners and teachers of skills. At the same time, the benefits of economic and social development seem to have by passed them.[15]

In India, several attempts have been made for alleviation of rural poverty. A systematic effort towards rural development started after India attained her Independence. During the initial period of development the Government neglected the participation of people in the policy formulation as well as in the implementation of different developmental programmes. It is an established fact that the success of any development programme largely depends on the active participation of the people alone.

Indian experience with Self Help Groups with a focus on women is emerging as a promising financial innovation with great potential to reach the poor and marginal workers in a cost-effective way to the lender and with many spin-offs to the needy and vulnerable, who are outside the economic arena.[16]

EMPOWERMENT OF WOMEN IN DEVELOPMENTAL ASPECTS

Development programme should be based on felt needs of the people in order to achieve greater people's participation and sustainability. The programmes should make people aware about the benefits they will receive in the form of irradiating rural poverty and illiteracy. Incentives in the form of certificates, trophies, cash prizes should be given to those participating in order to motivate people to take part in rural development programmes.

Development programmes exclusively for women should be conducted so as to increase the level of confidence and achieve orientation as well as improve management development skill to enable them to successfully run their business.

Women and development should be linked together. In the context of development women's empowerment is a key goal but it is achieved only to the extent they strive for it. It has been a truism to state that in the early decades of

Table 6.1 Participation in Women Development Programmes

Sl. No.	*Programmes*	*Kurnool Division-I*	*Nandyal Division-II*	*Adomi Division-III*
1.	Social Awareness	22(44)	20(40)	23(46)
2.	Health Programme (including immunisation programme)	9(18)	8(16)	8(16)
3.	Adult Literacy Programme	6(12)	8(16)	6(12)
4.	Promotion of Savings	9(18)	10(20)	12(24)
5.	Family planning programme	4(8)	4(8)	1(2)

Note: Figures in parentheses indicate percentages to total.

Source: Field Data.

Graph 6.1 Participation in Women Development Programmes

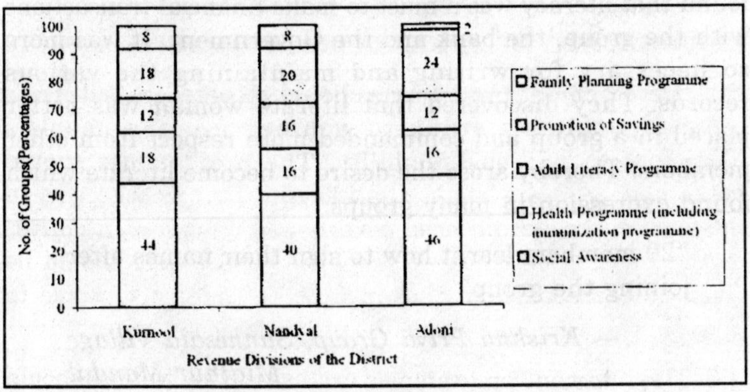

planning in Independent India as in almost all other countries, women were only looked at as a component of social welfare programmes and not of development. We have by now gone through the phase of looking at women segment from a welfare approach to equity approach for finally from a management approach.[17]

Empowerment of rural women would in real sense hasten the pace of economic development. Empowering women with economically productive work will enhance their contribution to rural development.

44, 40 and 46 per cent of SHGs are directly concerned with the promotion of social awareness in the three divisions of the district. Social awareness is an elastic term and embraces activities and concerns pertaining to the whole gamut of social evils and traditions that work against perpetuation of social and gender inequality such as casteism, untouchability, child marriages, beliefs in efficacy of 'mantram' as a cure for chronic disease and several other allied issues of community living. In the same way 18, 16 and 16 per cent of SHGs are participating in the Health and immunisation programmes to promote the health status of the community. 12, 16 and 12 per cent of SHGs are participating in Adult literacy programme. Women felt the need for literacy much more after joining the groups. The illiterate women hither confined to four walls of household found that literacy was a must to make financial transactions with the group, the bank and the Government. It was more so necessary for writing and maintaining the various records. They discovered that literate woman was better placed in a group and commanded more respect from other members. Thereby arose the desire to become literate which found expression in many groups:

> "20 members learnt how to sign their names after joining the group"
>
> — *Krishna Priya Group, Sunkesala Village Midthur Mandal*

> "All 15 members are now literate whereas earlier only 2 members were literate"
>
> — *Razia Sultana Group, Gudur Village*

18, 16 and 16 per cent of SHGs are participating in the Health Programme to increase the health status of their communities. They are discussing regularly in their group meetings to keep their surroundings clean and creating more awareness about hygienic conditions and prevention of various diseases.

Another area in which there was significant achievement was in the area of immunisation of children (0-5 years) and enrollment of children in Anganwadi centers. Various rounds of pulse polio immunisation programme conducted in the district. The group members conducted rallies in the villages, conducted house to house enumeration of 0-5 year children and brought the children for administering polio drops on the designated PPI days. The results were spectacular. This achievement was only with full and active participation of the women themselves and not under any target oriented approach of the Government.

Similarly as shown in the Table 6.1, 18, 20 and 24 per cent of the groups are actively participating in the promotion of savings. As an entry point and binding force for the groups, thrift was the most important parameter for group formation and sustenance. It promoted habit of savings amongst the members. All the members save uniformly at the rate of Rupee one per day and the amount saved by the groups increased month by month. With 1.3 lakh women joining the movement, it grew by Rs. 1.3 lakhs per day amounting to Rs. 39 lakhs per month.

Group savings led to a reinforcement of mutual trust that served the twin purpose of credit without conventional collateral and an inbuilt mechanism to ensure timely repayment through peer monitoring. Reactions from some of the group leaders bear testimony to this:

> "Before joining the groups, we had to approach the landlord who made us to wander around him and now, loan is easily available. Rate of interest was 48-60 per cent earlier and now it is available for 20-24 per cent"
>
> — *Bhagyalakshmi Group, Nakkavagulapalli Village Dhone, Mandal*

> "Earlier some valuable ornaments and articles must be kept as surety and now we just have to sign on the promissory notes for getting loans".
>
> — *Teja Group, Gudur Mandal.*

> "Timely loan was not available earlier and now we get loans whenever we require."
>
> — *Mother Teresa Group, Nandikotkur*

And the groups gave loans to members for various purposes right from consumption to income generating activities.

8 per cent, 8 and 2 per cent of SHGs are actively participating in the family planning programme. The small family norm was emphasized in group meetings and mandal conventions by Government officials and NGO's. Women having 2 or more children were identified in the group

meetings and mandal conventions and were motivated to undergo family operations.

REMOVAL OF UNTOUCHABILITY

Untouchability is one of the social evils of Hindu society. Purity and pollution are the two features of Hindu tradition and they are being followed despite the impact of modernisation. The rural society is more rigid and hierarchical based not only on caste but also on economic status, mostly on the basis of land holding and cropping pattern. Assetlessness both in physical and in human terms has perpetuated the tradition of untouchability despite the constitutional guarantee of equality of all castes and communities in India. Due to inadequate social protest and moments in the rural society untouchability based on caste in its various dimensions is evidenced in the reports of the commissioner of scheduled castes and tribes of the Government of India (1998-99)[18]. We present in Table 6.2 the activities undertaken by the SHGs regarding the removal of untouchability in our study area.

Table 6.2 Efforts Towards Removal of Untouchability

Sl. No.	*Programmes*	*Kurnool Division-I*	*Nandyal Division-II*	*Adomi Division-III*
1.	Common cup at tea shop	30(60)	19(38)	18(36)
2.	Drinking water supply	14(28)	21(42)	20(40)
3.	Social dining	4(8)	7(14)	8(16)
4.	Temple entry	2(4)	3(6)	4(8)

Note: Figures in parentheses indicate percentages total

Source: Field Data

Untouchability and social discrimination towards the SC's and ST's of rural society is glaring and manifested in the system of two glasses service at the tea shop of the village. But with the advent of the women SHGs, some protest meetings are conducted in order to remove this system.

60, 38 and 36 per cent of SHGs are in the forefront of this protest and struggle in the three divisions of the district. The awareness and protest in this regard is positively correlated with the level of development of our sample districts.

Similarly access to drinking water especially during summer season is limited to the depressed groups. Women folk are compelled to walk long distances stretching over several kilometers to fetch a pot of water from the agricultural wells often situated away from the village. Women groups have fought for greater access in terms of provision of bore wells and taps near their habitations and having a common dependable source of water supply for all caste groups in the habitation panchayat. 28, 42 and 40 per cent of the sample SHGs were involved in this struggle for improving access to drinking water supply in our study area. Temple entry movement was a part of the freedom struggle but has been confined to well known temples in urban locations. But at the village level, separate temples are often erected and maintained by the inhabitants of the main village who often belong to upper castes and the so called harijans have their own separate temples or have to adjust without any temple. But the SHG groups are seeking entry into the main temple of the village, though this aspect of activity is rather negligible as seen from the statistics of the table. Social dining especially at the time of marriage and other functions promotes social harmony and inter course. But even here, it is generally caste exclusive at the village level. Since most of the SHGs are homogeneous both socially and economically, social dining is often restricted to those who are members of the SHGs. Therefore, the role of the SHGs in fighting against untouchability is at the initial stage and it is long drawn out battle.

ROLE OF WOMEN IN DECISION-MAKING

Contemporary rural India is still predominantly a society based on the norms of patriarchy and an ideology of female subordination. It is this subordination of women, which has been identified as the dominant obstacle in women's development.[19]

"Human development encompasses elements that constitute the critical issues of gender and development. There are four major elements in the concept of human development, productivity, equity, sustainability and empowerment. Through enhanced capabilities, the creativity and productivity of people must be increased so that they become effective agents of economic growth. Economic growth must be combined with equitable distribution of its benefits. Equitable opportunities must be available both to present and future generations resulting in sustainability. And all people, women and men must be empowered to participate in the design and implementation of key decisions that shape their lives."

When gender determines the access to resources and power to individuals, empowerment begins when the individual recognizes and opposes the forces that deny such access. Power accrues to those who gain control over the distribution of resources. This control in turn confers the power of decision-making. In India women in general, poor rural women in particular are relatively powerless with no control over resources and little decision making power. Often the decisions are imposed on them. The prevailing patriarchal ideology, which demands values of submission sacrifice and silent suffering often, undermines their capability and deprives them of their share of resources. The process of challenging existing relations and gaining greater control over the forces of power may be termed as empowerment.[20]

After joining the groups, the literacy and awareness of women increased and so they are now playing an important role in decision making of their families. Decision of the mother with regard to the education and health of the child is more vital than that of the father in our empirical study. We have represented the role of women in decision making of sample SHGs in the Table 6.3.

Table 6.3 Decision Making in Their Household

Sl. No.	*Response*	*Kurnool Division-I*	*Nandyal Division-II*	*Adomi Division-III*
1.	Education of children			
	(a) Improved	36(72)	33(66)	30(60)
	(b) Not improved	14(28)	17(34)	20(40)
2.	Healthcare of family members			
	(a) Improved	42(84)	40(80)	38(76)
	(b) Not improved	8(16)	10(20)	12(24)
3	Other matters			
	(a) Improved	43(86)	40(80)	37(74)
	(b) Not improved	7(14)	10(20)	13(26)

Note: Figures in parentheses indicate percentages to total.

Source: Field Data.

Graph 6.2 Decision Making in Their Household

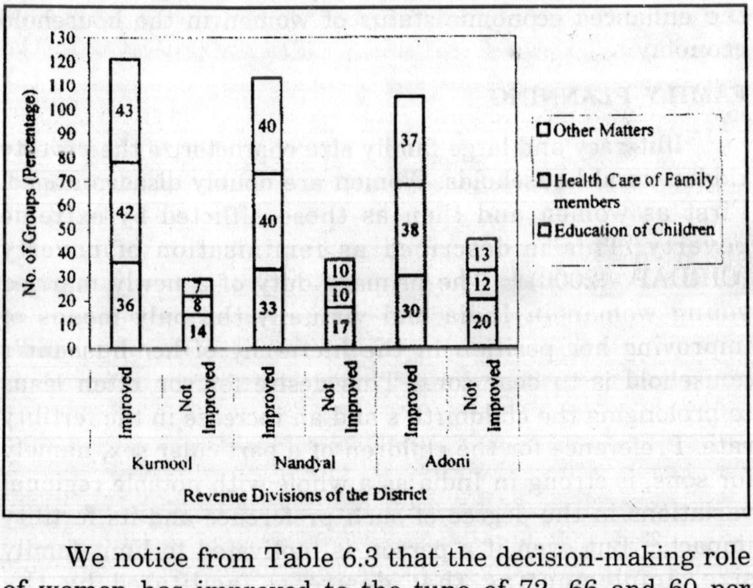

We notice from Table 6.3 that the decision-making role of women has improved to the tune of 72, 66 and 60 per cent in respect of the education of children in the three divisions of the district. Enrollment and retention of children at the primary school constitute the most formidable problems of universalisation of primary education especially in rural sector (IX Plan 1997-2002).[21] Therefore this finding relating to the improved role of women members which is also positively related to the economic status of the study divisions, holds a ray of hope for universal enrollment of children and thereby improving the literacy rate. Just as in the case of children's education, in the domain of health care of the family members also, the decision making role of women of our samples has improved in respect of 84, 80 and 76 per cent of SHGs in the three divisions of the respect of 84, 80 and 76 per cent of SHGs in the three divisions of the district which is again positively related to the level of development of the sample mandals. Similarly, the decision-making role of women of our samples has improved in respect of 86, 80 and 74 per cent of SHGs with regard to other matters. Thus it is clear from the above analysis that the decision making power of women improved due to the enhanced economic status of women in the household economy.

FAMILY PLANNING

Illiteracy and large family size characterize the poverty ridden rural households. Women are doubly disadvantaged. First as women and then as those afflicted by extreme poverty. This is described as feminisation of poverty (CIRDAP - 2000).[22] The primary duty of a newly married young woman in India and virtually the only means of improving her position in the hierarchy of her husband's household is to bear sons. This desire for son often leads to prolonging the childbirth's and an increase in the fertility rate. Preference for the children of a particular sex, namely for sons, is strong in India as a whole with notable regional variations in the degree of such preference and its fertility impact.[23] But even if a person is motivated to limit family size, implementing that desire is facilitated by the accessibility of effective means of fertility control. Accessibility includes knowledge of methods what is available, where to get them, how to use them—making it possible for them to use a method. In rural areas often such knowledge is missing, because of lack of exposure of rural women to mass media.

The small family norm was emphasized in group meetings and mandal conventions by Government officials and NGO's. Women having two or more children were identified and were motivated to undergo family planning operations.

A practice was established by which women having 2 or more children were asked to raise their hands in the meetings and it was quite heartening to note that women having more children were hesitant to identify themselves in the meetings, thereby implying that there was some thing wrong in having more children. This was in marked contrast to earlier days when it was difficult to convince women about the small family norm. Motivation of women by other women in the group yielded better results.

> "5 women have undergone family planning operation after joining the group."
>
> — *Jhansi Group, Vengalampally Village, Peapully Mandal*

> "8 women have undergone family planning operation after joining the group."
>
> — *Lakshmi Group, Tatipadu Village, Jupadu Bunglow Mandal*

We have restricted our scope to the family planning operation encouraged by the SHGs and the relevant data shown in Table 6.4.

It may be noted from the Table 6.4 that 4 per cent of SHGs in Nandyal Division undergone family planning operations is not so popular in our study area. The reason is still the rural society was dominated by traditions and customs. 5, 10 and 14 per cent of SHGs undergone family planning operations for two children. 36, 46 and 52 per cent

Table 6.4 Mobilisation Towards Family Planning

Sl. No.	*Response*	*Kurnool Division-I*	*Nandyal Division-II*	*Adoni Division-III*
1	Family Planning Operations undertaken:			
	(a) 1 child	-	2(4)	-
	(b) 2 children	5(10)	10(20)	14(28)
	(c) 3 children	18(36)	23(46)	26(52)
	(d) 4 children	27(54)	15(30)	10(20)

Note: Figures in parentheses indicate percentages to total.
Source: Field Data.

Graph 6.3 Mobilisation Towards Family Planning

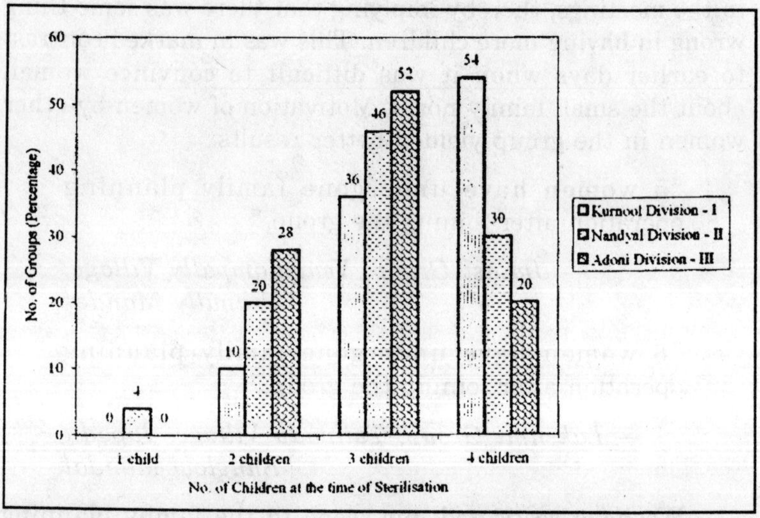

of SHGs undergone family planning operations for 3 children. Similarly 54, 30 and 20 per cent of SHGs undergone family planning operations for 4 children. As the small family norm was emphasized by SHGs recently, the number of families undergone family planning operations for 3 and 2 children is increasing. However this process is very slow and lack efficiency. This leads to slow decline in the birth rate. More efforts are being carried on by the group leaders in our study area to make effective control of birth rates.

HEALTH AND HYGIENE

Discussion on health and various health problems being faced by the women formed a major topic of discussion in group meetings and mandal conventions. Many of the Podupulakshmi groups have become depot holders for supply of ORS packet and essential medicines to the other women in the village. And closely related to the health aspect was availability of clean drinking water was brought to the notice of various officials in the group meetings and mandal conventions. Women took various steps to improve the sanitation and hygiene in the villages.

> "We have dug soakpits in front of our houses. We are keeping our houses and streets clean."
>
> — *Teja Group, Pesaravai Village, Gadivemula Mandal*

> "Our group has passed a resolution that all the members must plant and grow at least one tree for better health of our children."
>
> — *Sri Lakshmi Venkata Ramana Group, Peapully*

> "We have cleaned the village drains streets."
>
> — *Divya Group, Nandikotkur*

The need for individual sanitary latrines was felt by women and it was very common to find women demanding the same in every meeting. The State Government came forward with a scheme to construct individual sanitary latrines on a large scale. And the Podupulakshmi women utilised the scheme well.

ADULT LITERACY PROGRAMME

Women felt the need for literacy much more after joining the groups. They discovered that literate woman was better placed in the group and also in the society. Many groups started their own Adult Literacy Centres by appointing a person to teach them. While many women could not become literate themselves because of age factor and other problems, they however realized the importance of education and started sending their children to school. However they learnt how to sign and participated in the discussion of various social evils faced by them in their communities. Efforts will also be made to find some remedial measures.

Table 6.5 Mobilisation Towards Adult Literacy

Response		*Kurnool Division-I*	*Nandyal Division-II*	*Adoni Division-III*
Benefited from Adult Literacy Programme				
(a)	1-5 persons	15(30)	18(36)	12(24)
(b)	6-10 persons	25(50)	18(36)	28(56)
(c)	l 1-15 persons	6(12)	8(16)	8(16)
(d)	16 and above	4(8)	6(12)	2(4)

Note: Figures in parentheses indicate percentages to total.

Source: Field Data.

Graph 6.4 Mobilisation Towards Adult Literacy

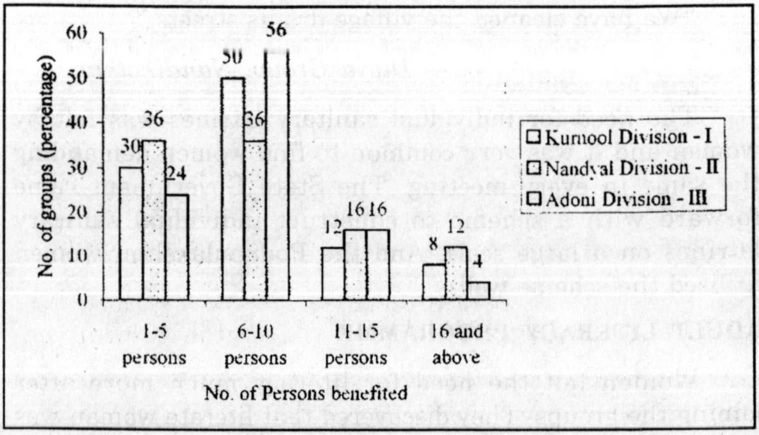

As seen in the above Table 6.5, 1-5 persons benefited from adult literacy programme in respect of 30, 36 and 24 per cent of SHGs. 6-10 persons benefited from adult literacy programme in respect of 50, 36 and 56 per cent of SHGs. Similarly, 11-15 persons benefited in respect of 12, 16 and 16 per cent of SHG groups. 16 and above number of persons benefited in respect of 8, 12 and 4 per cent of SHGs. The coverage of 6-10 persons under the adult literacy programme is more prominent in all three divisions of the district.

Thus it is clear from the above analysis that the response for adult literacy programme from the side of SHGs in our study area is very encouraging and they are trying their level best to promote their literacy levels and increased contribution to the development of their rural communities.

CHILD EDUCATION

After joining in the SHGs, many women realized the importance of education and thereby encouraged child education by sending their children to primary schools. As a result the enrollment in the schools started picking up:

> "In S.Gundala village of Dhone mandal, most of the children used to go for work earlier, but after formation of the groups, all the children who are in the school going age are being sent to school."
>
> "13 more children were admitted in the school after formation of the group."
>
> — *Shanti Group, Thanda Village, Pathikonda Mandal*
>
> "15 more children are being sent to school."
>
> — *Pragati Group, Nannur Village, Orvakal Mandal*

The primary school teacher and Anganwadi teacher who used to attend group meetings encouraged women to send their children to school. This subject used to be discussed in group meetings and mandal conventions. The Mandal Education Officer and the Mandal Development Officer spoke about the need for primary education in these meetings. The message of universalisation of primary education was spread to each and every group. Village Education Committees were constituted in each and every village. A massive publicity campaign was undertaken to spread the message to each and every village.

The "Mid-Day Meal" was a step in the direction of Universalisation of Primary Education. The district was also implementing "National Child Labour Project" aimed at rehabilitating 10,000 children working in hazardous occupation special schools were set up as a part of the project. The response is very encouraging to these child labour schools. The number of child labour has been decreased considerable in the rural areas after the child labour project started.

More and more children in the age group of 0-5 years started going to Anganwadi centers:

> "5 children started going to the Anganwadi centre after formation of the group."
>
> — *Lakshamma Group, Tadakanapalli Village, Kallur Mandal.*
>
> "No child was going to Anganwadi centre."
>
> — *Teja Group, Sunkesula Village, Midthur Mandal*

The need for Anganwadi centers was felt by women in those habitations where there were no such centers. In some of these habitations, women started their own Anganwadi centers and called them "Ammavadi" (creche center). They contributed one rupee per day per child, took a building on rent and appointed a teacher to take care of their children. They would leave their children in such centers before going for work and pick them up after returning from work. And the women proudly say that their centers are better than government run centers because the teacher owes the appointment to them and not to the government and hence takes better care of their children.

It is evident from the table 6.6 that the average attendance of boys in the three divisions is 71.6 per cent. That means 71.6 per cent of children (6-10 years) of the members of SHGs are going to schools. 60.6 per cent of children (6-10 years girls) of the members of SHG are going to schools. It is clear from the above analysis that the average attendance of boys is more than girls in the age group of 6-10 years.

Table 6.6 Mobilisation Towards Primary Education

Sl. No.	*Children's Age (in years)*	*Attendance at schools %*					
		Kurnool Division-I		*Nandyal Division-II*		*Adoni Division-III*	
		Boys	*Girls*	*Boys*	*Girls*	*Boys*	*Girls*
1.	6-10	70	61	73	62	72	59
2.	11-14	73	60	71	61	70	58

Source. Field Data.

71 per cent of children (11-14 years boys) of the members of SHGs are going to schools. 60 per cent of children (girls) of the members of SHGs are going to schools. As in the first age group in this age group also the average attendance of boys to schools is more than girls. So more emphasis should be laid down on girls education.

Table 6.7 Attendance at Anganwadis

Children's Age (0-5 ears)	*Kurnool Division-I*	*Nandyal Division-II*	*Adoni Division-III*
Attending	55	53	56
Not attending	45	47	44

Source: Field Data.

It is clear from the above table 6.7 that 55 per cent of children of the members of SHGs are going to Anganwadi centers. The percentage of children going to Anganwadi centers is almost the same for both boys and girls.

EARLY GIRL CHILD MARRIAGE

Early Girl Child Marriage is a major social evil in the entire Rayalaseema region of Andhra Pradesh. Despite the legislation and years of sustained efforts by the Government and the NGOs, the average age of girl child marriage in these parts is around 12-14 years. This is primarily because of the age-old custom of treating girl child as a burden on family and subsequently sending her away from the family as early as possible. Most of the girl children were not being sent to school and even if they were sent to schools, they dropped out of the schools by the time they attained puberty. Thus, an adolescent girl sitting idle at home was a burden to the family and hence they were married off early. There seemed to be no solution to this problem as changing the mind-set of the people was not an easy task.

But, a ray of hope kindled with the formation of the Podupulakshmi groups. Organized and enlightened women realized the wrongs they are doing by marrying their daughters at a young age. The women were explained about the concept of safe motherhood and the risks associated with early pregnancy in the group meetings and the mandal conventions.

And the women could relate their horrid experiences as most of them were also married at a young age. They were told not to repeat the mistakes which had been committed earlier with them. Slowly, a change began to appear. In many groups, the women decided to marry their daughters only after they attained the age of 18 years. The decision of these groups was spread to other groups through the mandal conventions and many groups started taking the same decision. In many of the groups adolescent girls were identified and organized into groups so that they can take up some activity. It was realized that one of the major reasons for early marriage was that most of these adolescent girls were sitting idle at home, hence, there was more pressures to marry them off especially from the old generation people. Therefore many of the groups decided to organize some sort of activity like tailoring etc., to keep them busy. And women discovered that they could face the pressure in the house because of the combined strength of the group.

The life of Nagamani, a 12-year old girl belonging to Scheduled Caste in Kalva village of Orvakal mandal bears testimony to this new found power of women groups.

Nagamani is the third daughter of a poor Scheduled Caste family having four daughters. She was a victim to all prevailing girl child discrimination since childhood. At the tender age of 9, she was married to a boy 15 years older to her against her wishes. The entire expenditure of the marriage was borne by Nagamani's in laws. The boy was suffering from skin disease and it was his second marriage. After marriage, she was sent to her in-law's house in another village. Unable to bear the trauma of early marriage and sexual harassment of the husband, she ran away from the inlaw's house and came back to her parents. Her parents promised her in-law's that she would be sent back after she attains puberty, a condition which they accepted.

Nagamani stayed with her parents in Kalva for three years. She gradually forgot that nightmare. She made it a habit to attend each and every SHG meeting in the village. She was mainly inspired by two aspects namely: (a) Girl child education and (b) marriage age. Her intention to study and to stand on her own feet grew day-by-day. But as soon as she attained the age of twelve, she was again set back to her husband's house forcefully by her parents. Nagamani protested, refused and cried but all in vain. In the darkness of the night, she ran away from her husband's house. She met the women SHG members and pleaded them to rescue her. Podupulakshmi women with the help of all the groups in the village approached the local Tehsildar and police for help. They were threatened with dire consequences by Nagamani's in-laws but they were firm in their plan. After facing several problems, they could finally rescue Nagamani from the clutches of her husband and in-laws by repaying them the marriage expenses. The marriage was broken and Nagamani returned to her village.

Through this incident, the women gained confidence that they can solve any social problem unitedly. With this inspiration, 500 adolescent girls in the village were organized into "Balika Sanghams". These girls are being educated in the night schools. They are learning tailoring, embroidery, etc., and have taken an oath that "we will not get married until we become 18 years old." And Nagamani is the leader of this revolution in the village today.

Thus, the women are trying to eradicate an age-old social evil and all this was again possible because of their collective strength and enhanced awareness as a result of Podupulakshmi.

Table 6.8 Early Girl Child Marriage

Sl. No.	*Girls age at the time of marriage*	*Kurnool Division-I*	*Nandyal Division-II*	*Adoni Division-III*
1.	12-14	20(40)	19(38)	15(30)
2.	15-16	18(36)	15(30)	20(40)
3.	17-18	8(16)	10(20)	11(22)
4.	Above 18	4(8)	6(12)	4(8)

Note: Figures in parentheses indicate percentages to total.
Source: Field Data.

As seen in the table 6.8, 40, 38 and 30 per cent of SHGs are performing the marriage of their girl child in the age group of 12- 14 years. Again this percentage is more in the other age groups also (15-16 and 17-18 years). However the percentage of groups in the age group above 18 are very less when compared to other groups. Such

Graph 6.5 Early Girl Child Marriage

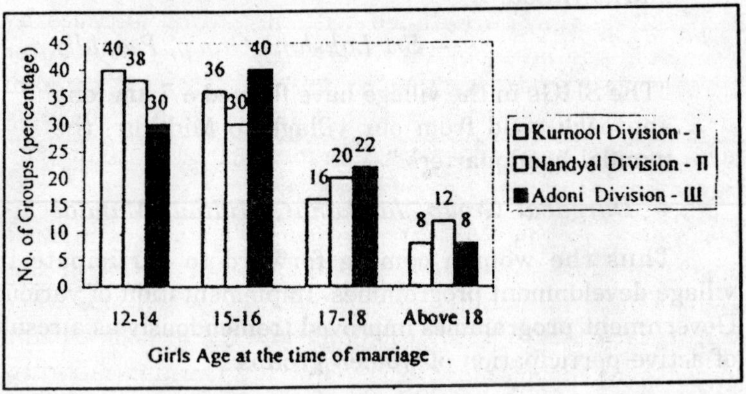

analysis indicates that rural community is favouring more the early marriages because of various social and institutional factors. However, at present the SHGs are making efforts to organize and enlighten women to realize the fault or mistake they are doing by marrying their daughters at a young age.

JANMABHOOMI PROGRAMME

To enable people to participate in the developmental programmes meant for them, the previous Government (TDP) launched another programme named "Janmabhoomi" in January 1997. It was a people's oriented developmental process. People were encouraged to take up community works like construction of roads, school buildings, drains and repairs to irrigation channels etc., themselves by contributing 30 per cent of the total cost by way of cash contribution or 'Shramadanam' (labour contribution). The idea was to involve people in community works and do away with the system of contractors and middlemen.

The women groups came forward in large numbers in many villages to take up community works by contributing their labour.

> "We have participated in all the rounds of Janmabhoomi. We whitewashed school building

and PHC building, and undertaken cleaning the Harijanwada."

— *Sri Lakshmi Group, Peapully*

"The SHGs in the village have formed a 7 km long approach road from our village to Midthur, the mandal headquarters."

— *Durgabai Group, Jalakanur, Midthur Mandal*

Thus the women coming forward to participate in village development programmes. Implementation of various Government programmes improved tremendously as a result of active participation of women groups.

The Government of Andhra Pradesh launched another novel programme of "Prajala Vaddaku Palana" (Government at the doorsteps of people) in November 1995. Under this, a team of Government officials visited all the habitations in a mandal once in three months. Gram sabhas were conducted in all the habitations and people were asked to represent their grievances to the officials. Women came out in large numbers to represent their individual as well as community needs to the officials. It was a common sight to see the women sitting in front rows in large numbers during the gram sabhas. Many of women's problems got solved in the process.

NATIONAL SOCIAL ASSISTANCE PROGRAMME

This programme introduced by the Government of India in August 1995. It was one of the programmes which saw very active involvement of the groups. The women groups took upon themselves the task to publicize the programme as it was a new scheme. The groups identified the old and destitute women in the villages eligible for old age pension, widows who were eligible for Family Benefit Scheme and the pregnant women eligible for maternity assistance scheme. The groups sponsored their applications to the concerned officials in the mandal level conventions. Some of the groups went a step ahead. Wherever, there was a delay on the part of the administration in sanctioning the cases, the groups sanctioned the amount to the eligible women immediately and later on the money was recouped to the group fund, once the cases were sanctioned by the Government. Some of the groups even donated a part of their savings to the "Chief Minister's Relief Fund" for victims of cyclones and earthquakes.

Similarly, functioning of many village level government institutions like primary schools, anganwadi centers, fair price shops, medical subcentres and veterinary dispensaries improved because of the increased participation of women as they were the one who were utilizing the services of these institutions.

Thus, the SHGs have become the nodal point for dissemination of information on health education, small family norm etc. A convergence of all basic services is taking place at the group level.[24]

PERCEPTIONS OF MEMBERS ON WOMEN DEVELOPMENT ACTIVITIES

Self assessment and self criticism are the best means of improvement in individual as well as group activities and performance. We were interested in understanding whether the members of SHGs were satisfied with their participation in various developmental as well as awareness building activities undertaken by them. We outline their responses in Table 6.9.

Table 6.9 Groups Satisfied with Participation in Women Development Programmes

Sl. No.	*Response*	*Kurnool Division-I*	*Nandyal Division-II*	*Adoni Division-III*
1	Satisfactory	49(98)	48(86)	46(92)
2.	Not satisfactory	1(2)	2(4)	4(8)

Note: Figures in parentheses indicate percentages to total.

Source: Field Data.

An overwhelming majority 98, 96 and 92 per cent are satisfied with their performance in different activities related to women development in the three divisions of the district. This feeling forms a solid foundation for building up their self-confidence and for venturing into several other challenging tasks that are ahead of them.

When the poor organize themselves and adopt various programme strategies, they are actual participants of and a subject in the whole process. While evolving into SHGs, they gradually learn to take decisions for themselves and also develop the capacity to exercise certain amount of control over the social, economic and political conditions that determine their immediate lives.

CONFLICT RESOLUTION

Disputes on a multiplicity of issues tend to rise in any human group. In this context, we have considered not merely disputes pertaining to group activities but also those that belong to the household domain but have a social bearing like alcoholism, dowry issues. Disputes among the members about non-payment of monthly savings contribution, members to be selected for loaning, non-repayment of loan instalment, and such other issues are a common feature. Lack of perception about the regulations, procedures and protocol of the programme are the causes of many of these disputes. For most groups which do not have a well defined arrangement for dealing with disputes, each situation presents itself as a crisis to be debated and resolved afresh. It is observed that the groups in a vast majority of the cases prefer to discuss the issue within the group forum itself and threw it out. It is a positive outcome of the group processes.

> "This programme creates good relationship among members and it makes them rescue each other."
>
> — *Rajeswari Group, Panyam*

> "The loans taken from the group are being repaid properly just because of social pressure. We feel

that the money is our own and it sets in the group only"

— *Bhagyalakshmi Group, Dhone Mandal*

We incorporate the responses regarding conflict resolution by the groups themselves in Table 6.10. The responses to the specific questions and during extended interviews provide eloquent pointers to the changes in women's perceptions of themselves as individuals and as members of the family and community.

Table 6.10 Means of Conflict Resolutions

Sl. No.	*Disputes over*		*Kurnool Division-I*	*Nandyal Division-II*	*Adoni Division-III*
1.	Group activities				
	(a)	Yes	48(96)	43(86)	38(76)
	(b)	No	2(4)	7(14)	12(24)
2.	Child development and marriages				
	(a)	Yes	45(90)	42(84)	46(92)
	(b)	No	5(5)	8(16)	4(8)
3.	Domestic violence and alcoholism etc.				
	(a)	Yes	45(90)	49(98)	47(94)
	(b)	No	5(10)	1(2)	3(6)

Note: Figures in parentheses indicate percentages to total.

Source: Field Data.

It is evident that 96, 86 and 76 per cent of the groups in the three divisions resolve conflicts that arise over group activities. However, this percentage is less in case of Adoni division. These figures imply that in the relatively developed areas conflict resolution regarding group activities is mostly done by the groups themselves. In case of underdeveloped area reliance is placed on the intervention of an external agency which is sponsored and facilitated group formation. However, in matters of child development and child marriages an overwhelming proportion of SHGs, 90, 84 and 92 per cent, take decisions by themselves. The same is the case with regard to matters of domestic violence, alcoholism of men where 90, 98 and 94 per cent of SHGs resolve the complicated issues by themselves as observed in our study area respectively.

REACTION OF HUSBANDS AND OTHER MALE MEMBERS

In patriarchal societies, the domination of men over women takes several forms and is manifested in thousand ways. Husbands have an inbuilt superiority complex and cannot accept the equality of their wives. Violence against women is perpetuated mostly by men. Violence against women has its roots in the subordination of women at the social level and their vulnerability has not decreased but increased in developing economies as a consequence of social disruptions, and a general degeneration of values. Every seventh minute, the National Crime Records Bureau finds that a woman is subject to some criminal offence or the other (Government of India, 1985).[25]

We have collected the opinion of members of SHGs — an organized, articulate women were making an effort to change their destiny. But the husbands of these women did not lag behind. They encouraged their wives to join in the groups.

> "The husbands are fully co-operating with us and encouraging us to do thrift."
>
> — *Mary Group, Adoni*

> "In the beginning the husbands were not even willing to send the women to meetings, but now they are ready to look after their kids and are sending the women to exposure visits also."
>
> — *Durgabai Group, Jalakanur Village, Midthur Mandal*

Initially the husbands used to insult the women saying that they don't know anything. Now they are respecting these women and they say that:

> "men should also have such groups so that they can also get organized like these women."
>
> — *Shanti Group, Peruru Village, Rudravaram Mandal*

> "Earlier husbands used to wander around the banks for loans but now they are not going to the banks. They are encouraging us to take loans from the group."
>
> — *Bhagyalakshmi Group, Nakkavagulapalli, Dhone*

We have captured from our interviews and focus group discussions from the members of SHGs, the reaction of their husbands towards their participation, leadership in community development programmes, group activities, visits outside the village and in securing benefits under different schemes of women development and classified their responses into two categories as shown in Table 6.11. *(See on next page).*

From the data shown in the table 6.11, it is quite evident that there has been a significant change in the reaction of husbands towards their wives participating and deriving benefits from different programmes and activities. 94, 90 and 98 per cent of SHGs are playing leading role in activities and programmes of community development. It is clear from our observations in the study area, that more encouragement was given to rural women by their husbands and other family members to participate in community development activities. So also is the case with regard to group activities. 100 per cent encouragement is given to the group activities in all the three divisions of the district. Similarly, regarding visits to offices situated outside the village, the reaction is favourable, encouraging and is positively correlated with the level of development of the division in the district, 84, 90 and 76 per cent of SHGs are being encouraged and supported in respect of their visits the offices outside the village. In the same way 98, 80 and 96 per cent of SHGs are deriving benefits under different welfare schemes formulated and implemented by the

Table 6.11 Reaction of Males Regarding the Participation of Women

Sl. No.	Items	Kurnool Division-I	Nandyal Division-II	Adoni Division-III
1	Leadership role in community development:			
	(a) Encouraging	47(94)	45(90)	49(98)
	(b) Not encouraging	3(6)	5(10)	1(2)
2	Group activities			
	(a) Encouraging	50(100)	50(100)	50(100)
	(b) Not encouraging	-	-	-
3	Office visits outside the village			
	(a) Encouraging	42(84)	45(90)	38(76)
	(b) Not encouraging	8(16)	5(10)	12(24)
4	Accessing of the benefits under welfare schemes of government			
	(a) Encouraging	49(98)	40(80)	48(96)
	(b) Not encouraging	1 (2)	10(20)	2(4)
5	Response of male members to group activities			
	(a) Favourable	49(98)	46(92)	42(84)
	(b) Not Favourable	1(2)	4(8)	8(16)

Note: Figures in parentheses indicate percentages to total.

Source: Field Data.

Government. The reaction of other male members of the household is quite favourable to women's participation and is positively correlated with the level of development of the division concerned.

Thus we can see favourable atmosphere to the group activities that are undertaken by rural women. Such rural atmosphere certainly will be helpful in increasing their economic and social status.

REACTION FROM LOCAL ELITE

The local elite of the rural society often belong to the upper castes and hold political offices in panchayat raj institutions co-operative bodies and other allied organisations. Members of the SHGs are mostly from the weaker sections of the community and often from the ranks of the SCs and STs and encounter several handicaps. More specifically they are handicapped because of the low caste status, being women and being poor. Things have been slowly changing. Today they all aspire to more comfortable material circumstances; all demand more dignity (Delege, 1999).[26] Whatever might have been the case in the past, there would be very few among the untouchables today who would regard themselves as impure or justify their low status on grounds of their misconduct in some previous life, a 'fact of nature' (Charlsley and Karanth, 1998),[27] with the active participation of women SHGs, the attitude of local elite towards women leadership is undergoing a slow but steady change. Even the manner in which the women members of the groups are addressed is undergoing the change for better due to the assertiveness and awareness of women regarding their rights and entitlement.

Their new found economic power enhanced their image in the eyes of their family, community and society. With money in their hands, women commanded more respect as they discovered:

> "When we formed into groups many people in the village tried to make fun of us but after seeing our development and awareness, everybody is respecting us and also approaching us for suggestions on various aspects."
>
> — *Jagadamba Group, Owk Mandal*

> "Previously, we were confined to houses only. Now our status is elevated. Almost all development programmes in the village are being done with our participation. Both the officials and villagers are treating us with respect."
>
> — *Bangaru Lakshmi Group,*
> *Kolimigundla Mandal*

We incorporate the findings relating to the reaction of the local elite in Table 6.12.

Table 6.12. Reaction of the Local Elite

	Response	*Kurnool Division-I*	*Nandyal Division-II*	*Adoni Division-III*
Yes		9(18)	8(16)	12(24)
No		41(82)	42(84)	38(76)
If yes, area of criticism:				
(a)	Moving freely with men	34(68)	30(60)	28(56)
(b)	Interacting closely with officials	13(26)	16(32)	15(30)
(c)	Discouraging group activities	3(6)	4(8)	7(14)

Note: Figures in parentheses indicate percentages to total.
Source: Field Data.

We find from the table 6.12 that 82, 84 and 76 per cent of SHGs were refrained from the criticism of local elite in the three divisions. 18, 16 and 24 per cent of SHGs were facing criticisms from the local elite. The area of criticism levelled against SHGs by the local elite is classified into three categories. In cases, where there is criticism it pertains to the free movement of members of SHGs inside and outside the village with the male folk. 68, 60 and 56 per cent of SHGs are facing criticism from local elite in respect of their free movement with male folk. 26, 32 and 30 per cent of SHGs are facing criticisms from local elite in respect of their close interaction with the officials. Similarly, 6, 8 and 14 per cent of SHGs are facing such criticism which is discouraging their group activities. It implies that the attitude of the local elite towards the developmental activities of women is positively correlated with the level of development.

POLITICAL PARTICIPATION

Poverty and development are ultimately issues of structures of power. There is substantial evidence to indicate that micro-credit recipients, through their increase in economic well-being, through their participation in public space, through their negotiations with external agents have felt empowered to the extent that they have, at times, even confronted local power structures. However, the state presence at the local level, through the police and judiciary have been one of coercion, one of imposing law and order and the status quo, rather than supporting initiatives for economic and social development of the rural poor (Rahman, 1998).[28]

Political marginalisation of the poor is an all pervasive phenomenon all over the world. The key determinant of the distribution of income and welfare in a society is government. Typically the poor are not represented in the government structures adequately. That is why their voice is hardly heard in the corridors of power. This is unlikely to change unless they are empowered. Wherever decentralisation took firm root, it has led to certain amount of 'power shift' in favour of poor people to claim, assert and depend their rights and access resources and opportunities in order to achieve their livelihood capabilities. The decentralisation would also promote improved accountability, transparency, participation, ownership and sustainability. Political empowerment is necessary for sustainable development of the SHGs as instruments of social mobilisation. According to UNDP (1994)[29] sustainable human development is the development that not only generates economic growth but distributes its benefits equitably, that regenerated the environment rather than destroying it, that empowers people rather than marginalizing them. It is the development that gives priority to the poor, enlarging their choices and opportunities and providing for their participation in decisions that affect their lives. It is the development that is pro-people, pro-nature, pro jobs and pro-women.

Participation of political activities and institutions is the surest means of taking their voice to the corridors of power and thereby overcome political marginalisation. It is observed in our field investigations that leaders of SHGs are getting elected to Panchayat Raj institutions.

Though Kurnool district is known for its factions and factions dominate village economy and politics, it was heartening to note that all the political representatives cutting across functional and political lines extended whole-hearted support to the movement. There was no political interference in the whole movement right from formation of the groups to sanction of DWCRA and IRDP to these groups.

Reservation of one-third of the seats in local bodies for women was a step in the direction of political empowerment of women. The women who got elected as sarpanches and members of Mandal Praja Parishad and Zilla Parishad played a crucial role in the process of women's empowerment. Being women themselves, these elected women representatives could readily understand the various problems being faced by women and gave priority for solving these problems. They are actively attending the group meetings and mandal conventions actively. They served as a role model for other women. Some of these elected women representatives, especially those belonging to the weaker sections were members of Podupulakshmi group themselves. Thus the process of political empowerment of women had set in.

Political empowerment of the poor is the foundation of rural poverty alleviation. The poor peoples chance to influence rule and to control organisations depend on the power and influence. Therefore, it is necessary for the poor to seek empowerment at the political level to restrain the non-poor from arranging things to their own advantage and the rural elite from wielding decentralize power (IFAD, 2001).[30] We have classified the responses of our members of SHGs regarding their interest in elections to Panchayat Raj bodies and incorporated these responses in Table 6.13.

Table 6.13 Attitude Towards Political Participation

Sl. No.	*Response*	*Kurnool Division-I*	*Nandyal Division-II*	*Adoni Division-III*
1.	Yes	42(84)	40(80)	20(40)
2.	No	8(16)	10(20)	30(60)

Note: Figures in parentheses indicate percentages to total.
Source: Field Data.

Graph 6.6 Attitude Towards Political Participation

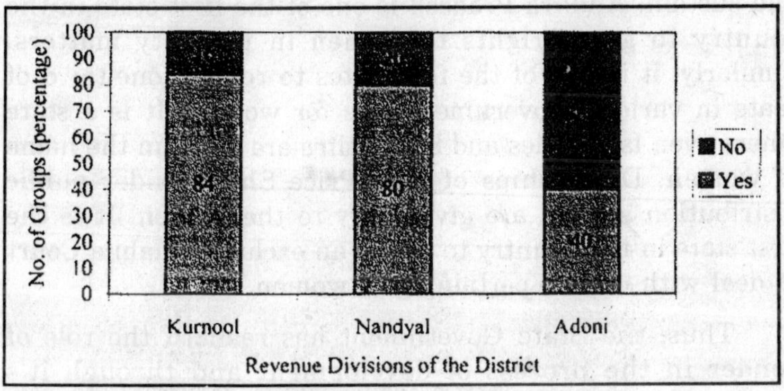

It is obvious from the information given in table 6.13 that the 84 per cent of SHGs are more interested in political participation in the first division followed by second and third divisions. However the percentage of group political participation is less in the third division. Probably this is due to the better political access of their male counterparts in the comparatively developed divisions on one hand and the awareness created and sustained by promoting agency of the SHG and the other. There is a scope for further research on these issues and processes of political emergence of SHGs and thereby their sustainability in all dimensions namely political, social, cultural, psychological and economic as poverty is something more than all these dimensions put together.

THE ROLE OF STATE GOVERNMENT

Thus the rural poor women of Kurnool district were making an attempt to change their destiny by organising themselves into SHGs. But the process of social mobilisation which is resulting in many benefits for the women is not a spontaneous process and it is made possible by the lead role played by the State Government and district administration.

The State of Andhra Pradesh has taken up the theme of women's empowerment as a main agenda to tackle the issue of poverty. The State Government, through its various policies has created a conducive environment for social mobilisation and women's empowerment process to emerge and sustain. Andhra Pradesh is one of the first state in the country to grant rights to women in property matters. Similarly, it is one of the few states to reserve one-third of seats in various Government jobs for women. It is a state where even land titles and house-sites are given in the name of women. Dealerships of Fair Price Shops under public distribution system are given only to the women. It is the first state in the country to set up an exclusive Mahila Court to deal with crimes pertaining to women.

Thus, the State Government has realized the role of gender in the process of development and through it's various legislative and executive policies, is making an attempt to empower women.

Summing Up

Social mobilisation is the surest means of women empowerment. Poor have to be mobilized and empowered so that they can effectively participate in the programmes meant for them. Women have been traditionally bypassed in the process of development. Women SHGs have initiated programmes of awareness building and assertive action regarding access to public places like temples, drinking water, wells and participating in social sector development activities as well as infrastructure building and maintenance.

An organized, aware and empowered women has realized the importance of various socio-developmental indicators like literacy, family planning, children's education, health, sanitation etc.

Thus, formation into SHGs by women resulted not only in their economic development, but also development in other fields such as literacy, children's education, family planning, health, sanitation etc. The social mobilisation movement had transformed the lives of the women. DWCRA/SHG was not merely an economic programme for them. It was a programme which had changed their lives:

> "This programme is like God, which came to save women. It is a weapon in the hands of women"
>
> — *Krishna Priya Group, Midthur Mandal*

> "This programme is a boon for us. Because of this, we are exposed to the society. We know about various Government programmes and schemes. This has improved our social and economic status."
>
> — *Rajeswari Group, Orvakal Mandal*

The women are making an attempt to see that at least their future generation does not suffer from capability deprivation. They are mostly satisfied in the type of participation they are initiated into and are able to resolve conflicts regarding group activities as well as social issues like child marriage, alcoholism, domestic violence. The reaction of husbands and other male members of the household as well as the local elite is quite favourable to their activities and participatory processes including visits to offices outside the village. They are favourably disposed towards the political participation at the level of local government with a view to bring about a power shift in their favour which is critical for sustaining and improving the status of women SHGs.

Thus the voiceless, assetless and powerless women caught in the triad of economic, human and environmental poverty before social mobilisation. But one must be very clear that it is social mobilisation alone which is the answer to the problem of poverty. However one must also bear in mind that is not the panacea for all the problems being faced by the poor. It will help in mobilisation of the poor and enable them to solve their problems themselves. The process of social mobilisation is indeed difficult and may not result in success everywhere, but one should realize that the present way of dealing with the problem of poverty will not result in success anywhere. So a beginning should be made somewhere. The Kurnool experience has shown that Government can initiate and sustain large scale programme that is based on social mobilisation. The centerpiece of a policy framework for poverty alleviation has to be mobilisation of the poor as social mobilisation and social mobilisation alone is the sine-qua-non for all development.

REFERENCES

1. Kumaran, K.P. (1994), Self-Help Groups and Development of the Rural Poor, Unpublished, NIRD, Hyderabad.
2. Reddy, G.N. (1987), 'Participation to Promote Collective Self-reliance of the Rural Poor,' *Journal of Rural Development,* Vol. 6, No. 3, May.
3. Mukherji, P.N. (1984), 'Women's Movement Studies—A Methodological Note,' *Samya Sakti, Vol.* 1, No. 2.
4. IDS, Jaipur, (1991), WDP—Emerging Challenges, Institute of Development Studies, Jaipur.
5. Deepti Aggarwal, (2001), Empowerment of Rural Women, Intensive Agriculture, March-April.
6. Sakuntala Narasimhan (1999), Empowering Women: An Alternative Strategy from Rural India, *Sage Publications*, New Delhi.
7. Amartya Sen (1995), *The Hindu,* 6th November, Interviewed by Ramamanohar Reddy, Chennai.
8. Frenchie Fournier (1997), Foreword, Poverty and Participation in Civil Society, Edited by Yogesh Atal of Else Oyen, *Abhinav Publications,* New Delhi.
9. A.C.Pigou (1960), The Economics of Welfare, *Macmillan & Co Ltd,* London.
10. IFAD (1996), The State of World Poverty, Rome for a Discussion on the Process and Structural Causes of Poverty, See

Rovert Chambers (1983), Rural Development, Putting the Last First, London, Longmans.

11. South Asian Association for Regional Cooperation (SAARC) (1992). Meeting the Challenge, Report of the Independent South Asian Commission on Poverty.

Haq Mahbub Ul (1997), Human Development in South Asia, *Oxford University Press,* New York.

Holcombe, Susan (1995), Managing to Empower the Grameena Banks, Experience of Poverty Alleviation, *Oxford University Press,* Dhaka.

12. Amitava Mukherjee (1999), Out of the Abysis. The Challenge Confronting Some Civil Society Actors, *Indian Economic Association,* 82 Conference, Amritsar.

13. Holcombe, Susan (1995), Managing to Empower. The Grameena Banks' Experience of Poverty Alleviation, *Oxford University Press,* Dhaka.

14. Karmakar, K.G. (1999), Rural-Credit and Self-Help Groups, Micro-Finance Needs and Concepts in India, *Sage Publications,* New Delhi.

15. N. Lalitha, Rural Women Empowerment and Development Banking, *Kanishka Publishers,* New Delhi.

16. Ch.Appa Rao, 'Women Empowerment Through SHG and DWCRA—A Study in Andhra Pradesh.'

17. 'Empowerment of Rural Women' *Monthly'Public Opinion Survey,* December 2001.

18. Government of India (1998-99), Reports of the Commissioner of SC and STs, New Delhi.

19. CIRDAP (1998), Increased Household Income and Rural Women in Asia, Impact on Status and Activities, Dhaka, Bangladesh.

20. N. Lalitha, Rural Women Empowerment and Development Banking, *Kanishka Publishers,* New Delhi.

21. Ninth Five Year Plan (1997-2000).

22. CIRDP (1998), Poverty, Gender and Participation, Dhaka.

23. Bhat, Mazi, P.N. and et al (1999), Finding of National Family Health Survey, Regional Analysis, *Economic and Political Weekly,* Vol.XXXIV, Nos. 42 and 43, October 16-22/23-29.

24. Ajay Jain, Poverty Alleviation Through Social Mobilisation: The Kurnool Strategy.

25. Government of India (1985), Five Year Plan Documents (The Seventh and Eighth Five Year Plans 1985-95, New Delhi, The Planning Commission).

26. Delige, R. (1999). The Untouchables of India, Berg, New York.

27. Charsely, S.R. and G.K.Karanth (1998). Challenging Untouchability, Dalit Initiative and Experience from Karnataka, *Sage Publications,* New Delhi.

28. Rahman Hossain Zillus (1998), Poverty Issues in Bangladesh, Power and Participation Research Centre, Mimeo.

29. UNDP (1994), Human Development Report, *Oxford,* New York.

30. IFAD (2001), Rural Poverty Report, the Challenge of Ending Rural Poverty, *Oxford,* New York.

7

Problems of Women Development with Reference to the DWCRA/SHG Approach

LACUNAE IN THE GROUP APPROACH (OR) DRAWBACKS IN THE APPROACH (OR) PROBLEMS IN THE APPROACH

The programme launched by the district administration had achieved laudable objectives. But like any other programme of the government, it had certain drawbacks:

1. When the movement was launched, the women were encouraged to form into groups of 30 members each. This was because Kurnool strategy was based on Nellore experience wherein 30 member groups were formed. However over a period of time, it was realized that 30 member group was not a cohesive group and the ideal size of the group as expressed by the members themselves was 15-20;

   A large group made it difficult to conduct group meetings, as attendance often was not 100 per cent and there was no democratic functioning of groups because of non-participation of some of the members;

2. Another problem arose when it was decided to link the groups with the banks. NABARD guidelines prescribe that the group size should be below 20, if informal SHGs have to be financed. In case of more than 20 member group, it had to be formally registered;

3. A holistic approach to development was lacking on the part of the Government. Despite all the efforts made by the district administration, the different government departments continued their own sectoral approach to development. As a result, convergence of basic services could not be attained at the group level fully. It is indeed a paradox that though the aims and objectives of all the Government departments are the same and the people with whom they are working are also same, still each department prefers to form its own target groups. The Government is bogged down with target oriented approach so much that the real objective gets lost. Because of the success of group strategy, each department started forming its own groups. The women and child welfare department was organising women into "Mothers' Committees" while "Mahila Swastha Sanghams" were being formed by medical and health department. The Scheduled Caste Corporation preferred to have its own Scheduled Caste women groups, while tribal thrift groups were being organized in tribal areas. The same women were the members of Podupulakshmi group, mother's committee etc. This artificial compartmentalisation created by the Government departments was a major hindrance in achieving convergence of programmes;

4. In the beginning, all the Government departments took very active part in the formation and sustenance of the groups but slowly, many of the departmental officers began to withdraw from the programme. As the whole movement was co-ordinated by DRDA, other departments gained an impression that it was basically a DRDA programme and it is the responsibility of the DRDA officials to sustain and monitor the groups. Consequently, other officers started taking less interest in the programme and one could find many mandal level and village level functionaries not participating in the group meetings and mandal level conventions. What was surprising was that even women and child welfare

department, which took the lead in the movement started perceiving the DWCRA and SHG groups as DRDA groups and many CDPOs and ICDS supervisors did not evince keen interest subsequently. There were even instances where in the Anganwadi workers were told to close the groups. This short-sighted policy resulted in the disintegration of some of the groups especially in those areas, where there was no AGS/VDO(W)NGO to monitor the groups;

5. The sectoral approach of Government departments was again visible when funds from different departments could not reach these groups. While DRDA was trying to link up all its programmes with the SHGs, the respective corporations namely the SC Corporation, BC Corporation, Tribal Welfare Corporations continued to have their own individual beneficiary oriented programmes. Thus there was an imbalance. On one hand, because of a massive social mobilisation movement, SHGs were formed and readied to handle more money and utilize properly and most of the money of the Government departments went elsewhere in the same traditional manner;

   And even when the money was spent on the women, there was no uniform approach. The women and child welfare department gave its "income-generating revolving fund" to its own "Mother's committees." Similarly SC Corporation selected its own SC groups for giving funds. There was no uniform procedure of selection of the groups with the result, lot of duplication took place. The same SC woman got DWCRA as a member of Podupulakshmi group, income generating fund of ICDS as a member of "Mothers' Committee" and revolving fund from SC Corporation;

6. The priority of the Government also changed during the period. While SHGs and DWCRA movement were given lot of importance during 1995-96, less attention was paid to them during 1996-97 but again the social

mobilisation became the top most agenda during 1997-98. As a result, the interest taken by the district administration also varied during the period;

7. The success of the programme and the sustenance of the groups depend to a large extent on the presence of Non-Government Organisations who have a crucial role to play in the whole process. But the presence of NGO is limited. This was a serious constraint in sustaining the movement in remote and backward areas;

8. The campaign approach followed by the district administration resulted in the formation of a large number of groups. What could not be done in years was achieved in months by this approach but it had its own disadvantages and limitations. Some of the groups formed were not homogeneous groups. In some of the groups, not all the members were poor. Subsequently, such groups could not sustain themselves for long as the needs of the poor were vastly different from the needs of the well-off. The sustenance as well as monitoring of such a large number of groups was a Herculean task since a large number of groups were formed in such a short time frame;

9. The basic data pertaining to all the groups regarding their thrift, credit, meetings, records maintenance and other socio-developmental indicators like literacy, family planning, children's education, etc., was not collected in the beginning of the movement. In the absence of the bench-mark survey, it was not possible to have a scientific evaluation of the programme at successive intervals and take corrective steps;

10. It was observed that the participation of women groups in the watershed programme was minimal, except in the case of a few watersheds;

Thus, some of the loopholes in the implementation of Government sponsored programmes came up in this movement also. Though it was not meant to be a Government programme, it turned out to be so in certain aspects, and consequently had the weaknesses of a Government sponsored programmes.

Constraints or Problems Faced by Women in Their Economic Activities

Some of the constraints faced by women at large in matters of securing credit and employment or better life are as follows:

1. Vested interest to exploit women's work cheaply;
2. Women's limited skills and exposure;
3. Women's incompetence in formal dealings;
4. Insensitivity of policy-makers;
5. Erosion of women's economic activities;
6. Insufficient collective strength;
7. Women members were irregular in repaying the loan. They were not adhering to the norm set for repayment of loan and interest;
8. Mobilising the rural women into cooperatives is very difficult;
9. Low literacy;
10. Traditional women oriented activities such as rope making, mat weaving, hand-made papads, agarbatti making may not strictly require group loan. In case of weaving, sewing of ordinary garments, leather products etc., where equipment can be individually owned, group loan is not imperative. Thus group credit that is being extended by the banks is creating a hurdle to these women who want to start their business venture on an individual basis;
11. The women members of SHGs are expressing that the loan amount that is being provided by the commercial

banks is not sufficient to establish productive asset on profitable basis;

12. There is a greater time lag between the identification of the beneficiaries and disbursement of loan to them. Due to such delay in the disbursement of the loan, they are loosing interest in starting the business unit;

13. The rate of interest charged by the commercial banks is considered to be high which may not be more beneficial and encouraging to the women entrepreneurs. Payment of higher rate of interest reduces the returns of the women earned in their productive activities;

14. The commercial banks are not giving financial assistance to all SHGs. They are favouring more the SHGs which are performing well (success groups). But they are totally neglecting and are not coming forward to extend financial help to the SHGs which are not performing well (failure groups) in their productive activities. What is more important is good support shall be given to the failure groups so that they can achieve success or develop in future;

15. Lack of capital is a serious constraint to the development of women particularly in rural areas. If credit or finance can be effectively delivered to women, it will help them to make a meaningful improvement in their economic and social conditions. But unfortunately women are facing so many problems in getting finance to take up self employment opportunities, particularly women in informal sector;

16. Most of the women, particularly in rural areas are not aware of the facilities that are being extended by the Government, banks and other organisations to their development. Because of such ignorance, they are devoid of financial help and so they are not in a position to start any productive activity irrespective of their capabilities;

17. Lack of raw materials and infrastructural facilities is another important problem faced by women in their economic activities;

18. Due to low returns in their economic activities, women are facing the difficulty in the repayment of the loan to the banks;

19. The time allowed for SHGs by the banks for repayment of the loan is very short. It is not more than 10 months. The SHGs of our study area are expressing that they find it difficult to repay the entire loan within the 10 months (10 equated instalments). If once they fail to repay the entire loan amount within the stipulated time, they will not be given any type of financial help further by the banks. Such procedure of the banks is depriving the SHGs from improving their productive activities;

20. The middlemen provide raw materials on credit—leading to low profit and marginal subsistence for women vendors;

21. No guarantees are extended on behalf of the groups to enable them to get additional resources from the banks;

22. There is a political meddling in the selection of both members of the group and the activity to be undertaken by it.

Marketing Problems

1. Women lack bargaining power.

2. Direct access to transport and markets is also crucial if women are to maintain control over the products of their labour.

3. Where the women are not permitted in the market place, male family members who sell their goods receive the cash.

4. For example, in the silk weaving industry in Banaras, cloth produced at home and sold by the husband to

intermediaries leaves the women "no control nor separate share of the earnings."

5. Women have low mobility, less scope for information seeking, hence less experience.
6. Women were unable to face the competition in the urban markets.
7. Lack of salesmanship.
8. Lack of publicity or advertisement
9. Inadequate demand and low prices in the market.

Women, when given a chance or whenever they had an opportunity have proved in many places that they are better and more conscious managers than men.

Due to lack of financial and other resources at their command, women often fail to maintain certain minimum standards of their families. They need a certain amount of credit which could enable them to secure raw materials. But such sources are scarce for women.

OVERCOMING THE PROBLEMS

What was perhaps required was a change from 'Programme Approach' to 'process approach.' If the social mobilisation were to succeed institutionalisation of the whole process had to take place. Institutions should be developed and strengthened so that the process continues.

An attempt was made in May 1997 to overcome the above problems in the approach:

1. It was realized that 30 member group was not a cohesive group. Hence, women were encouraged to reorganize themselves into groups of 15-20. This was achieved by dividing the original group into two or by dropping some unwilling members from the group. The process of reorganisation of the groups was done over a period of 5-6 months and by December 1997 almost all the groups have been reorganized and are below 20 member groups;

2. 'Capacity building' and 'Human Resource Development' of the Government officials, NGOs, group leaders, members and everybody else involved with the programme is the single most important factor for the success of the movement. Though a large number of training programmes, workshops were conducted for all those involved in the programme, there was no fixed annual training calendar. The conduct of training programmes depended on the decision taken by the District Collector and Project Director, DRDA depending on their availability of time. Similarly, though mandal level conventions were planned every 3 months, they could not be conducted many a time because of busy schedule of collector and PD, DRDA. What was required was a fixed annual training calendar to be decided in the beginning of each year itself in consultation with those involved in the process.

   Therefore, a District Resource Team was constituted in August 1997 consisting of Project Director, DRDA, Project Director, Women and Child Development Agency, District Medical and Health Officer, AGM, NABARD and NGOs actively associated with the programme. The team was entrusted with the task of formulating the annual training calendar, identifying the training centers in the district, identifying the resource persons for imparting training and finalising the training curriculum. A similar team was constituted at the mandal level to organise mandal level trainings.

   Similarly, dates were fixed for organising mandal level conventions and cluster level training programmes. Even if the district officials are busy with some other engagements eg., elections, relief work, law and order etc. The training programmes must continue as per schedule. Then only one can talk about a sustainable model of development, a model which is not based on "personality cult" but based on an institutional framework," which sustains itself irrespective of any individual occupying a particular post;

3. A bench-mark survey of all the groups was carried out in November 1997. The data pertaining to all the

groups in, terms of savings, credit, meetings and other socio-developmental indicators like literacy, family planning, children's education etc., was gathered. The entire data was computerized and MIS was developed for all the groups. This data is updated once in 3 months. The MIS enables one to know the strengths and weaknesses of all the groups. Training programmes can be developed as per the needs of the groups. MIS provides an important tool for evaluation of the groups;

4. A uniform set of guidelines was prescribed for till the SHGs. It was decided that henceforth, the women thrift and credit groups would be the nodal points for convergence of basic services of all the government departments. Each department instead of forming it's own groups would strengthen the existing women groups and implement their programmes through them;

5. Action plans of various departments like DRDA, ICDS, SC Corporation, BC Corporation, Tribal Welfare etc., were dovetailed in such a manner that maximum funds of these departments go to these groups and no duplication would take place;

6. To increase the participation of women groups in the watershed programme, priority in sanctioning of new watersheds was given to those areas where the social mobilisation was good, that is wherever SHGs were doing well, those areas were selected for sanction of new watersheds. The women SHGs became the members of "Watershed Committee." The involvement of these groups in the programme increased tremendously and so the quality of the programme;

7. Banks are not following the proper criteria in extending credit facilities to benefit the poorest of the poor. Banks should identify the areas where women's employment and income is low and special agencies may be set up for extending credit facilities to the SHGs in such areas.

8

Summary and Conclusions

Women constitute half of the human population and rural women in India constitute nearly 77 per cent of the total female population. They contribute significantly to agriculture and allied activities etc., and also artisanal activities, apart from the household activities. About 79 per cent of rural women workers are involved in agriculture related pursuits as cultivators and labourers. Farm and home are integral parts in the rural society in India and the farm housewife often plays multiple roles as producer, entrepreneur, worker, consumer and house maker. Women engaged in the secondary and tertiary sectors account for 5 per cent and 16 per cent respectively. In India, poverty in general and extreme poverty in particular has a significant gender dimension. Women are the most vulnerable group affected by poverty.

The rural women play a critical role in the process of moving their families out of poverty. Around 30 per cent to 35 per cent of the rural Indian households are estimated as headed by women. Even when there is a male earner, women's earning form a significant part of the income of poor households. Thus, enhancing women's economic productivity is an important strategic necessity for improving the welfare of the estimated 60 million Indian households which are still below the poverty line. Thus the most feasible option to generate their own income is through self-employment, despite the problems they face in gaining access to assets and resources.

It is a known fact that women as a part of the factor of production have equal capacity of adding to the national income and hence contributing to the economic development. However, the capacity of female population has been largely ignored over the years and hence resulted in the low economic position and status of women in general. To contribute to economic development, women must engage themselves in what is called economic or gainful activity.

A micro enterprise suits the life style of Indian women, but caught up in the dual responsibility role, her entry into the business needs to recognize the quantum of time. However, in recent times women engage themselves in micro enterprises both in rural and urban areas. Women found themselves with less risky business like trade and service units rather than manufacturing. So, self-employed women and those employed in the informal or agricultural sectors often work in small enterprises, which provide them with little access to the credit and information needed to manage and market their products effectively (Young 1994-96). The two strategies are of special importance for increasing women's economic participation namely, increasing access to credit and capacity building regarding organisational and work skills together with information provision. There is an imperative need to develop rural entrepreneurship with a special focus on women. Micro enterprises have great potential for generating productive employment especially in rural areas. NABARD and SIDBI have launched schemes for promotion of Self-Help Groups and NGO's as a channel for flow of funds to micro enterprises.

It is true that credit programmes are being launched to help women in micro enterprises both by the government and non-government organisations. Many NGO's have an excellent track record in incorporating women into their programmes designed to assist under micro enterprises. Efforts such as IRDP, DWCRA and TRYSEM, to encourage entrepreneurship in micro enterprises have not achieved a break through.

Group entrepreneurship in the form of self help group in which the women savings are pooled together and on the basis of the performances of repayment of their own savings-credit, a tie up may be created with the banks in future for starting micro enterprises suitable to the rural environment, utilizing the local raw materials by carefully analyzing and assessing the market for such products. However, it may not be the overall solution but only a little attempt, which are being followed by the NGO's and Government Organisations in the recent past.

Indian experience with self help groups with a focus on women is emerging as a promising financial innovation with great potential to reach the poor and marginal workers in a cost effective way to the lender with many spin-offs to the needy and vulnerable, who are outside the economic arena.[1]

There are broadly three approaches that have been evolved over time to attack extreme poverty. It is realized that the operation and the outcome of the three approaches namely, (a) The welfarist approach, (b) The Service Delivery Approach and (c) Empowerment Approach proceed on an understanding of the characteristics of poor. It is realized and agreed, vulnerability, isolation, alienation and dominance and dependence affect the poor and their capacity to take decisions. Assetlessness, powerlessness and material deprivation take away from the poor their capability to take decisions. Lack of participation in the political process, lack of freedom of choice and insecurity militate against the creation of an enabling environment that facilitates and encourages the poor to take decisions. The distinction between capacity and capability is fundamental. Capacity relates to the cerebral attributes of human beings, a healthy mind for instance. Capability is in relation to physical attributes of people, a healthy body. Capacity building is an important plank on which the superstructures of SHGs activities are supposed to be built. The three-pronged approach of the World Bank to attack poverty comprises, (a) Promotion of opportunities, (b) Facilitating empowerment, (c) Enhancing security for the poor.

Poverty can be viewed as, (a) Economic poverty, (b) Environmental poverty, (c) Human poverty. 'Economic poverty' basically means that the poor lack income generating resources and the purchasing power to earn enough to meet their subsistence. 'Environmental poverty' deals with the physical environment in which the poor lives. The poor do not have access to basic minimum needs of life like safe drinking water, shelter, sanitation, roads etc. 'Human poverty' relates to the socio-cultural environment of the poor. The deprivation relates to socio-developmental indicators like literacy, primary education, primary healthcare, family welfare etc.

Thus, poverty is not merely a problem of low income and less purchasing power of the poor as is general prevalent notion, it encompasses a wide gamut of physical and socio-cultural environment in which the poor lives. Any poverty alleviation programme has to take into account all the above three aspects of poverty as removal of one type poverty may not result in improving the living conditions of the poor.

Government launched various programmes to bring the people above the poverty line. While programmes like IRDP, TRYSEM, DWCRA, PMRY and other programmes by SC, ST, BC and Minorities corporations etc., attempted to provide income generating assets to the poor so as to increase the purchasing power, other subsidy programmes like PDS were an attempt to provide the poor food security. Funds were also earmarked for social service schemes to benefit specific needy sections of society like old, physically handicapped, destitute, widows and pregnant women etc., various wage employment programmes were started to provide employment to poor during the lean seasons. The objective of all the programmes was to eradicate the economic poverty by increasing the income of the poor.

There was also an attempt by the Government to improve the physical environment of the poor by providing basic minimum needs. Programmes like MNP, IAY, EAS and JRY were an attempt to provide the basic minimum needs in the villages where the poor mostly lived.

Government also started various programmes to increase the capability of the poor by providing literacy, primary education, primary healthcare, family welfare etc. Thus it is clear from above that poverty alleviation programmes started by Government tried to cover all the three aspects of poverty. The question then arises is: where have we gone wrong? Why the nation continues to be in poverty despite massive investments made in anti-poverty programmes?

The answer to the above question is that despite all its best intentions, Government failed to implement poverty alleviation programmes successfully because of number of reasons:

1. There is no continuity in Government sponsored programmes;
2. Lack of commitment on the part of Government machinery to implement anti-poverty programmes;
3. In Government set-up, there are leakages while delivering goods and services;
4. Though the nature of the problems differs from region to region and people to people, Government offers the same solution everywhere. The present set-up simply cannot respond to the wide diversity and magnitude of the problems being faced by poor in the country;
5. The approach of the Government has been target oriented, 'Time Bound' and 'Top-Down' approach;
6. Lack of people's participation in Government sponsored programmes is often quoted as the primary reason for failure of anti-poverty programmes;

7. Most of the Government programmes at the field level have been 'Personality based' rather than 'institutional based' meaning thereby that the success of the programmes revolved around the top man in the field and the moment there was a change in the leadership; the programmes collapsed;
8. There have been plethora of programmes and multiplicity of schemes with the result that many of the schemes do not simply take-off in the field;
9. Every new Government or administration initiates a new programme. Funds are earmarked for schemes, which are not suited to local needs;
10. Government programmes are poorly planned and more so poorly implemented;
11. There is lack of coordination amongst various Government departments, resulting in overlapping of funds and areas;
12. Government programmes are based on distrust on Government functionaries as well as distrust on the people for whom it has to deliver the goods;
13. There has been no serious attempt to train, educate and sensitize the people about the various Government schemes. Lack of proper awareness about the programmes is one of the main reasons for the failure of many Government Programmes;
14. The 'subsidy-culture' being continued by successive Governments has made the people totally dependent on Government support. People have lost the initiative to do things themselves. The 'dependency syndrome' is responsible for making the people wait for the Government schemes/grants for years rather than doing the things themselves;
15. Failure of certain Government departments to provide the necessary extension services in certain critical areas

like agriculture, sericulture, horticulture, fisheries, animal husbandry etc., is responsible for failure of many programmes;

16. Failure of delivery system is one of the reasons for the failure of Government programmes;

17. Little attention paid to human resource development is one of the primary reasons for failure of many programmes. People were perceived to be the 'objects' and not the 'subjects' in the development;

18. The feudal power structure in our villages was responsible for much of the benefits being cornered away by ineligible and undeserving people;

19. The skewed and unequal distribution of resources amongst areas was also responsible for unequal development;

20. Public servants are not accountable to the people at large but owed their loyalty to the political masters and higher bureaucracy;

21. The delay in implementation because of various administrative bottlenecks was responsible for failure of many schemes.

The reasons for failure are endless but the basic fact remains that the Government did not succeed in eradicating poverty from this country.

The question then arises is: Is there a solution for all these problems? Can we ever bring people above the poverty line? A close look at the above problems will show that in the present set-up, there is really no ready-made solution for these problems. The system improves to some extent if only committed political leadership and a committed bureaucracy exists or else same condition retains.

After years of experience, Government realized that if its programmes have to be a success, people should be involved in planning and implementation, bureaucratic procedures have to be simplified and funds should be directly transferred to the people. An organized community has to be involved in planning, implementation and monitoring of the programmes. Poor have to be mobilized and empowered so that they can effectively participate in the programmes meant for them.

The development paradigm today puts the focus of development on people and their participation. However, to pursue a development strategy without gender as a category is a wasteful and self-defeating exercise. This is because development has not paid attention to women. Women have been traditionally bypassed in the process of development.

Poor women's voices are seldom heard in the corridors of power. Plans and policies are invariably made at high levels where women's representation is very low. Unless poor women have access to decisions that affect and influence their lives, policies and programmes will continuously fail to integrate poor women into the mainstream of development.

Thus women are central to the success of poverty alleviation efforts. This realisation brings women at the center stage of development efforts. The goals of poverty eradication and empowerment of women can be effectively achieved if poor women could be organized into groups for community participation as well as for assertion of their rights. Today, self help groups with an accent on savings, credit and financial resources for development is seen as an effective strategy for empowerment of women. Organising women into groups is also perceived as a viable strategy for over all development.

The District administration of Kurnool district of Andhra Pradesh has adopted the Podupulakshmi strategy as an instrument for poverty eradication since 1995. The district administration realized that an alternate strategy has to be adopted if a serious dent has to be made on the problem of poverty. Rural poor have to be mobilized and empowered so that they can effectively participate in the Government Programmes meant for them.

Experience of NGO's and successfully run Government schemes show that if poor people are mobilized, they will be able to access and utilize resources which are meant for them in a much better manner. In fact, efforts to organize poor people, particularly women have been going on in the district. Under the programme of Development of women and children in Rural Areas, Organisation of rural poor women into groups had been going on in the district since 1991. But DWCRA remained merely a programme and could not become a vehicle of socio-economic upliftment of women. However one time assistance under DWCRA does not ensure that the groups could really overcome economic poverty. Therefore these groups linked to the banks directly, which would ensure flow of regular credit to the groups forever, enabling them to undertake their economic activity.

It is interesting to note the reasons quoted by the groups for forming themselves into Self Help Groups.

"To become organized"

— *Bhagyalakshmi Group, Dhone Mandal*

"For mutual help and co-operation"

— *Satya Sai Group Kolimigundla*

"To eradicate poverty"

— *Mother Theresa Group, Nandikotkur Mandal*

"To take loans from the group for income generating activities"

— *Devi Group, Kodumur Mandal*

"To set up self employment ventures"

— *Indira Group, Pattikonda*

"The problems which cannot be solved individually can be solved by forming into groups"

— *Mary Group, Atmakur Mandal*

DESIGN AND METHODOLOGY OF THE STUDY

The Area of present study covers the Kurnool district. The district is divided into three revenue divisions. In order to present the three divisions we have randomly chosen five mandals from each division Ten Women Self-Help Groups from each mandal are chosen randomly from the universe. Thus we have arrived at a total sample of 150 SHGs. The statistical data for the study are collected with the help of systematically designed schedule. The data collected are analyzed and presented in suitable tables. We met the leaders, members of each group and elicited responses and observed the activities that were undertaken by the groups. It has been a great experience and exposure to grasp the realities of the rural poor and their ways of adoption to survive under conditions of economic distress and social oppression. Thus, our data collection involved not merely the conventional questionnaire, but also participant observation and focus group discussion with the group members.

The present study is discussed under eight chapters.

WOMEN AND DEVELOPMENT

In this chapter the problem of women development in a developing economy has been stated. It includes the role of women in the third world. Women are central to the success of poverty alleviation efforts. This realisation brings women at the center stage of development efforts. Since 1950's when development planning first came into the international spot light, a number of approaches having different effect on women have been tried. It also includes employment and occupational structure in India. Tribal women contribute to the workforce in a more substantial way. The National Commission for Women, a statutory body set up in 1992 to safeguard the rights and interests of women. It also includes the role of rural women. The problem that India faces with female poverty is much more severe and brutal. The government completely neglects the poverty of women and the vicious cycle of problems.

The above study proves that poorer the family, greater is the dependence on women's income despite the triple burden of reproduction, domestic labour and productive labour. Moreover compared to men, women contribute a large share of what they earn to basic family maintenance. However the emergence and progress of the DWCRA and SHG movement is expected to bring about greater social mobilisation through economic empowerment and capacity building.

DESIGN AND METHODOLOGY OF STUDY

In this section review of literature, the objectives and hypothesis of the study are specified. It also includes the sample design, size, field work plan, source of data collection and statistical tools used in the collection, analysis of data and design of dissertation. It also includes district profile.

WOMEN DEVELOPMENT AND FIVE-YEAR PLANS

In this chapter various schemes introduced by the Government during five year plans exclusively for women to increase their meaningful participation in the economy are analyzed. The policies and programmes relating to women are confined to areas like health, education and social welfare, till the fifth Five-Year Plan. But from the sixth plan a separate chapter on women development programmes is included and the plan envisages the measures needed for employment generation for women.

In the Sixth plan a new scheme namely DWCRA was started, which has proved quite popular. In the seventh plan a significant step taken to improve women status was the identification of a number of beneficiary oriented programmes under various sectors of development. Developmental programmes like CAPART, rural sanitation programme, JRY, NRY were launched during this period.

A major thrust in the strategy for women development during the eighth plan was on the formation and strengthening of grassroot level women's groups. More emphasis is laid on vocational training of women and encouraged, in new areas of technical education such as electronics, computer systems, bio-engineering, communications. Developmental programmes like Mahila Samridhi Yojana, Indira Awaas Yojana were started for economic betterment of women. National Commission for Women set up to protect women's rights. Rashtriya Mahila Kosh was set up in 1993 to provide credit to poor women for income generation activities.

The Government of Andhra Pradesh has also implemented several developmental schemes like Mahila Samakya Scheme, Podupulakshmi scheme Arogya Deepam, construction of working women's hostels, establishments of creches, Balwadi's, women welfare centres, service homes, vocational training centres, Anganwadi centres for providing better education, nutrition and to improve their skills and economic status. Andhra Pradesh Women's Cooperative Finance Corporation was established by the Government of Andhra Pradesh to introduce various economic programmes for women.

Thus the government has given more importance to various developmental programmes during various five year plans particularly in the sixth, seventh, eighth, ninth and tenth five year plans to help women in the country.

PROGRESS OF SHGs

DWCRA groups are more than two decades older in India. They are conceived as an effective instrument of fighting feminine poverty on the one hand and child poverty on the other. The rural women are handicapped in many ways. Their burden of work is more than that of men. The chemistry of sociology and the social factors like class, gender, caste, religion, age etc., play an important role in determining women's access to and control over resources, which are central to the issue of empowerment of women in a given society.

Due to the efforts of governmental and non-governmental agencies, SHGs have become a major movement particularly among women. Such movement by and large, is restricted to certain pockets of the country.

Therefore, there is an urgent need both at governmental and non-governmental levels to activate this movement and spread it in different parts of the country where the poor are largely concentrated.[2]

When the poor organize themselves and adopt various programme strategies, they are actual participants of and a subject in the whole process. While evolving into self-help groups, they gradually learn to take decisions for themselves and also develop the capacity to exercise certain amount of control over the social, economic and political conditions that determine their immediate lives.

The SHGs though formed on and based around economic activities, are not confined to just being that. In fact, these activities were carried out under the aegis of various NGOs. The spread of concept, however, has been patchy and the process of linking up SHGs with the banks needs to be developed with systematic efforts. However the concept of the SHGs is gradually spreading as this brings the benefits of flexibility and responsiveness to the needs of the rural poor women. Income-spending patterns as well as preferences in the use of productive resources are different for women. Men spend more on status consumer goods, whereas women spend the income mostly on families, especially children's basic needs and for general household consumption (Binu Agarwal, EPW, 1998).[3] SHGs are an effective tool for the empowerment of women in the real sense. The viability, sustainability and empowerment depend to a large extent on the grassroot process and praxis rather than conceptually sound rationale. Women can be empowered not by an external agency but by themselves, through capacity building to take up challenges and to question all types of exclusion and exploitation. Thus, formation of SHGs is not the end in itself but the means to facilitate the process of empowerment. A number of NGOs have helped in facilitating this process. The repayment rates in such groups are very high. We therefore need to spread the success stories to emphasize the point that women are creditworthy.

STRUCTURAL CHARACTERISTICS OF SAMPLE SHGs—PERFORMANCE OF SAMPLE SHGs

The Self-Help Groups are of small sizes and possess a high degree of social and economic homogeneity. The natural groupings based on caste, sub-group, occupation or heritage consist of about 10-15 members. The number of members in each group varies, the maximum is 16 and the minimum is 7 and the average number of members is 11. Mean age among the members varies from 20 to 41. The average family size among the group varies from 3 to 6 and average family income per month varies from group to group. The maximum and minimum are respectively Rs. 980 and Rs. 355. These small groups were socially functional in the sense that the members worked easily together because of mutual understanding. Their rules were normally standardized and did not allow for flexibility and adjustment. However, the SHGs evolved their own rules and regulations including the rate of interest, schedules of payment and recovery. Saving has been the prime activity of these groups right from their inception. The saving is made on monthly basis and the monthly contribution for each group is fixed and it varies from group to group that is Rs. 30 to Rs. 100. Interest rate for the loan varies from group to group, the maximum being 20 per cent and minimum 10 per cent per month. Decision regarding the disbursement of loan to its members is decided by the members themselves, depending upon the nature of their needs.

DRDA had promoted 57 per cent, while the NGOs have facilitated 33 per cent, UNDP facilitated 9 per cent and the others 1 per cent of SHGs in our sample. Our sample groups are composed of poor assets. Their asset base is very slender. 82 per cent of households within our sample mandals possess assets worth Rs. 50,000 and below.

We summarize the findings of our empirical investigation and the statistical computations with regard to

Table 8.2 Income and Employment Generation and Capacity Building

Sl. No.	Characteristics	Kurnool Division		Nandyal Division		Adoni Division	
		Mean	SD	Mean	SD	Mean	SD
1.	Impact of Group Activity on net income generated (in '000 Rs)	3.80	2.13	3.80	2.42	3.83	2.80
2.	Employment generation (number of days in a year)	154.3	103.60	176.32	116.30	122.22	96.00

opportunities created for the unemployed women, greater the scope for the generation of additional income and overall development of the society.

SOCIAL MOBILISATION

Women members of DWCRA, SHGs as well as other groups are victims of subordination within and outside the household. They are deprived not only in terms of assets but also subjects of violence and atrocities in the domestic and social contexts. Gender gap and discrimination are more pronounced in the context of the hierarchical, patriarchical rural society with built-in gender bias against women. Individual efforts in such a context cannot succeed in overcoming the variety of social oppressions and economic deprivations and political marginalisation. Empowerment approach is the best strategy of fighting poverty in all its dimensions. More than economic empowerment self-confidence, awareness and group strength are to be inculcated by the facilitating agencies at the initial stages. The participatory approach is assumed to develop self-confidence, competence and managerial capacity. With reference to awareness, empowerment has deeper meanings not just an understanding of situation but an ability to act.

Empowerment of rural women would in real sense hasten the pace of economic development. Our sample SHGs have undertaken a variety of campaigns against social evils such as child marriage, alcoholism, dowry system, untouchability and participated in a variety of community development programmes ranging from sterilisation of the eligible couple to adult literacy. Access to public places, temples, drinking water wells and community functions is increasing and in the process, untouchability is apparently getting diluted. After joining the groups, the literacy and awareness of women increased and so they are now playing an important role in decision-making of their families. It is clear from our sample study that the decision-making power of women improved due to the enhanced economic status of women in the household economy. Similarly more efforts are being carried on by the group leaders in our study area to make effective control of birth rates. In the same way SHG women took various steps to improve the sanitation and hygiene in the villages. After joining in the SHGs, many women realized the importance of education and thereby encouraged child education and adult education. Thus women are trying to eradicate an age old social evils and all this was again possible because of their collective strength and enhanced awareness as a result of DWCRA and SHG movement.

Political empowerment is necessary for sustainable development of the SHGs as instruments of social mobilisation. The women who got elected as sarpanches and members of Mandal Praja Parishad and Zilla Parishad played a crucial role in the process of women's empowerment. They serve as a role model for other women. The State Government also through its various legislative and executive policies is making an attempt to empower women.

HOW CAN THE STRATEGY LEAD TO POVERTY ERADICATION

As discussed earlier, poverty consists of (a) economic poverty, (b) human poverty and (c) environmental poverty. Thus, it is important to understand as to how social mobilisation and empowerment of community can lead to eradication of all the three aspects of poverty.

The rural poor women organized on the platform of thrift and credit are able to access various anti-poverty government programmes like DWCRA, IRDP, funds from various government departments and bank loans directly. They are progressing from one step to another and are able to improve their economic status by proper utilisation of the funds. By forming into networks, they are able to access more resources and are confident of overcoming their economic poverty by various income generating activities being undertaken with these resources.

An organized, aware and empowered woman has realized the importance of various socio-developmental indicators like literacy, family planning, children's education, health, sanitation etc. The women are becoming literate, sending their children to schools, adopting small family norm and keeping their environment clean. They are making an attempt to see that at least their future generation does not suffer from capability deprivation.

The Government delivery system in key areas of health, public distribution system and education has failed to a certain extent primarily because of absence of demand from the local people. The delivery of services can be improved tremendously, if the demand for these services can be generated from those using them. The functioning of various departments has improved tremendously because of the keen interest shown by these women groups. The village level networks which are emerging can gradually take over several local functions of the government.

The encouraging response to the "Janmabhoomi Programme" launched by the previous Telugu Desam Party Government has raised a hope that an empowered community can solve their basic minimum needs themselves without middlemen provided government comes forward positively to solve their problems. The women groups have actively participated in the programme and have constructed roads, drains etc. They are also participating in watershed programmes and other wage employment programmes. Thus the involvement of an empowered community will go a long way in solving the basic minimum needs of the poor.

The above examples, in brief, show how the empowered community can handle all the poverty alleviation programmes. So one must be very clear that it is social mobilisation alone, which is the answer to the problem of poverty. However, one must also bear in mind that it is not the panacea for all the problems being faced by the poor. It will help in mobilisation of the poor and enable them to solve their problems themselves. The process of social mobilisation is indeed difficult and may not result in success everywhere, but one should realize that the present way of dealing with the problem of poverty will not result in success anywhere. So a beginning should be made somewhere. The Kurnool experience has shown that the Government can initiate and sustain large-scale programme that is based on social mobilisation. The centerpiece of a policy framework for poverty alleviation has to be mobilisation of the poor as social mobilisation and social mobilisation alone is the sine-quo-non for all development.

BEFORE SOCIAL MOBILISATION

Voiceless, assetless and powerless women caught in the triad of economic, human and environmental poverty.

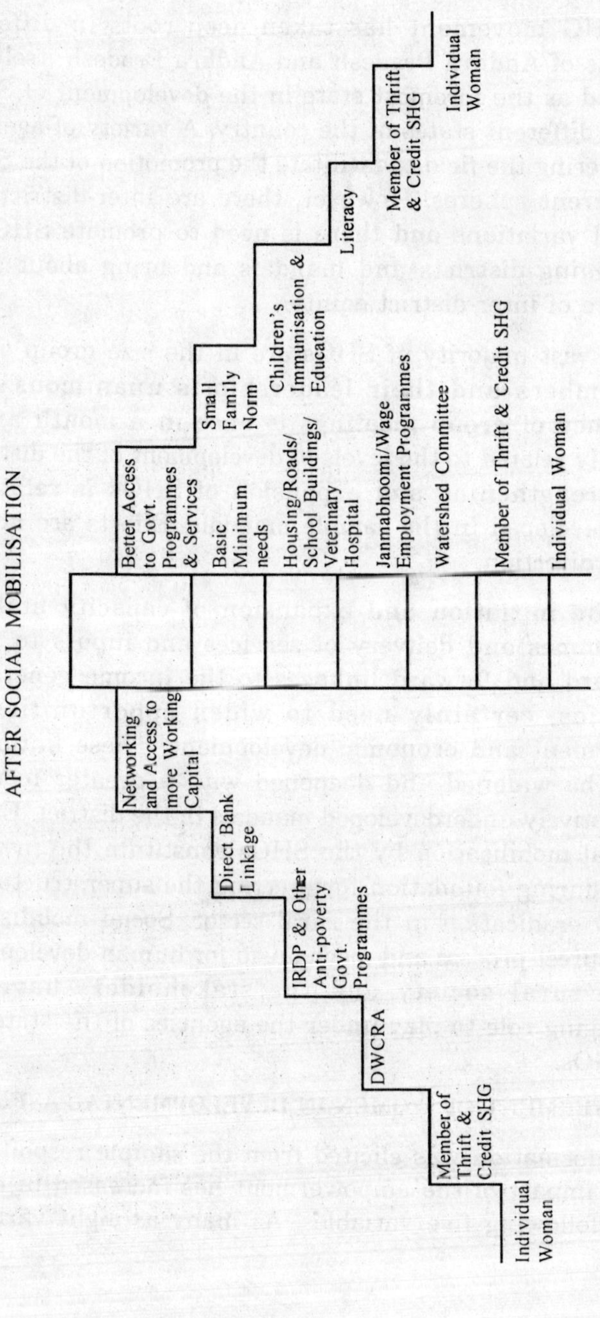

Women overcoming their poverty through Self-Help

POLICY IMPLICATIONS OF THE FINDINGS OF THE STUDY

SHG movement has taken deep roots in different districts of Andhra Pradesh and Andhra Pradesh itself has emerged as the foremost state in the development of SHGs among different states of the country. A variety of agencies are entering the field to facilitate the promotion of the SHGs in different spheres. However, there are inter-district and mandal variations and there is need to promote SHGs in the lagging districts and mandals and bring about some measure of inter-district equity.

A vast majority of SHGs are in the size group of 10-15 members and their leadership is unanimous. The frequency of group meetings is once in a month and is inversely related to the levels of development of the districts. The strengthening and expansion of SHGs is relatively underdeveloped in the sample mandals. Efforts are needed in this direction.

The initiation and expansion of capacity building programmes and delivery of services and inputs to forge backward and forward linkages to the income generating activities; certainly need to widen opportunities for employment and economic development. These initiatives are to be widened and deepened with a greater focus in the relatively underdeveloped mandals in the district. Efforts of social mobilisation by the SHGs constitute the invisible and enduring foundation for erecting the superstructure of poverty eradication in the rural sector. Social mobilisation is the surest process and mechanism for human development at the rural society and the stakeholders have the challenging role to play under the agencies of the state and the NGOs.

EMPOWERMENT OF WOMEN IN DEVELOPMENTAL ASPECTS

Information was elicited from the sample respondents on the impact of the empowerment has increased in terms of the following five variables. As many as eight variables were used for social development, seven variables for economic development, six variables were included in social empowerment, six variables for self-confidence and four variables for development of skills.

Table 8.3 Percentage Distribution of Member's Empowerment Regarding the Impact of Participation in Group Activities: Social Development

Sl. No.	Item	Kurnool Division		Nandyal Division		Adoni Division	
		SHG	DWCRA	SHG	DWCRA	SHG	DWCRA
	A. Social Development						
1.	Adoption of small family norm	44.75	38.68	43.25	38.75	45.25	39.58
2.	Discontinuation of early marriages	27.15	15.75	26.25	14.75	25.15	16.67
3.	Discontinued child labour	39.58	25.12	40.25	24.78	38.79	24.75
4.	Improvement in girl child education	74.25	52.20	75.00	52.08	73.75	50.55
5.	Improvement in children education	80.38	77.15	81.25	76.25	79.25	76.22
6.	Improvement in sanitation	85.62	46.25	84.56	47.23	85.15	46.00
7.	Improvement in personal hygiene	75.67	40.65	76.50	41.67	75.15	40.25
8.	Decrease in social inequality	58.42	20.05	58.25	21.72	59.15	20.33

Among SHGs, the social development is higher in the items like improvement in personal hygiene (75.77%), improvement in sanitation (85.11%), improvement in children education (80.29%) and improvement in girl child education (74.33%).

In case of economic development, there is a significant change in credit worthiness (95.02%), freedom from moneylenders (94.7%), increase in self-employment potential (81.96%), improvement in banking habits (81.19%), control over resources. All the seven variables in

Table 8.4 Percentage Distribution of Member's Empowerment Regarding the Impact of Participation in Group Activities: Economic Development

Sl. No.	*Item*	*Kurnool Division-I*		*Nandyal Division-II*		*Adoni Division-III*	
		SHG	*DWCRA*	*SHG*	*DWCRA*	*SHG*	*DWCRA*
1	*2*	*3*	*4*	*5*	*6*	*7*	*8*
	B. Economic Development						
1.	Control over resources	78,27	46.92	79.17	47.91	78.35	45.55
2.	Credit worthiness	95.15	63.58	94.58	64.15	95.33	63.75
3.	Freedom from moneylenders	94.25	81.55	95.75	82.00	94.15	80.55
4.	Improvement in banking habit	80.58	69.17	81.25	70.55	81.75	65.08
5.	Increase in self-employment potential	83.55	72.58	81.58	73.75	80.75	72.53
6.	Access to markets	46.92	39.75	47.15	38.55	47.25	37.65
7.	Increase in mobility	65.42	63.33	64.58	63.45	65.38	64.15
	C. Social Empowerment						
1.	Able to sign	32.25	12.50	31.50	13.25	31.25	12.25
2.	Aware of women's rights	42.75	27.08	42.00	26.55	41.25	26.75
3.	Awareness of property rights	43.25	22.92	42.75	23.90	42.50	21.75
4.	Improvement of status in the family	78.15	69.75	79.25	70.15	75.65	70.58
5.	Improvement of status in the group	90.17	75.25	91.25	76.75	92.55	78.56
6.	Improvement of status in the society	82.33	60.42	80.55	61.58	83.58	60.16
	D. Self Confidence						
1.	Awareness	84.25	58.25	85.42	60.56	83.75	59.75
2.	Increase of bargaining power	57.33	22.92	58.35	23.95	57.25	22.25
3.	Self confidence	94.25	83.33	93.58	82.56	92.75	81.56
4.	Access to information about government programme	78.75	66.75	77.25	65.55	73.25	63.28
5.	Participation in the development programme	92.15	83.33	91.58	84.00	90.75	82.15
6.	Able to meet government officials	80.25	81.15	80.75	80.58	81.75	82.55

(Contd...)

1	*2*	*3*	*4*	*5*	*6*	*7*	*8*
	E. Development of Skills						
1.	Productive skills	37.50	22.92	38.15	23.25	37.00	24.25
2.	Marketing skills	38.15	23.15	37.75	22.33	36.75	24.75
3.	Decision making improvement in the family	70.05	55.15	71.25	57.25	70.75	57.78
4.	Decision making improvement in the group	75.83	58.33	74.25	59.15	76.15	58.15
5.	Communication skills	55.08	38.50	54.68	37.15	51.25	38.25

economic development were higher for SHGs compared to DWCRA groups.

Regarding social empowerment, six items are covered, out of these six, three variables have a positive sign (more than 60 per cent) between SHG and DWCRA.

Self-confidence is examined with the help of six variables. Six variables show a significant impact on self-confidence among SHGs compared to DWCRA.

Development of skills is analysed through five variables. Across groups, DWCRA groups are lagging behind in all these aspects. The respondents of SHG as well as DWCRA reported that decision-making power has improved in the group and in the family and also in communication skills.

PROBLEMS OF WOMEN DEVELOPMENT WITH REFERENCE TO THE DWCRA/SHG APPROACH

An examination of the problems of women development with reference to financing women development programmes indicated that credit can play an important role in providing funds for developmental activities but unfortunately the women, particularly women belonging to weaker sections are facing several problems in securing such finance or credit to finance their productive economic activities.

- The complicated procedures of lending, higher rates of interest, inadequate dispersal of bank branches particularly in rural areas, provision of providing guarantees and securities for bank lending of money, failure to get further financial help from the bank if they do delay in repayment of loan. All such factors are restricting the women development and thereby to generate more and more income.

- A holistic approach to development was lacking on the part of the Government. Many of the departmental officers began to withdraw from the programme. There was no uniform procedure of selection of the groups with the result, lot of duplication took place.
- Women spend more income on her family than on herself. Cash in the hands of women often mean more nutrition and education for children. On this basis more emphasis is given to expand income generating schemes through bank credit. It was found that at the end of each plan, there has been substantial addition to the backlog of unemployment of women. The problem has been further aggravated by the increasing number of educated women.

SUGGESTIONS

In the light of the foregoing analysis the following measures are suggested for improving the functioning of the women devclopmont programmes and to achieve better results in general and for the proper and better use of the female labour force in particular:

1. The state has to take lead action in the form of enabling policies, provision of resources for the establishment of support mechanism which can multiply and monitor the process and monitor the devolution of powers and responsibilities to local communities and the poor. Social mobilisation and people's participation should be the key strategy of the government for poverty eradication. It should occupy the highest priority of the Government;
2. The process of empowerment of women at the political level has already begun, but it needs to be carried forward

into the social and economic spheres as well. Special emphasis would have to be placed on ensuring that control of social infrastructure in the public domain is vested in women and women's organisations;

3. The Government should formulate a "National Women's Empowerment Policy" by drawing various experts working in this field. Various interventions which are required at the macro and micro level should be worked out and suitable amendments can be carried out in existing laws, rules, regulations, procedures and Government orders which come in the way of poverty alleviation;

4. There is a need for more and better coordination between the Government and the NGOs working in this area. Both should be partners in development. The role of the Government and the NGOs has to be clearly defined and understood by both the partners. Both have their own advantages and limitations. The NGOs should not undertake specialized programmes which the Government is already undertaking eg., construction of houses, sanitary latrines, wasteland development etc. NGOs should concentrate on social mobilisation;

5. There should be a common set of guidelines for all the SHGs;

6. All the Government functionaries should be trained and sensitized on the processes involved in social mobilisation and community empowerment. There is a need to have a conceptual clarity amongst all Government officials regarding the approach to be followed. Similarly all the NGOs including their community volunteers should be exposed to social mobilisation process. The media which plays an important role should also be sensitized on the concept;

7. Continuous training, motivation and exposure of the community volunteers, network leaders, group leaders

and members is required to sustain the groups. A fixed annual training calendar should be designed by identifying proper training centres and resource persons. NIRD and SIRDs should draw up exclusive training programmes for social mobilisation and community empowerment;

8. Banks and implementing agency should take steps to avoid under financing and for verification of assets periodically. This type of verification helps the misuse of funds by the beneficiaries;
9. While selecting the groups, preference may be given to those groups, in which the members have crossed the eligible age limit to secure government jobs;
10. The rate of interest charged by commercial banks is considered very high therefore, it may be reduced for the benefit of the poor entrepreneurs;
11. The major problems of raw material shortage, lack of common work-shed, irregular marketing etc., need to be solved for the steady growth and successful functioning of the units;
12. A common work-shed can be provided to enable the women to keep their produce safely and also perform the work in groups which automatically raises the competitive spirit and ultimately production. The shed can also act as a market place;
13. If more and more financial, infrastructural and marketing facilities are given at the right time and place, these self employed units may become highly enterprising units;
14. Preference should be given to the literate women in the training programme. The Government should take various steps to promote women education, training and skill especially women of lower strata of the society;
15. To improve the economic status of women and to bring them into mainstream of national development a

combination of multiple policy strategies to be adopted such as (a) Boosting of productivity in women's work, (b) expansion of women's employment opportunities, (c) raising of income levels in women's jobs and (d) mobilisation of women into participatory groups;

16. The rural women should be helped to get into non-traditional activities through the provision of credit facilities and entrepreneurial skill development programmes;
17. More training centres should be established with marketing links;
18. Delays should be avoided at every stage;
19. Continuous follow-up should be exercised to monitor the programme and to help them wherever necessary;
20. A women's forum should be formed to discuss the SHG activities;
21. Due to the efforts of governmental and non-governmental agencies, SHGs have become a major movement particularly among women. Such movement by and large, is restricted to certain pockets of the country. Therefore, there is an urgent need both at governmental and non-governmental levels to activate this movement and spread it in different parts of the country where the poor are largely concentrated;
22. The group members should be properly guided about the maintenance of accounts and investment;
23. More emphasis should be laid upon capacity building and skill development of the group members;
24. Groups should be formed on the basis of inherent binding force already prevailing among the members;
25. Heterogeneous groups tend to break away in the long-run, hence, the groups should be as homogeneous as possible. The most important factor is commonness of

issue/problem or interest. If groups are formed around a common interest, self-help groups are called 'Interest groups.' Interest groups tend to be more sustainable than merely credit groups;

26. Steps shall be taken to see that group functioning should be democratic, otherwise non-participating members might distance themselves away from the groups;
27. There should be rotation of group leadership so that all members of the group get an opportunity to play managerial role. In case of constant leadership in the same person, it will have concentration of power in a very few persons which is potential danger for the group;
28. The government should recognize the groups as suitable platform for dissemination of knowledge or information;
29. The government will have to consider the groups as a two-way link between villagers/people and it;
30. Efforts should be made to provide economic independence which leads to the increase in the status of women, consequently that should help in decreasing frequency of child marriages;
31. Multipurpose training centres in rural and urban areas would provide a self-reliant approach to life;
32. Women are not only users but also providers of health care, so they have to be fully informed and become active participants in health planning and decision-making process at all levels;
33. Rural industrial products, handicrafts by women should be promoted and supported by adequate marketing arrangements;
34. Encouragement of co-operative ventures will promote and secure greater female participation at all levels.

At present, the climate in India is ripe for promoting the economic status of women. It is widely believed that with the growth of education and communication, opening up of new employment opportunities, Indian women will move steadily towards more equal status with men.

Women is the pivot of a family around which revolve the whole activities of men and children. She is responsible for a family's happiness, health and prosperity. So how can a nation ignore her existence? She should be treated with equality of opportunities and it is the sole responsibility of the government to protect her interests in the wake of liberalisation.

The above analysis leads to the conclusion that the quotation given by Swami Vivekananda is true.

> "Just as a bird could not fly with one wing only,
> a nation would not march forward, if the women
> are left behind."

REFERENCES

1. Ch.Appa Rao, 'Women Empowerment Through SHG and DWCRA—A Study in Andhra Pradesh,' *Indian Journal of Regional Science,* Vol.XXXV, No. 1, 2003.
2. K.P.Kumaran, 'SHGs of the Rural Poor in India: An Analysis.' *Journal of Rural Reconstruction,* Vol. 32, July-Dec. 1999, No. 2.
3. Agarwal, Binu (1918), A Field of One's Own: Gender and Land Rights in South Asia, Cambridge, *Cambridge University Press.*

Bibliography

BOOKS

Awasti, D.S. "Role of Women in Economic Development," Kanpur, Indian Economic Association.

Awasti, S.K. "Economic Development and Planning in Retrospect," *Vikas Publishing House Pvt. Ltd,* New Delhi, 1983.

Ahluwalia Montek, S. (1985), "Rural Poverty, Agricultural Production and Prices: A Re-examination in John Mellor and Desai Gunvant, M. (eds), "Agricultural Changes and Rural Poverty," *The John Hopkins University Press,* London.

Appadorai, A. "Status of Women in South Asia," *Orient Languages Ltd,* Calcutta, 1954.

Asthana Prathima, "Women's Moment in India," *Vikas Publishing House,* New Delhi, 1974.

Ajit Mazumdas, "Problems of Unemployment in India," 1997.

Ashok, K.Arora. "Financing of Small-Scale Industries," *Deep & Deep Publications,* 1992.

Ashok Mitra, Lalit Pathak, Shekar Mukherji, "The Status of Women Shifts in Occupational Participation," *Abhinav Publications,* 1980.

Arun Kumar, "Social Characteristics of Working Women," *Sarup and Sons Publishers,* New Delhi.

Beard, Mary, R. "Women as Force in History: A Study in Traditions and. Realities," *The Macmillan Company,* New York, 1946.

Boser Up, E. "Women's Role in Economic Development," George Allen, London, 1970.

Bela Rani Sharma and Raj Pusti, "Encyclopaedia of Women Society and Culture Series—Post Independence India and Women," *Anmol Publications Private Ltd,* New Delhi.

Betellei, A. "Chronicles of Overtime, *Penguin Books,* New Delhi, 2000.

Chakaravarthy Sukamay, "Development Planning: The Indian Experience," *Oxford University Press,* New Delhi, 1989.

Charsely, S.R. and G.K.Karanth, "Challenging Untouchability, Dalit Initiative and Experience from Karnataka," *Sage Publications,* New Delhi, 1998.

Carr, Mary et al., "Speaking Out, Women's Economic Empowerment in South Asia," *Vikas Publications,* New Delhi.

Dantwala, M.L. "Dilemmas of Growth: The Indian Experience," *Sagar Publications,* New Delhi, 1996.

Desai, Deera, "Women in Modern India," Vora Anand Company, Bombay, 1959.

Desai, A.P., "Essays on Modernisation of Under-developed Society," Thzekar and Company Limited, Vol. I & II, 1971.

Dinakar Rao, K. "Women's Development: Linkages for Credit," New Delhi.

Desai, B.M. and N.V.Namboodiri, "Rural Financial Institutions: Promotion and Performance," *Oxford and IBH Publishing Company Pvt. Ltd,* New Delhi.

Desai, S.S.M, "Rural Banking in India," *Himalaya Publishing House,* Bombay, 1983.

Delige, R, "The Untouchables of India," Berg, New York, 1999.

Dev, S. Mahendra, "State Interventions and Women's Employment," in T.S.Papola and Alakh N.Sharma (Eds), "Gender and Employment in India," *Vikas Publishing House Pvt. Ltd,* New Delhi, 1999.

Dharm Narain and Sen, A.K. et al, "Studies on Indian Agriculture, *Oxford University Press,* New Delhi, 1989.

Engles, E. "The Origin of the Family, Private Property and State," Reprinted by *Progress Publishers,* Marlow, 1994.

Frencine Fournier, "Foreword, Poverty and Participation in Civil Society," Edited by Yogesh Atal of Else' Oyen, *Abhinav Publications,* New Delhi, 1997.

Gandhi, M.K. "To the Women," Anand T. Hingorani, Karachi, Bharatiya Vidya Bhavan, Bombay.

Gandhi, M.K. "Role of Women and Social Justice," *Navjeevan Publishing House,* Ahmedabad, 1958.

Gunner Myrdal, "Economic Theory and Underdeveloped Regions," Vora and Company, Bombay, 1958.

Gunner Myrdal, "Asian Drama—An Enquiry into Poverty of Nations," Pantheon, New York.

Gunner Myrdal, "The Challenge of World Poverty: A World Anti-Poverty Programme in Outline," Pantheon, New York, 1970.

Ghosh, S.K., "Women in a Changing Society," *Ashish Publishing House,* New Delhi, 1984.

Gupta, D. "Interrogating Caste: Understanding Hierarchy and Difference in Indian Society," *Penguin Books,* New Delhi, 2000.

Griffin, "The Political Economy of Agrarian Change," *The Macmillan Press Ltd,* London, 1979.

Griffin Keith, "International Inequality and National Poverty," *The Macmillan Press Ltd,* London, 1978.

Griffin Keith, "Land Concentration and Rural Poverty," *The Macmillan Press Ltd,* Hongkong, 1981.

Haleh Afshar, "Women, Work and Ideology in the Third World," Tavistock Pup, London and New York, 1985.

Hathi, J.L., "Problems of Unemployment in India," 1974.

Harper, M. "Profit for the Poor," *Oxford and IBH Publishing Co.,* Delhi, 1998.

Haq, Mahabub Ul, "The Poverty Curtain: Choices for the Third World," *Oxford University Press,* Bombay, 1978.

Haq, Mahabub Ul, "Human Development in South Asia," *Oxford University Press,* New York, 1997.

Heggade, Odeyar, D., "Women and Economic Development: A Study of the Different Facets of Their Role in 'India," *Ramya Roopa Prakashan,* Bangalore, 1984.

Holcombe, Susan, "Managing to Empower: The Grameen Bank's Experience of Poverty Alleviation," *Oxford University Press,* Dhaka, 1995.

IFMR, "An Economic Assessment of Poverty Eradication and Rural Unemployment Alleviation Programme and Their Prospects," Madras, 1984.

Jackson Dudley, "Poverty, Macmillan Studies in Economics," *Macmillan,* London, 1972.

Jain Devaki, "Indian Women," Ministry of Information and Broadcasting, Government of India, 1975.

Jawaharlal Nehru, "Women of India," The Director, Publications Division, Ministry of Information and Broadcasting, Government of India, Delhi, 1958.

Jaya Kumar G.Stanley, "Status of Women in Male Dominated Society," *ISSR Publishers,* Vellore, 1992.

Kamatha Prasad, "Planning for Poverty Alleviation," *Publishing Academy* 208, Defence Colony, New Delhi.

Kalbagh, C, "Women in Enterprise and Profession," *Discovery Publishing House,* New Delhi.

Karmakar, K.G. "Rural Credit and Self-Help Groups, Micro-Finance Needs and Concepts in India," *Sage Publications,* New Delhi, 1999.

Lalitha, N, "Rural Women: Empowerment and Development Banking," *Kaniska Publishers,* New Delhi.

Kaushik Dasu, "The Development Economy: A Critique of Contemporary Theory," *Oxford University Press,* Delhi, 1984.

Kuznets, S. "Economic Growth and Structure," Heinemann, London, 1965.

Lewis, A, "Development Planning," Allen & Unwin, London, 1966

Mahajan, V.S., "Women's Contribution to India's Economic and Social Development," *Deep & Deep Publications,* New Delhi.

Maheswari, S.R, "Rural Development in India," *Sage Publications,* Delhi, 1985.

Minhas, R.S. "Planning and the Poor," *S. Chand & Company Limited,* New Delhi, 1974.

Mukta Mittal, "Women Power in India," *Anmol Publications Pvt. Ltd,* New Delhi, 1995.

Myrdal Gunner, "Asian Drama," Volume III, Twentieth Century Fund, New York, 1968.

Manohar and Murali, "Socio-economic Status of Indian Women," *Seema Publications,* Delhi, 1983.

Murthy, S. and Gaur, K.D. "Women Work Participation and Empowerment: Problems and Prospects," *RBSA Publishers*, Jaipur.

NABARD, "NABARD and Micro-Finance," Mumbai, 1999-2000.

NCERT, "Human Development in South India," *Oxford*, New Delhi, 2000.

Nanda, Y.C. "Role of Banks in Rural Development . in the New Millennium, National Bank for 'Agriculture and' Rural Development, Mumbai, 2000.

Padmini Sen Gupta, "Women in India," Information Services' of India, New Delhi, 1964.

Pandya, B.A., "Women Organisations and Development, *Illustrated Books Publishers*, Jaipur, 1994.

Parthasarathy, G. "Integrated Rural Development Concepts: Theoretical Base and Contradiction in Development Planning and Policy," edited by Gupta, D.B., et al., Wiley Eastern, New Delhi, 1982.

Pigou, A.C. "The Economics of Welfare," *Macmillan & Co. Ltd*, London, 1960.

Rai and Tandon, "Voluntary Development Organisation and Socio-Economic Development," Indian, Economic Association, 82nd Conference Volume, Amritsar, 1999.

Romy Borooah, "An Inter-disciplinary Look at Women, Households and Development," Edited by Romy Borooah and Others," *Sage Publications*, New Delhi, 1994.

Sapru, R.K. "Women and Development," *Ashish Publication*, New Delhi, 1989.

Sahai, "Women in a Changing Society," *Mittal Publications*, New Delhi, 1985.

Sakuntala Narasimhan, "Empowering Women: An Alternative for Strategy from Rural India," *Sage Publications*, New Delhi, 1999.

Sen, A.K. "Poverty and Famines: An Essay on Entitlement and Deprivation," *Oxford University Press*, Delhi, 1984.

Todaro Michael, P. "Economics for a Developing World," *Longmans* London, 1977.

Todaro Michael, "Economics for a Developing World," Second Edition, *Longman,* New York.

Tokli, M.R. and Sharma, D.P., "Rural Banking in India," *Oxford & IBH Publishing Company,* New Delhi.

Thakur, R.N. "Education and Political Status of Indian Women: Key to Economic Development," Women and Economic Development, A. Banerjee and R.K.Sen (ed). 2000.

United Nations Development Fund for "Women—An End to Debt: Operational Guidelines for Credit Projects," UNLHEM, New York, 1993.

Venkata Reddy, K. "Rural Development in India," *Himalaya Publishing House,* Bombay, 1988.

Vasanth Desai, "Indian Banking Nature and Problems," *Himalaya Publishing House,* Bombay.

Von Pischke J.D. et al, "Rural Financial Markets in Developing Countries: Their Use and Abuse," John Hopkins University, Baltimore, USA, 1983.

Yogesh Atal, "Poverty and Participation in Civil Society," *Abhinav Publications,* New Delhi.

Zweig, F. "Women's Life and Labour," Victor Gollanz, London, 1952.

JOURNALS

Aggarwal, P. 'Role of Women in Socio-Economic Development," *Social Welfare,* March, 1987.

Aziz Wahida, 'The Place of Women in National Life,' *Social Welfare,* Vol. IX, No. 24, March 23, 1945.

Awasthi, P.K. et al., 'IRDP: Receptivity and Reaction,' *Indian Journal of Agricultural Economics,* Vol. 41, No. 4, October-December.

Arunachalam, Jaya and Azad Nandini, 'Role of Women and Children in the Informal Sector,' *Productivity,* 26 (3), 1985 (Oct-Dec.)

Aggarwal, Deepti, 'Empowerment of Rural. Women,' *Intensive Agriculture* 39(1-2), 2001 (March-April): 3-5.

Amod Kumar, 'Towards Women's Empowerment: The Equation of Education and Economics,' *Women's Link,* 6(3), 2000 (Jul-Sept): 15-19.

Azim, Shaukath, 'Gender Empowerment: Where Does India Stand?' *Social Welfare,* 48(2), 2001 (May): 9-11.

Barik, B.B. and Vannan, P.P, 'Promoting Self-Help Groups: As Sub-System of Credit Cooperatives,' *Cooperator,* 38(7) 2001 (January): 305-312.

Berger, Marguerite, 'Giving Women Credit: The Strengthens and Limitations of Credit as a Tool for Alternating Poverty,' *World Development,* 17(7), 1989 July.

Behra, L, 'Success Story: Self Help Groups in Sati (Orissa) Making Rapid Progress,' *Cooperator,* 34(1), 1996 (July): 18.

Bagchee Sandeep, 'Poverty Alleviation Programmes in Seventh Plan: An Appraisal,' *Economic and Political Weekly,* Vol. XXII, No. 4, January 24, 1987.

Bardhan, P.K. 'On the Incidence of Poverty in Rural India of the Sixties,' *Economic and Political Weekly,* Feb 1973.

Copertake James, G. 'The Resilience of IRDP: Reform and Perpetuation of an Indian Myth,' *Development Policy Review,* 1996, 14.

Dhar, Gauri, 'DWCRA Programme in Andhra Pradesh, *Gramin Vikas Newsletter,* January 1985.

Dighe, Anitha, 'Women's Employment in the Urban Informal Sector: Some Critical Issues,' *Social Change,* 15(2), June 1996.

Deshmukh Durga Bai, 'New Dimensions of Women's Life in India,' *Social Welfare,* Vol. III, No. 9, Dec. 1956.

Dantwala, M.L. 'Rural Development: Investment Without Organisation,' *Economic and Political Weekly,* 1983.

Desai, A.R. 'Rural Development and Human Rights in Independent India,' *Economic and Political Weekly,* Vol.XXII, No. 31, 1987.

Datta, Rekha. 'On Their Own: Development Strategies of the Self-Employed Women's Association (SEWA) in India, *Development* (43(4), 2000 (Dec): 51-55.

Devasia, Leelamma, 'Rural Women's Empowerment: A Grassroot Level Experiment,' *Social Welfare,* 48(4), 2001 (July): 5-10.

Empowerment of Rural Women—A New Dimension, *Monthly Public Opinion Surveys* 47(3),'2001 (December) 4-6.

Everett, Jana and Savara, Mira. "Bank Loans to. the Poor in Bombay: Women Benefit, *SIGNS,* 10(2), 1984 (Winter), 272-290.

Gartner, Audrey, 'Professionals and Self-Help: The Uses of Creative Tension,' *Social* Policy, 27(3), 1997 (Spring), 47-51.

Ghosh, D.K. 'Group Cohesiveness in DWCRA Groups: An Application of Sociometric Approach;' *Kurukshetra,* May-June, 1995.

Ghosh, D.K. 'DWCRA: Programme and Its Impact,' *Gramin Vikas Newsletter,* 1993 (Aug.-Sept).

Gupta, K.N. 'Women's Empowerment and Protection of Their Rights,' *Social Welfare,* 47 (12), 2001 (March): 22-28.

Harper, Malcolm, 'Self-Help Groups: Some Issues from India,' *Small Enterprise Development* 7(2), 1995 (June): 36-41.

Hassan, Abul, 'Self-Help Groups and Access to Rural Credit,' *Cooperator,* 34(6), 1996 (Dec): 237.

Humphreys, Keith, 'Individual and Social Benefits of Mutual Aid/ Self-Help Groups: A Summary of Data on the Effectiveness of Self Help Groups,' *Social Policy,* 27(3), 1997 (Spring): 12-19.

Haskar, Nandita, Draft Perspective Plan for Women, *Mainstream,* 26(38), 1988 (July 2).

Haque, Farhana, 'A Loan to a Woman—A Direct Way to Address Poverty,' *CERES,* 21(1), 1988 (Jan-Feb): 27-31.

Hara Gopal, G. and Balaramulu, Ch. 'Poverty Alleviation Programmes: IRDP in an Andhra Pradesh District, *Economic and Political Weekly,* Vol.XXIV, Nos. 35 & 36, Sep. 2-9.

lyengar, Ashok, K. 'Credit Facilities for Rural Women,' *Social Welfare,* 29(9), 1982 (Dec.)

Jain, S.C. 'Poverty Alleviation Programmes in India: Some Issues of Micro *Policy,' Indian Journal of Agricultural Economics,* Vol.XLI, No. 3, Conference Number, July-Sept. 1986.

Jain, A.K. and P.K. Bhargava, 'Role of Women in Economic Development: The Case of Women Workers in India,' *The Indian Journal of Economics,* April 1989, p.440.

Joshi, Soneha, and Pushpanadham, K. 'Empowering Women for Educational Management,' *University News,* 39(4), 2001 (Jan): 4-7.

Jessintha, N. 'APSSS and Women's Development,' *Caritas India,* 4, 1985 (Oct-Dec.): 21-25 & 46.

Jose, A.M. 'IRDP and Employment Generation for Women: A Micro-Level Study in Kerala,' *Man and Development,* 11(2), 1989 (June).

Kabeer, N. 'Conflicts over Credit: Re-evaluating the Empowerment Potential of Loans to Women in Rural Bangladesh,' *World Development,* 29(l),2001 (Jan): 63-84.

Kulkarni, D.Vijay, 'Empowerment of Women Through Self-Help Groups,' *Janata,* 56(23), 2001 (Aug): 12-15.

Kulshrestha, R. Laxmi and Gupta, Archana, 'Self-Help Groups: Innovations in Financing the Poor,' *Kurukshetra,* 2001 (Nov.): 26-29.

Kumaran, K.P. 'Self-Help Groups: An Alternative to Institutional Credit to the Poor: Case Study in Andhra Pradesh,' *Journal of Rural Development,* 16(3), 1997 (July-Sept.): 515-530.

Kalpagam, U, 'Women, Informal Sector and Perspectives on Struggles,' *Social Scientist;* 15(6), 1987 (June) 33-44.

Kabir, M. and Others. 'Participation of Women in Cooperative Programmes, Economic Activity, Social Change and Family Planning,' *Social Action,* 37(2), 1987 (April-June): 163-173.

Kumar Rajinder, et al 'Impact of Credit on Income Employment and Capital Formulation of Rural Poor,' *Indian Journal of Agricultural Economics,* Vol. 41, No. 4, Oct-Dec. 1986.

Kallur, M.S. 'Empowerment of Women Through NGOs: A Case Study of MYRADA Self-Help' Groups,' *Indian Journal* of *Agricultural Economics,* Vo1. 41, No. 4, Oct-Dec, 2001.

Lakshmikanthan, K.R. 'Self Help Groups in the Life of Rural Poor: A Pilibhit Case Study,' *Women's Link,* 6(2), 2000 (Apr-June): 10-16.

Launch of Certificate Programme on Empowering "Women Through Self Help Groups, *Social Welfare,* 47(7), 2000 (Oct.): 30-31.

Levy, Leon, H. 'Self-Help Groups: Types and Psychological Processes,' *Journal of Applied Behavioural Science,* 12(3), 1996 (JulyAug-Sep), 310-322.

Lokayan, 'Workshop on Empowerment of Women in Household Space,' *Women's Link,* 6(4), 2000 (Oct-Dec): 46-48.

Mohanan, S. 'Micro Credit and Empowerment of Women—Role of NGOs,' *Yojana,* 44(2), 2000 (Feb): 21-23.

Lalit Kumar Tyagi, 'Poverty Eradication Through Self Help Promotion,' *IASSI Quarterly,* Vol. 18, No. 1, 1999.

Murugan, K.R. and Dharmalingam, B, 'Self-Help Groups: New Women's Movement in Tamilnadu,' *Social Welfare,* 47(5), 2000 (Aug): 9-12.

Madeley, John, 'Hill Women of Nepal Take the Credit, *'Development and Cooperation,* 4, 1991: 16-17.

Mohammadi, Pari, 'Women in National Planning: False Expectations,' *Development,* 4, 1984: 80-81.

Mohiuddin, Asghari and Others, 'Evaluation of Preparedness Status of State Governments for Implementation of DWCRA Programme in the Field,' *National Bank News Review,* 4(1), 1988 (March): 29-32.

Marina Rinta, 'Development Through Empowerment of Women in India,' *Kurukshetra,* August 1995.

Narayan Reddy, G, 'Integrated Approach to Women's Development and Health Delivery Systems in Rural Areas, NIRD Experiences,' *Journal of Rural Development,'* September 1992.

Naib, V.P, 'Self-Help Groups in Rural Development,' *Panchayat Aur Insan,* 6 & 7 (12&1), 1995 (March & April): 5-6.

Nanda, Y.C. 'Linking Banks and Self-Help Groups in India and the Role of NGOs: Lessons Learned and Future Perspectives,' *National Bank News Review,* 15(3), 1999 (Jul-Sep): 1-9.

Narayanswamy, R. and Roy, A.K, 'Women Empowerment Through Cooperatives: A Case Study of Mahila Vikasa in Andhra Pradesh,' *Cooperative Perspective,* 34(5), 2000 (Jan-Mar): 63-68.

Ojha, R.K. 'Self-Help Groups and Rural Employment,' *Yojana,* 45(5), 2001 (May): 20-23.

Owusu, K. Opoku and William Tetteh, 'An Experiment in-Agricultural Credit: The Small Farmer Group Lending Programme in Ghana,' *Savings and Development,* Vol. 1, No.1, 1982.

Patel, I.G., 'Promotion of Credit to Women Entrepreneurs,' *Reserve Bank of Indian Bulletin,* 1981. Dec. 35(12): 1059-1064.

Patel, A.R, 'Entrepreneurship and Small Business Development for Women,' *Kurukshetra,* August 1995.

Rajeswari, G. and Manimekalai, N. 'Empowerment of Women Through Self-Help Groups (SHGs), *Margin,* 32(4), 2000 (Jul-Sept): 74-87.

Ramesh, Ashwini, 'Self-Help Groups and Small Village Co-operatives for Rural Development: A Critical Perspective Vision,' *Indian Cooperative Review,* 18(1), 2000 (July): 30-37.

Ramesh, Ashwini, 'Why Self-Help Groups and Why Not the Village Cooperatives for Rural Development: A Critical Perspective Vision,' *Cooperative Perspective,* 35(3), 2000 (Oct.Dec): 30-35.

Rani, T. Usha and Others, 'Role of Women in Dairy Development—A Case Study,' *Yojana,* 35(16), 1991 (Sep.15): 26.

Role of Women Central to Population and Development Issues, *Asian-Pacific Population. Programme News,* 11 (1&2), 1982 (Quarterly): 11-13.

Ranjan Kackar, 'DWCRA—Andhra Women March Towards Employment,' *Gramin Vikas Newsletter,* July 1995.

Raka Gupta and Bipin Kumar Gupta,. 'Role of Women in Economic Development,' *Yojana,* August 1987.

Rajaram Das Gupta, 'Working and Impact of Rural Self-Help Groups and Other Forms of Micro Financing,' *Indian Journal of Agricultural Economics,* Vol. 56, No. 3, 2001.

Satyanarayana Reddy and Renuka, 'DWCRA: A Boon for Rural Women,' *Yojana,* 1994 (Dec.).

Sadeque, Syed. 'The Rural Financial Market and the Grameen Bank Project in Bangladesh—An Experiment in Involving Poor and Women in Institutional Credit Operations,' *Savings and Development,* 2, 1986, 181-196.

Sivaram Reddy, C, 'Development of Women and Children in Rural Areas—An Appraisal,' *Kurukshetra,* 1988, February.

Satya Sundaram, 1, 'Education and Empowerment of Village Women'.

Scheyvens, Regina and Leslie, Helen, 'Gender, Ethics and Empowerment: Dilemmas of Development Fieldwork,' *Women's Studies International Forum,* 23(1), 2000 (Jan-Feb): 119-130.

Sengupta Milanjan, 'Empowerment: A Socio-psychological Approach to Self Help Group Formation,' *Prajnan,* 26(4), 1998 (Jan-March): 523-534.

Sharma, S.L. 'Empowerment Without Antagonism: A Case for Reformulation of Women's Empowerment Approach,' *Sociology Bulletin,* 49(1), 2000 (March): 19-40.

Singh Mor, D.P, "Issues and Initiatives in Women's Empowerment, *Social Welfare,* 48(6), 2001 (Sep): 22-27.

Singh, J.P, "Indian Democracy and Empowerment of Women," *Indian Journal of Public Administration* 46(4) 2000 (Oct-Dec) 601-616.

Singh Sukhpal, "Self Help Groups in Indian Agri-business: Reflections from Case Studies, *Artha Vijnana,* 37(4), 1995 (Dec): 380-388.

Srinivasan, N, "Why Self Help Groups: Borrower's Point of View," *National Bank News Review,* 12(1), 1996 (Jan-Mar): 18-19.

Suguna, B, "Women's Empowerment: Concept and Framework," *Social Welfare,* 48(9) 2001 (Dec): 3-7.

Surikanthi A, "Literacy: Essential for SHGs," *Social Welfare,* 47(6), 2000 (Sep): 32-34.

Saibaba G, "Pattern and Problem of Women Employment," *Eastern Economist,* Vol. 65 No. 1,. July 4 No. l and 2, 1975, New Delhi.

Thakurela, S.K, "DWCRA and Credit for Women," *Gramin Vikas News Letters,* 1993 (Oct-Nov).

Thangamuthu, C and Manimekalai N, "Generation of Employment for Women Through DWCRA, *Journal of Rural Development.*

Tyagi, Ombeer Singh, "Women's 'Empowerment: A Micro Perspective, *Women's Link,* 6(1), 2000 (Jan-Mar): 37-39.

Thakur, D.S, 'Rural Development in India: Past Experience and Tasks Ahead,' *Indian Journal of Agricultural Economics,* Vol XXXII, No. 3 July-Sep. 1977.

Usha Rao, N.J, "Development Strategy for Scheduled Castes, Scheduled Tribes and Women in Karnataka's Seventh Plan: Some Perspectives.

Uma Joshi, "Rural Women: A More Purposeful Role, *Kurukshetra,* August 1997 p. 94.

Verma, G.L, "Women Beneficiaries and IRDP,' *Journal of Rural Development,* 1986 July.

Vajpaye, A.B, Women's Empowerment Year "Give Women the Freedom of Choice," *Social Welfare,* 47(11), 2001 (Feb): 5-12.

Venkata Ravi and Venkataramana, M, 'Self Help Among Scheduled Caste Women, *Indian Economic Panorama,* 9(4), 2000 (Jan): 36-42.

Venkata Subramanian, K "Women Empowerment,' *University News,* 39(42), 2001 (Oct) 14-17.

Viswanathan, K.S, 'Self' Help Groups—Their Role in Irrigation Development and Management,' *National Bank News Review,* 81 (11-12) 1993 (Jan-Feb) 36-37.

Wickrama K.A.A and Keith, Pat. M, 'Savings and Credit: Womens' Informal Groups as Model for Change in Developing Countries,' *Journal of Developing Areas,* 1994 April.

Wadhwa, Subhash, C, "Self Help Groups for Reaching the Poor,' *Financing Agriculture,* 27(3), 1995 (July-Sep): 4-12.

Yaron. J, "Successful Rural Finance Institutions. World Bank Discussion Paper, 150, Washington, D.C. USA, 1997.

REPORTS

APDPIP, on Andhra Pradesh, District Poverty Initiatives Project Appraisal Document (PAD). Report No. 20089 South Asia Regional Office, 2000.

Chief Planning Officer, Handbook of Statistics. 1993-94, Kurnool District.

CIRDAP, Increased Household Income and Rural Women in Asia, Impact on Status and Activities, Dhaka, Bangladesh, 1998.

CIRDAP, Poverty, Gender and Participation, Dhaka, 1998.

CIRDAP, Rural Development Report, Center on Integrated Rural Development for Asia and Pacific, Dhaka, 1999.

Government of Andhra Pradesh, Annual Report of the Commission of the Rural Development, Hyderabad, 1998.

Government of Andhra Pradesh, Annual Report of the Commission of the Rural Development, Hyderabad, 1999.

Government of Andhra Pradesh, Provisional Population Totals, Series 29, Hyderabad, 2001.

Government of Andhra Pradesh, Statistical Abstract, Hyderabad, 2001.

Government of India, Census of India, Registrar General, New Delhi, India, 1991.

Government of India, Seventh Five Year Plan, New Delhi, 1985-90.

Government of India, Eighth Five Year Plan, New Delhi, 1990-95.

Government of India, Ninth Five Year Plan, New Delhi, 1997-2002.

Government of India, Provisional Population Totals, New Delhi, 2001.

Government of India, Towards Equality Committee on the Status of Women in India, 1974.

Government of India, Tenth Five Year Plan, Planning Commission, New Delhi, (2002-2007).

Government of Andhra Pradesh, Vision-2020, Hyderabad, India, 1999.

Government of Andhra Pradesh, Strategy Paper, 2001.

IFAD, The State of World Poverty, Rome for a Discussion on the Process and Structural Causes of Poverty, See Rovert Chambers (1983), Rural Development, Putting the Last First, London, Longmans One of the Best Discussions on How These Perpetuate Poverty, 1996.

IFAD, "Rural Poverty Report, The Challenge of Ending Rural Poverty," *Oxford,* New York, 2001.

International Fund for Agricultural Development .(IFAD), "The State World Rural Poverty—An Inquiry Into Its Causes and Consequences, New York University Press, New York.

NABARD, Annual Report, Mumbai, 1999.

NABARD, Annual Report, Mumbai, 2000.

NABARD, Annual Report, Mumbai, 2001.

NIRD, Rural Development Report; Rural Employment, Hyderabad, Andhra Pradesh, 1994.

NIRD, National Conference on SHG Movement in the Country and Swarnajayanti Gram Swarozgar Yojana (SGSY), National Institute of Rural Development, Hyderabad, Andhra Pradesh, 2001.

South Asian Association for Regional Cooperation (SAARC), The Independent Source Asian Commissions of the SAARC on Poverty Alleviation, Dhaka, 1992.

South Asian Association for Regional Cooperation (SAARC), Meeting the Challenge, Report of the Independent South Asian Commission on Poverty, 1992.

The World Bank, World Development Report, *Oxford,* New York, 1990.

The World Bank, Gender and Poverty in India, Washington DC, 1991.

The World Bank, World Development Report 1999-2000, *Oxford University Press,* New York.

The Hindu, April 27, Chennai, 2002.

The Hindu, Vision-2020, 2002.

UNDP, Human Development Report, *Oxford,* New York, 1994.

UNDP, Human Development Report, *Oxford,* New York, 1996.

UNDP, Human Development Report, *Oxford,* New York, 1997.

UNDP, Human Development Report. *Oxford,* New York, 2000.

OTHERS

Government of India, Report of the Committee on the Status of Women in India, Ministry of Education and Social Welfare, New Delhi, 1974.

Government of India, Fourth World Conference on Women, Beijing, 1995, Country Report, Department of Women and Child Development, Ministry of Human Resources Development.

APDPIP, on Andhra Pradesh District Poverty Initiatives Project Appraisal Document (PAD), Report No. 20089, South Asia, Regional Office, 2000.

The Hindu, April 22, Sunday 2002.

The Hindu, Vision 2020, [illegible].

Index

A

Activities, 23
Analysis of data, 17
Andhra Pradesh, 77
Annual Plans 1990-1992, 36
ANP, 26

B

Bank (facilitating agency), 112
Bank-NGO-MFI-SHG, 112
Bank-SHG-member, 112

C

Capacity building, 158-189
Contribution of women, 5
CSWB, 24

D

Design and methodology of study, 253
Design and methodology of the study, 252
Development Commissioners, 25
Developmental policies, 4
DWCRA, 29, 37, 246
  background for the origin if SHGs, 94-95
  basic problems, 87-90
  case for SHGs formation, 95-96
  causes for the failure of DWCRA programme, 94
  credit, 83-85
  critical review, 90-91
  definition of SHG, 99
  emergence of SHG for banking with the poor, 101-102
  experience of training through SHGs, 107-108
  formation of SHGs, 105-107
  introduction, 81-83
  NABARD and SHGs, 114-117
  need for gender centred development, 109-110
  objectives, 85
    activities covered, 85
    financial pattern, 86
    group strategy, 85
    marketing of products, 86-87
    organisational set-up, 86
    selection activity, 85-86
  origin and progress, 81-120
  progress of SHGs, 111-112
  role of SHGs, 103
  self help groups, 100-101
    characteristics, 104-105
  strengthening DWCRA, 91
  strengthening SHGs, 117-118
  why self-help groups, 96
    access to credit, 96-97
    borrower transaction costs, 97-98
    confidence in won abilities, 98

equality, 98
freedom to the borrower, 98
improved loan recoveries, 98-99
lender of the last resort, 97
overcoming asymmetric information problems, 99
promotion of thrift and savings, 99
take up various development activities, 99
women movement, 110-111
DWCRA and SHGs, 121-157
allocation of credit, 150-152
distribution of SHGs by financial transactions, 144-148
facilitating agencies, 132
financial functions of SHGs, 152-154
group meetings, 139-142
household assets, 144
introduction, 121-122
linkage with the bank, 123-128
movement in Andhra Pradesh, 122-123
networking of the groups, 128-130
NGO network in the district, 132-133
occupational status of group leaders, 142-144
rules, regulations and working norms, 130
selection of group leader, 136-139
SHG member beneficiaries under IRDP, 142
size of sample SHGs, 130-131
transaction costs, 148-150
UNDP assistance, 133-136

E

Economic obstacles, 13
Employment generation, 158-189
Empowerment of women, 43, 264

F

Five year plans, 22-80
FWPR, 9

G

Gram Sevikas, 25

I

IADP, 25
ICDS, 66
Income and employment generation and capacity building, 158-189, 257
asset status, 177-181
capacity building, 181-184
decision-making within the household, 169-172
economic activities undertaken by groups, 159-160
employment generation by sectors and gender, 172-177
findings, 184-186
introduction, 158-159
method of tackling problems or remedies, 167-169
probelms faced by the groups, 160-164
– of marketing the product, 164-167
India women, 2
Indira Mahila Kendras, 68
Indira Mahila Yojana, 68
Infant Mortality Rate, 57
International Women Year, 76
IRDP, 29, 37, 158

J

Jawahar Rozgar Yojana, 36

K

Khadi and Village Industries, 34, 48
Krishi Vigyan Kendras, 29
Kurnool strategy, 190

M

Mahila Samriddhi Yojana, 68
Male dominated society, 1

N

NABARD, 111, 126, 127
National Commission for women, 11
National Commission on Labour, 4
National Policy for Empowerment of Women, 54
Nehru Rozgar Yojana, 36

O

Objectives, 14

P

Panchayat, 23
Participation of women, 1
PMRY, 246
Policy implications of the findings of the study, 264
Poverty alleviation through social mobilisation, 190-232
  adult literacy programme, 207-209
  approaches to development of the poor, 192-193
  child education, 209-212
  conflict resolution, 218-220
  early girl child marriage, 212-215
  empowerment of women in developmental aspects, 196-200
  family planning, 204-207
  health and hygiene, 207
  introduction, 190-192
  Janmabhoomi programme, 215-216
  national social assistance programme, 216-217
  perceptions of members on women development activities, 217-218
  political participation, 224-227
  reaction from local elite, 222-224
  – of husbands and other male members, 220-222
  removal of untouchability, 200-201
  replication of the grameena bank model, 193-195
  role of SHGs in women development issues, 195-196
  – – state government, 227-230
  – – women in decision-making, 201-204
Poverty eradication, 1-21, 260
  data base, 16-17
  development policies for women, 5
    anti-poverty, 6
    efficiency, 6
    empowerment, 6
    equity, 5-6
    welfare, 5
  empowerment, 2-3
  female work participation rate, 9
  gender inequality, 3
  how to focus on women, 7-8
  hypotheses, 15
  magnitude and characteristics of women in poverty, 12-13

National Commission for Women, 11-12
– machinery for empowering women, 11
percentage of female workers, 10-11
poverty eradication through women development, 12
research design and methodology, 15
RMK, 11
sample design and size, 15-16
statement of the problem, 13-14
why do women lag behind, 6
– focus on women, 7
– women work why do women seek employment, 8-9
women and development, 3-5
Pradhan Mantri Gramodaya Yojana, 57
Problems of women development, 233-242, 267
constraints or problems, 237-239
lacunae in the group approach drawbacks, 233-237
marketing problems, 239-240
overcoming the problems, 240-242
Progress of SHGs, 254
Rashtriya Mahila Kosh, 69

S

Self Help Groups, 55, 105-107, 114-117, 142, 256
in India, 116
MSHAKTI, 37
a Mahila Block Societies, 68
al mobilisation, 259
Structural characteristics of sample SHGs, 256

T

Teresa, Mother, 83
Total literacy campaigns, 43
TRYSEM, 29, 37, 246

U

Universal immunisation programme, 38

V

Vocational training of women, 40

W

Women and development, 252-253
and five-year plans, 253
Women development centres, 38
Women Development Corporations, 49
Women development programmes and five year plans, 22-80
all women police stations, 71
A.P. State Social Welfare Advisory Board, 73
– – – Financial Corp., 74
– – Women Co-operative Finance Corp., 76
commitments of the ninth plan, 4445
– – – tenth plan to empower women, 56
co-operative development fund, 70-71
education and training, 46-48
eighth plan, 39, 41
education, 40-41
employment, 39-40
Mahila Samridhi Yojana, 41
establishment of Mahila Courts and family courts, 71
fifth plan, 26-28
first plan, 24

fourth plan, 26
girl child protection scheme, 70
health and family welfare, 45-46
incentive awards to mahila mandals, 26
Indira Mahila Yojana, 68
institutional services, 62
introduction, 22
liberation, 75-76
local leadership, 26
Mahila Samriddhi Yojana, 68
ninth plan, 43
nutrition, 46
participation of NGOs in women and child welfare activities, 74
promotion of women entrepreneurship, 69-70
Rashtriya Mahila Kosh, 69
rehabilitation, 75-76
schemes for training for employment, 42
second plan, 25
seventh plan, 31-32
Council for Advancement of Peoples Action and Rural Technology, 36
education, 32
employment, 33
health, 32-33
Jawahar Rozgar Yojana, 36
Khadi and Village Industries, 34
Nehru Rozgar Yojana, 36
rural development, 33
– sanitation programme, 36
voluntary organisations, 35
sixth plan, 28-31
special scheme to prevent child labour, 70
– schemes in the world bank assisted ICDS projects, 67
support to employment programmes for women, 75
tenth plan, 53
third plan, 25-26
thrift promotion, 68-69
training of associate women workers were introduced, 26
vocational training courses for adolescent girls, 71-72
women as critical agents of change, 23-24
– component in the adult literacy programme, 74
– development corporation, 72-73
– welfare programmes in Andhra Pradesh, 61-62
work and employment, 48-50
Women movements, 110
Women rights, 3
World Bank Report, 121